CW01217980

History from the Sources
General Editor: John Morris

ARTHURIAN PERIOD SOURCES
VOL. 1

ARTHURIAN SOURCES

Vol. 1
Introduction, Bibliography, Notes, Index

ARTHURIAN PERIOD SOURCES

1 **Arthurian Sources, Vol. 1**, by John Morris
   Introduction, Notes and Index
      How to use *Arthurian Sources*; Introduction and Notes;
      Index to *The Age of Arthur*

2 **Arthurian Sources, Vol. 2**, by John Morris
   Annals (A) and Charters (C)

3 **Arthurian Sources, Vol. 3**, by John Morris
   Persons
      Ecclesiastics (**E**) (alphabetically listed)
      Laypeople (**L**) (alphabetically listed)

4 **Arthurian Sources, Vol. 4**, by John Morris
   Places and Peoples (P), and Saxon Archaeology (S)
      Places and Peoples (alphabetically listed)
      Saxon Archaeology:
         The Chronology of Early Anglo-Saxon Archaeology;
         Anglo-Saxon Surrey; The Anglo-Saxons in Bedfordshire

5 **Arthurian Sources, Vol. 5**, by John Morris
   Genealogies (G) and Texts (T)
      Genealogies
         Editions by Egerton Phillimore (1856-1937): *The Annales Cambriae* and Old-Welsh Genealogies from B.L. MS. Harley 3859; Pedigrees from Jesus College (Oxford) MS. 20; Bonedd y Saint from N.L.W. MS. Peniarth 12
      Texts discussed
         Gospel-books; Honorius's Letter; Laws; Martyrologies; Muirchú's Life of St. Patrick; *Notitia Dignitatum*; *Periplus*; Ptolemy; The 'Tribal Hidage'; Welsh Poems

6 **Arthurian Sources, Vol. 6**, by John Morris
   Studies in Dark-Age History
      Celtic Saints—a Note; Pelagian Literature; Dark Age Dates; The Dates of the Celtic Saints; The Date of Saint Alban; Christianity in Britain, 300-700—the Literary Evidence; Studies in the Early British Church—a Review; Gildas

7 **Gildas**, edited and translated by Michael Winterbottom
      The Ruin of Britain; Fragments of Lost Letters; Penitential or Monastic Rule

8 **Nennius**, edited and translated by John Morris
      'Select Documents on British History'; The Welsh Annals

9 **St. Patrick**, edited and translated by A.B.E. Hood
      Declaration; Letter to Coroticus; Sayings; Muirchú's Life of St. Patrick

ARTHURIAN SOURCES

Vol. 1
Introduction, Bibliography, Notes, Index

JOHN MORRIS

PHILLIMORE

1995

Published by
PHILLIMORE & CO. LTD.
Shopwyke Manor Barn, Chichester, Sussex

© Mrs. Susan Morris, 1995

ISBN 0 85033 755 0

Printed and bound in Great Britain by
HARTNOLLS LTD.
Bodmin, Cornwall

CONTENTS

	page
Preface by the literary executors of John Morris	vi
Publisher's note	vii
How to use *Arthurian Sources*	1
Introduction	2
Key to the abbreviation-system used in the notes	9
Works cited in the notes	11
Notes to *The Age of Arthur*	35
Notes to the maps in *The Age of Arthur*	107
Index to *The Age of Arthur*	122

PREFACE

In *The Age of Arthur*, the late Dr John Morris constantly referred the reader to an **A-T** series of appendices containing the detached results of those textual, bibliographical, historical and archaeological studies upon which were founded his knowledge and interpretation of the history of Arthurian times.

Unfortunately, death overtook him before he had completed the preparation of the schedules of notes which were to have become these appendices. Much of his intended annotation was, obviously, still in his mind; much was in the form of cryptic memoranda or marginalia and highly allusive remarks; much in various states of draft; some in a more finished typescript condition.

Fortunately—or, more truly, providentially—among his friends was Richard White, who bravely undertook to see what could be saved from disaster. With reverence for prevented intention balanced by a judicious recognition of practicality, he has had regard to the omission in bibliography, the unconfirmed judgement, the unfinished assessment of evidence, which any literary executor will find in the unfinished papers of one suddenly dead who can no longer be interrogated. For the space of several years on end, he has given generously of his already hard-pressed time and of his already heavily engaged energies, to rescue and present as much as could be recovered of John Morris's apparatus for *The Age of Arthur*.

This is a monument of scholarship, friendship and devotion in the highest degree worthy of honour, which we very sincerely, gratefully and respectfully commend to the approval of the reader.

In view of this, as John Morris's literary executors, we have insisted upon certain precautions for Richard White. Our late friend, a man of sincerity, warmth and temerity, was a scholar of polite and curious learning, of wide range but sometimes indifferent focus; of idiosyncratic method, approach and perception; his insights and interpretation often appear eccentric in relation to the current general opinions of historians. These qualities gave his work great value, but leave it exposed to debate. His opinions will eventually be proved 'right' or 'wrong' by the judgement, knowledge and taste of the historians of future times. Meanwhile, we have to ensure that Richard White's devoted act of friendship does not bring him into obloquy or suspicion because of any real or supposed 'heresy' which disputation or research may discern or reveal in John Morris's notes.

Accordingly, the editorial hand has been clearly signalled throughout every part of the work, so that what is John Morris's and what is Richard White's can be clearly perceived.

However, the editor's corrections to, and differences from, the work as the author left it, which are thus signalled by editorial convention, do not represent more than a small part of *this* editor's work. A very sensitive interpretation of John Morris's more cryptic or sketchy notes has had to be done. Some material was, eventually, found to be beyond the reach of sensible organisation, and was rejected from publication: but only after the most patient and diligent attempts to bring it into a presentable state had been made by Richard White and numbers of other experts and scholars to whom he has addressed the problems.

What is now presented to the reader, is the result of Richard White's heroic effort to repair, edit and preserve John Morris's notes. It would be monstrous if this tremendous labour were to be rewarded by blame or disparagement in the course of any criticism of Morris's views which might ensue upon the publication of the notes. We have sought to insure against that by requiring Richard White to leave the 'repairs' showing and to let John Morris speak for himself.

ROBERT BROWNING
JOHN McNEAL DODGSON

PUBLISHER'S NOTE

John Morris planned his six volumes of *Arthurian Sources* as a sectional work, with evidence gathered under a series of twenty lettered headings labelled **A-T**, as he made clear in *The Age of Arthur*, p. 519. When he died, his assembled materials were still in fragmentary condition. The only section which seems to have been more or less complete was **E**, 'Ecclesiastics', which occupies much of volume 3. But it is clear from this that in the course of execution his plan was already undergoing change. Entries originally intended for **F**, 'Foreign persons and places', had already found their way into **E** and elsewhere. The notes to *The Age of Arthur* suggest that he was in the process of abandoning **G**F 'Genealogies, Foreign', and perhaps other categories.

Among his publishable materials nothing remained of sections **D** ('Dedications'), **F** ('Foreign persons and places'), **I** ('Inscriptions'), **K** ('King Lists'), **M** ('Miscellaneous'), **O** ('Ogam Script'), **Q** ('Quotations from texts'), or **R** ('Roman institutions'). Incomplete (sometimes very incomplete) drafts existed for **A** ('Annals'), **C** ('Charters'), **G** ('Genealogies'), **L** ('Localities, Geography', now renamed **P**, 'Places and Peoples'), **P** ('Persons, laymen' now renamed **L**, 'Laypeople'), and **T** ('Texts discussed'), and have been published here, sometimes with additional textual material which (the Publisher hopes) may prove useful to the reader. Mere fragments remained of some other sections and these have been gathered into more complete sections in a position which has been thought helpful: **B**, materials relating to the battle of Mount Badon, now in **P**; **H**, Honorius's letter to the *ciuitates* of Britain, now in **T**; **J**, 'Jurisprudence, Law', now in **T**; **N**, 'Names of Places', now in **P**.

The most drastic loss was the absence from Morris's papers of any significant materials for **S** ('Saxon Archaeology'), although it is clear both that he had done much work on this subject and that he intended it to be one of the major sections of his *Arthurian Sources*. The Publisher has sought to fill this gap as far as possible by reproducing under **S** Morris's published papers on the subject, which have an importance of their own, providing a framework of interpretation and offering detailed surveys of two southeastern counties.

Assembly and editing of John Morris's *Nachlass* has been the work of many hands over many years. The Publisher believes that everything which is practicable to that end has now been done. These *Arthurian Sources* are therefore offered to the public both in the belief that they will be useful and to complete Morris's projected nine-volume series of 'Arthurian Period Sources', of which volumes 7–9 were published in 1978–80. They are issued as a tribute to the memory of a scholar who had a passionate conviction of the importance of bringing historical evidence before as wide a public as possible, an aim enthusiastically shared by Phillimore & Co., his publisher.

1995

HOW TO USE
ARTHURIAN SOURCES

These six volumes of *Arthurian Sources* were designed to offer detailed underpinning for the story presented in *The Age of Arthur*. They are organised into sections designated by **bold** capital letters, as follows.

A		Annals (vol. 2)
C		Charters (vol. 2)
E		Ecclesiastics (vol. 3)
G		Genealogies (vol. 5)
	GA	Armorican
	GB	British
	GE	English
	GI	Irish
L		Laypeople (vol. 3)
P		Places and Peoples (vol. 4)
S		Saxon Archaeology (vol. 4)
T		Texts discussed (vol. 5)

Volume 1 is the essential key to the rest of the series. The Notes (pp. 35–121) and the Index (pp. 122–152) provide the bridge which links *The Age of Arthur* to *Arthurian Sources*. For the present volume this material has been thoroughly revised to ensure the closest integration between text, notes, index, and sources. The crucial instrument of cross-referencing is the bold-letter series, **A**–**T**, which directs the reader to the relevant sections of volumes 2–5.

Volume 6 contains a series of detailed studies of sources and historical questions, whose findings also underpin parts of *The Age of Arthur*.

INTRODUCTION

The purpose of this collection of *Arthurian Sources* is to help to make the sources for the history of the British lands in the fifth, sixth, and seventh centuries easier to use.

Treatment of different kinds of sources has to differ, since the availability of published material varies, and so does the amount and value of work previously done. The texts of the Irish and Welsh annals are collated for two reasons: though all major texts have been printed, many are available only in a few specialised libraries, while some are occasionally offered second-hand at vast prices, while others cannot be acquired at all; and the half-dozen main texts have not yet been collated. It is not, however, necessary to treat the *Anglo-Saxon Chronicle* similarly, since its collated texts are readily available. All the annalistic texts are treated in volume 2.

All significant information about persons and places is given for reference (see volumes 3–4).

In some categories of sources, whose technicalities have been studied by a small number of specialists, most students are still to a large extent dependent on their conclusions, since it is not always easy to distinguish the evidence, and the ways in which it can be used – as with the charters of the five countries (Ireland and Scotland, England and Wales and Brittany), treated in volume 2, the growing volume of pagan Saxon archaeological material (considered in volume 4), and the genealogical literature (discussed in volume 5).

In addition, a small number of particular problems, as the battle of Badon (**P**), the letter of Honorius (**T**) and a few miscellaneous matters require separate brief discussion.

The score of headings into which the *Sources* are intended to be grouped was set forth on page 519 of *The Age of Arthur*. [The final version of these headings and their reference-letters is printed on page 1 of this volume. This list represents the subjects for which Morris left material suitable for press at the time of his death.]

The source-material for these centuries is circumscribed by two main difficulties, from which the evidence for the Roman centuries, and for medieval and modern history thereafter, is largely exempt. A high proportion of the texts was not written for the purpose, real or avowed, of giving a straightforward account of what happened, or how men lived, but was expressly composed to advance the interests of the authors or of the institutions which they served, or else for the instruction and edification of the reader; therefore, whereas copyists of Roman and of most later medieval texts regarded it as their proper business to copy their originals as exactly as they could, those who copied worn-out manuscripts of these centuries frequently considered it their duty to improve and alter the origins, leaving out what was barbaric in style or unedifying in content and modernising their matter for the benefit of their contemporaries. Moreover, much of the archaeological material lacks the abundance of coins, pottery, and other artefacts which makes the dating of the material remains of other ages relatively simple.

Secondly, modern study of the evidence has been much less. Both the texts and the material remains of the Roman period, and the documentation of later British history from Bede onwards, have been exhaustively studied over the centuries since the Renaissance. The sheer numbers of scholars engaged, and their successive improvements upon their predecessors' work, have refined away much of the inherent difficulties in their texts and of the shallow-based assumptions which are bound to afflict the earlier stages of the study of any historical period. Moreover, these long-continued studies have provided many of the essential tools of critical study, sound printed texts, easily available, to penetrate through the errors of manuscripts to reach back to what the author wrote, together with the analysis of why he wrote it; and handy reference-works, listing what is known of people, places, the development of languages, of familiar phraseology and much else, have also been produced. Since serious study of the period between the Roman and English mastery of Britain is much more recent, many of the tools have not yet been fashioned, and techniques at the historian's disposal are still raw and crude.

One of the main influences to have greatly benefited the study of other periods during the last hundred years has worked to the disadvantage of these centuries. The exact criticism of the great scholars of the Renaissance and the 17th century was set against a background of a highly-dramatised, personalised and uncritical outlook among the historians who used their labours just as the early stages of archaeology concentrated upon the antiquarian collection of objects and buildings. In the later 18th and early 19th century romanticism pervaded the study of the past, epitomised when the poet and historical dramatist Schiller was appointed professor of history at the University of Jena in 1789. Reaction against romanticism bred a sober reaction among historians, from the middle decades of the 19th century, who applied to the writing of history the critical canons developed by the great Renaissance editors of the texts of Classical antiquity. Niebuhr, Mommsen, Ranke, Stubbs and their many successors and contemporaries applied themselves to the single task of getting their facts straight, of collecting all the available evidence, of sifting error, invention and fancy from accurate record, and of establishing what actually happened and how.

In the last years of the 19th century the interest of critical scholars was increasingly attracted to constitutional history, and to the exploration of archaeological sites, rather than the collection of objects. Both studies required that the examination of crude facts, and the rejection of false or suspect evidence be developed to a new pitch. They therefore attracted men trained as lawyers, or whose cast of mind accustomed them to the lawyers' necessary suspicion that all witnesses are liars, in whole or in part, unless proved otherwise.

The major exponents of this severe criticism made an immense contribution to historical understanding, which can only be assessed against the clutter of fantasy with which they were faced, and which is now forgotten because they have cleared it away into the dustbin. When Haverfield undertook the study of Roman Britain in the 1890s, it was less than 25 years since Bertram's extraordinary forgery of a geographical account of the province, allegedly copied by the medieval monk, Richard of Cirencester, had been exposed, and accounts of Roman Britain were still plentifully peppered with traces of forgery. In addition, Haverfield had to cope with widespread beliefs that any place called 'Coldharbour' was, by its name alone, a Roman site, and even that places beginning with Ost-, as Osterley Park, owed their names to the Roman general Ostorius Scapula. Maitland and Vinogradoff faced beliefs, immoderately oversimplified by readers of Seebohm, that the discovery of Roman sites in or near modern villages indicated direct continuity of agrarian institutions from Roman times, or that modern parliament directly descended from the *witan* of the Saxon kings, with the ancestral *witan* depicted as remarkably similar to its modern descendant. Levison was confronted with an ill-sorted archive of early medieval European documentation, Saints' lives, grants of land and privileges, a disordered quarry wherein any man might select such items as suited the interest of his own assumptions and theories, and might at will reject evidence which displeased him.

Each of these scholars, and many of their contemporaries, made lasting advances of great importance in the study of their own subjects in their day. They were, however, exposed to a variety of risks. Their exact legal training was fitted to cope with evidence which claimed to give accurate accounts; it was much less adapted to the study of material which made no such claim, whose ill-informed propagandist purpose offended their assumptions. Most of them worked on their own, without peers, almost the only competent specialists in their own spheres. Isolation breeds fallibility; as one scholar remarked more recently of another, who was the only competent authority in this own field, 'He is a fine scholar, and I am sure he is right; but I would be happier if there were two of him to argue with one another'. Isolation overawed their successors. As they became the elderly acknowledged experts, more erudite than any younger man, they were subject to the insidious contagion of uncritical deference from their successors. The younger men found it

INTRODUCTION

hard to develop mature confidence in their own judgement, either smothering inferences which conflicted with their elders, or else giving way to saucy efforts to debunk the pundits, often by straining their own evidence. The solitary eminent authorities shared the common weakness of mankind, and risked issuing dogmatic pronouncements which were over-readily accepted with insufficient examination of the evidence upon which they rested; and such dangers grew greater in their later years.

The magnitude of their achievement to some extent stifled their successors and limited their possibilities. Their attitudes prevailed long after the job to which they were adapted had been accomplished, and their occasional misjudgements caused harm, because they were uncritically accepted. Haverfield properly placed great weight on the dating of Roman-British sites and objects by the pottery and coins found in them, normally providing a useful date-bracket when later coins were absent. But when he came to consider the end of Roman Britain, he rashly attributed the end of each site to a date soon after the minting of the latest coin there found. The outlook of the lawyer which prevailed in his day trained him not to go beyond the formal evidence. Evidence ended with coins which had ceased to be minted in the Western empire, a year or two after A.D. 400. The limitation of the lawyer, therefore, trapped him into an endless series of brash assertions that sites ended about 400, or earlier, if they had no later coins. Thus it was long maintained that Wroxeter and Hadrian's Wall were 'abandoned' in the 380s, and Verulamium had 'the appearance of a bombed city' at that date, and that the entire civilisation of Roman Britain collapsed 'about 400'. In spite of mounting evidence to the contrary, it was until very recently considered safe and scholarly to date the end of a site too early, rash speculation to date it later. The mere suggestion of a fifth-century date for pottery or sites marked a man as a daring rebel. It is only in the last ten years that the force of evidence has compelled the abandonment of these assumptions; but they still linger, blighting the understanding of many sites where they have not yet been formally disproved. Yet the assumptions never had any historical basis. Since almost no Roman coins minted later than about 402 ever reached Britain, the absence of non-existent coins could never have justified any assumption that sites ended with the coins. Yet this single legalistic assumption has stunted the interpretation of archaeological evidence for rather more than half a century.

The generalised assumption was matched by a number of small individual misjudgements which have done damage large and small. In the *Victoria County History of Warwickshire* Haverfield sharply dismissed the alleged Roman fort at Metchley, Edgbaston, on the southern extremity of Birmingham. The fort was not therefore recognised until the Medical School of Birmingham University was built upon it; and when recognised that portion of the fort not covered by the buildings was exposed and preserved. Yet the earlier sketches and plans of the earthwork, made before its surface traces had disappeared, were plainly Roman; had Haverfield's judgement been less intemperate, the Medical School would have been sited slightly to one side, and the fort would have escaped destruction.

The same over-severe attitude to formal evidence led sometimes to less severe suppression of evidence. In the *Victoria County History of Somerset* is printed the text of the Roman inscriptions of Bath; one of them, of the second half of the first century, was the memorial of a man named Vettius Benignus. So Haverfield printed the text: but in the translation, a slip of the pen caused him to write Vettius Bolanus. The slip reveals his thinking and his attitude to evidence. Vettius Bolanus was legate to Britain in A.D. 69–70; and a stone of approximately the same date naturally suggests that Benignus was in some way connected with Bolanus, either owing citizenship to him or, more probably, being his freedman. But the stone simply suggests the possibility—it does not prove it. The slip of the pen demonstrates that Haverfield recognised the possible connection; but because it was not formally proved, he thus concealed it from his readers, most of whom were unlikely to have heard of Bolanus. By modern standards, it would be considered his business to draw attention to the possibility in a footnote.

Similar oversights are more easily recognised in the expanding discipline of archaeology than in textual scholarship. But they are paralleled. One extraordinary mishandling of evidence by F.W. Maitland was examined at length by H.P.R. Finberg (*Lucerna* [London, 1964], pp. 131–143), who convicted him of acting as prosecutor, in the course of polemical controversy (p. 137). The pleas of an attorney are noticeable in many other passages; for example in *Domesday Book and Beyond* (Cambridge, 1897), p. 393, Maitland argued that a 'tendency to reckon 120 ... acres to the hide is plainly perceptible' in the 13th century. The evidence adduced is from the cartulary of Ramsey Abbey whose manors were 'scattered in the eastern midlands'. Thirty-one equations are cited from the cartulary; they range from 48 to 256 acres to a hide, and only seven of them give 120 acres to the hide. The comment, however, points out 'no other equation occurs more than twice' and that 'where the computation of 120 acres to a hide is forsaken, we see little agreement in favour of any other equation'. What is said amounts to special pleading. What is left unsaid is more so, for of the seven 120-acre equations, four are in Cambridgeshire, whose total is six, and two more are within five miles of its modern county boundary. Of the remaining 25 equations, 'scattered in the eastern midlands', only one gives the 120-acre equation, and several other equations occur twice. The special pleading disguises the fact that, in this cartulary, the 120-acre equation is a specific feature of the Cambridgeshire manors. The cause of the special pleading is revealed in the footnote, which mentions, but does not cite or discuss, a comparable discussion by Frederic Seebohm (*The English Village Community* [London, 1883], p. 37), based on the Huntingdonshire Hundred Rolls. The evidence which Seebohm cited in fact gives much stronger support to Maitland's contention, for of his eighteen equations, seven give 120 acres, with one double and one 1½ multiples of 120. Outside Cambridgeshire Seebohm logged traces of a 120-acre equation in half his instances, whereas the evidence which Maitland quoted to prove the same point records only one instance among 25 examples. Yet Maitland did not quote Seebohm, whose discussion of the figures is better balanced and easier to follow than his. The reason is simply that the principal purpose of Maitland's book is, in his own words, that 'in some sense I have been endeavouring to answer Mr. Seebohm', whose overall conclusions the work attacks, and adequately disproves without need of such special pleading.

Levison's work in a different field is magisterial; but in his later years he was particularly prone to the issue of authoritative pronouncements, and to sweeping unwelcome evidence out of sight. In an article published in *Neues Archiv der Gesellschaft für ältere deutsche Geschichtskunde* 29 (1903/4) 95–175, when he was comparatively young, he argued (pp. 128–9) that all passages, contained in the longer version of Constantius's *Life of St Germanus* of Auxerre, but not in the shorter version, were Carolingian interpolations. His arguments have not yet been examined in print by any other scholar, but some of the passages which he rejected, on grounds which do not carry universal conviction, have continued to be treated as part of the original fifth-century text by scholars who silently bypass his argument. When, twenty years later, he edited the *Life* for MGH, he left out the passages which he rejected; they are not even given in the footnotes, which briefly refer to *Neues Archiv*, a periodical not over-easy to obtain, and since the long version has been printed only by editors of the 16th and 17th centuries, it is a difficult labour to verify his argument. The normal standards of a modern editor would have required that he should at least have included in his notes or critical apparatus the text of the passages that in his view were interpolations. The detail is discussed below: see E Germanus (volume 3). A further instance of a prosecutor's zeal run riot in the course of controversy, in a work published in 1946, is discussed at length in volume 2, pp. 89–98.

Similar instances in the work of these men, and many more in the work of lesser scholars bred in the same school of thought, could be multiplied indefinitely. The work which these men did in their own days, chiefly in the first half of the 20th century, greatly advanced the study of the evidence for these centuries. The debt which we owe to their labours is not lessened because they occasionally gave way to the pressures bearing upon a man of lone eminence. But they need to be emphasised, because the dead hand of limited legalistic assumptions still lies heavily upon modern research.

What matters most is that younger scholars should free themselves of indecent respect for the authority of their elders. Often still a younger man learns to distrust his own judgement of the evidence, and may not command the confidence to challenge established pronouncements until he reaches middle years, if at all. What matters is that every item of evidence be scrutinised exactly, and not only is it right that the purpose and bias of its author, the reason why an archaeological site or object is as it was found, be closely examined, but also that each and every statement of every modern scholar be examined as searchingly as the evidence itself, constantly re-tested against new evidence and new views. The purpose of the survey and collation of sources brought together in this work is to make the close examination of both the evidence and of modern views thereon somewhat easier than it is at present.

JOHN MORRIS

KEY TO THE ABBREVIATION-SYSTEM
used in the Notes (pp. 35–121, below)

Roman numerals I, II and III refer to the sections of *Works cited in the Notes* below (pp. 11–34): I Sources (pp. 11–28), II Modern Works (pp. 29–33), III Periodicals (p. 34).

AA	I MGH	Beds.	Bedfordshire	ECE	I Charters
AASS	II Leeds	Berks.	Berkshire	ECEE	I Charters
AB	I *Vitae*; III	BG	I Procopius	ECHR	III
AC	I Annals	BGG	I Genealogies	ECMS	I
ACDS	II MacKinlay	BHL	II	ECMW	I
ACL	II Stokes	BICS	III	ECPMS	II Cruden
ACm	I Annals	BM	British Museum	ECW	I Charters
ACR	II Fox			ECWM	I Charters
Aethelbert	I LEEK	BNE	I *Vitae*	ed.	editor, edition
Aethelstan	I LEEK	Brev. Ab.	I *Vitae*		
AG	I *Vitae*	BT	I Welsh	Edward	I LEEK
Age	II Morris	BV	I Procopius	EETS	I
AHS	I	By S	I Genealogies	e.g.	for example
AI	I Annals	c.	circa, about	EHD	I
AIM	I Irish	CA	I Welsh	EHDS	I
ALE	I	CArch	III	EHR	III
Alfred	I; I LEEK	CASP	III	EHS	I
ALI	I	CEIS	II Hughes	EIHM	II O'Rahilly
ALW	I	cf.	compare	Ep(p).	Letter(s)
Ant.	III	CGH	I Genealogies	EPNE	II
Ant. Jl.	III	ch.	chapter	EPNS	II
AP	I Welsh	CHE	I Church	ERN	II Ekwall
APS	I Arthurian	Chron.	Chronicle	ESSH	I
Arch.	III	CIIC	I Corpus	EVC	II Seebohm
Arch. Ael.	III	CIL	I Corpus	EWGT	I Genealogies
Arch. Camb.	III	CLH	I Welsh		
Arch. Jl.	III	CPL	II Bieler	f.	filius, son of
ARS	I	CPNS	II Watson	FAB	I Welsh
ASch	I Charters	CPS	I Chronicles	ff.	following
ASE	II Åberg, Stenton	CR	III	FHG	I
		CS	I Annals	fig.	figure
ASH	I *Vitae*	CS	II Skene	FM	I Annals
ASP	II Myres	CSEL	I Corpus	FW	I
ASS	I *Vitae*	CSHB	I Corpus		
ASWi	I Wills	CSW	II Davies	GC	I ALW
ASWr	I Writs	CT	I Welsh	GCS	I
AT	I Annals	CTh	I Codex	Gesetze	I Liebermann, Schmid
AU	I Annals	DAB	II		
		DAS	I	GM	II Vinogradoff
BA	I Welsh	DB	I	GP	I MGH
BB	II	DBB	II Maitland	GPC	II Thomas
BBA	I	DC	I ALW		
BBC	I Welsh	DCB	II	H	I Genealogies
BBCS	III	DEPN	II	HA	I Bede
BCS	I Charters	DSB	II Leeds	HE	I Bede, Rufinus
BD	I Genealogies				

9

HF	I Gregory	NC	III	Sal.	I *Vitae*
HH	I	n.f	Neue Folge	SANHS	III
Hlothere	I LEEK	NH	I Pliny	SASI	II Chadwick
HMC	Historical Monuments Commission	NLA	I *Vitae*	SC	I
		Not. Dig.	I	SCD	II Arnold-Forster
		n.s.	new series		
HMSO	Her Majesty's Stationery Office	NS	I Charters	SCSW	II Bowen
		Occ.	West (cf. Not. Dig.)	SD	I
				SE	II Kemble
HS	I	OEN	II Chadwick	SEBC	II
HW	II Lloyd	OET	I	SEBH	II
HWL	II Parry	OIT	II Jackson	SEIL	II Thurneysen
HY	I	Or.	East (cf. Not. Dig.)		
				SG	I Irish
IANB	II Rivet			SILH	II Carney
i.e.	that is	p.; pp.	page(s)	SRA	I
ILS	I	*passim*	scattered (references)	SRG	I MGH
Ine	I LEEK			SRL	I MGH
Iolo	I Welsh	PE	I *Vitae* Brev. Ab.	SRM	I MGH
ITS	I Irish			SS	I MGH
IWP	II Williams	PFE	II Jolliffe	STS	I
		PG	I		
J	I Genealogies	PH	I *Vitae* Brev. Ab.	Sup.	Supplement
JBAA	III			SyAC	III
JCS	III	Pinkerton	I *Vitae*	Tac. Ann.	I
JEPN	III	PL	I	TCASL	II Seebohm
JRIC	III	pl.	plate	TCD	Trinity College, Dublin
JRS	III	PLAC	I MGH		
JRSAI	III	PLECG	II Chadwick		
JTS	III	PLRE	II		
		PNK	II EPNS	THS Cymm	III
KCD	I Charters	P and P	III	TRHS	III
		PP	II Wainwright	TRIA	III
LB	I	PPS	III	Triad	I TYP
LBS	II Baring-Gould	PRIA	III	TSW	II Seebohm
		PSA	III	TT	I *Vitae*
LC	I Charters	PSAS	III	TW	I Pennant
LEEK	I	PWP	I Welsh	TYP	I
LG	I				
LH	I	RBH	I Welsh	VC	I ALW
LHEB	II Jackson	RC	III	VCH	II
Lismore	I *Vitae*	RCHM	II	v., vita	Life of
LL	I	RGKB	III	VM	I Geoffrey
LRE	II Jones	RHS	Royal Historical Society	vol(s).	volume(s)
m	map, mac, son of			VSBG	I Genealogies; *Vitae*
		RIA	Royal Irish Academy		
M	I			VSH	I *Vitae*
MA	III	RIB	I	VT	I *Vitae*
MGH	I	RIS	I Muratori		
MHB	I	Rolls	I Chronicles	WBT	I Welsh
MHH	I *Vitae*	RS	Record Society	WEW	II Hoskins
MIAS	III	RV	II Ebert	WHR	III
Mon. Ang.	II Dugdale			Wihtred	I LEEK
MS(S)	Manuscript(s)	SAEC	I		
Myv. Arch.	I Welsh	SAL	Society of Antiquaries of London	YC	III
				ZCP	III

WORKS CITED IN THE NOTES
(pp. 35–121, below)

Space and time prevent the publication of a full bibliography. The works here cited provide a brief guide to the main printed sources; the modern works named are chiefly those which list, assess and discuss the sources, and which contain the fullest bibliographies. Many useful discussions are therefore excluded, but most of them are mentioned in the text or bibliographies of the works here cited.

1 **Sources and Collections of Sources**
Some of the printed texts are hard to find and difficult to use. It has therefore been necessary to consult the most accessible and useful editions (for example the volumes of the Loeb and Teubner series of editions of Classical texts); in a few instances it has been impracticable or inadvisable to cite the most recent publication.

Abingdon Chronicle	Rolls 2, 1858	
Adam of Bremen	*Gesta Hammaburgensis Ecclesiae Pontificum* MGH SS 7,267, ed. 2, 1876; PL 146, 451	
Aethelweard	*Chronicon* CHE 3; MHB 499; ARS	
Aetheriae *Peregrinatio*	CSEL 39, 35 ff.; cf. II Löfstedt	
Alcuin	MGH Epp. Karoli Aevi; HY 1,349	
Aldhelm	MGH AA 15; PL 89	
Alfred	*Alfred des Grossen Bearbeitung der Soliloquien des Augustinus* ed. W. Endtler, Bibliothek der Angelsächischen Prosa II, Hamburg 1922	
Ambrose of Milan	CSEL 73; PL 16	
Ammianus Marcellinus	ed. Teubner (C.U.Clark); ed. Loeb (J.C.Rolfe, 1935–40)	
The Ancient Laws and Institutes of England	ed. B.Thorpe, London 1840	ALE
The Ancient Laws of Ireland	ed. W.N.Hancock and others, 6 vols. Dublin 1865–1901; cf. p. 445 *Age*	ALI
The Ancient Laws and Institutes of Wales	ed. Aneirin Owen, 2 vols. London 1841. Vol. 1 contains the so called Demetian, Gwentian and Venedotian Codes; cf. p. 445 *Age*	ALW DC GC, VC
Anglian Chronicle	see p. 283 *Age*	
Anglicanae Historiae Scriptores	R.Twysden, 2 vols. London 1652	AHS
Anglicarum Rerum Scriptores post Bedam	H.Savile, London 1596; Frankfurt 1601	ARS
Anglo-Saxon Chronicle; see Saxon Chronicle		
Annales Fuldenses	MGH SS 1,343	
Annales Laurissenses (or *Regni Francorum,* or *Einhardi*)	MGH SS 1,126; SRG 1895	

II

ANNALS Irish (see **A**)
- *Annals of Inisfallen* — (1092) ed. S.MacAirt, Dublin 1951 — AI
- *Annals of Tigernach* — (1088) ed. W.Stokes RC 16, 1895, 375–419: 17, 1896, 6–33; 119–263; 337–420: 18, 1897, 9–59; 150–198; 267–303; 374–391 — AT
- *Annals of Clonmacnoise* — translated C.Mageoghagan (1627) from an original of c. 1408, now lost; ed. D.Murphy, Dublin 1896 — AC
- *Annals of Ulster* — (before 1498) ed. W.M.Henessey, Dublin 1887–1901, 4 vols. — AU
- *Annals of the Four Masters* — (1632–1636) ed. J.O'Donovan, 7 vols. Dublin 1851; ed. 2, 1857 — FM
- *Chronicum Scotorum* — (1660–1666) ed. W.M.Henessey, Rolls 46, 1866 — CS
- *Annals of Roscrea* — ed. D.Gleeson and S.MacAirt PRIA 59 C 1957–1959
- *Annals from the Book of Leinster* — VT 512–529

ANNALS Welsh (see **A**)
- *Annales Cambriae* — Rolls 20, 1860; YC 9, 1888, 152; MHB 830; *Nennius* ed. Morris, Chichester 1980; cf. Welsh Literature, Bruts. See vol. 5 below. — ACm

ANNALS English (see **A**) — see *Anglian Chronicle*; Saxon Chronicle; Florence of Worcester; Flores; Henry of Huntingdon; etc.

Anonymus Valesianus — ed. H.Valesius, Paris 1636; Muratori (ed. 1786) 25; (ed. 1913) 24, 4; MGH AA 9 (Chron. Min. 1) 7 ff. and 306 ff.; ed. Rolfe, *Ammianus* (Loeb); ed. J.Moreau (Teubner) 1961; etc.

Archiv: see III ACL

Arthurian Period Sources — gen. ed. J.Morris, 9 vols. Chichester 1978–1995 — APS

Asser — *Life of King Alfred* ed. W.H. Stevenson, Oxford 1904; MHB 467; SRA 2

Augustine of Hippo — PL 34 ff.; cf. *The Anti-Pelagian Treatises of St. Augustine* ed. F.W.Bright, Oxford 1880; *de Gestis Pelagii* CSEL 42

Ausonius — MGH AA 5; also Loeb

Barnabas — *Epistula Catholica* ed. A.Hilgenfeld, Leipzig 1866

Bede — *Opera Omnia* ed. J.A.Giles, 13 vols. London 1843–1845; PL 90 ff. *Opera Historica* ed. J. Stevenson, EHS London 1838–1841

WORKS CITED IN THE NOTES : 1, SOURCES

	Historia Ecclesiastica Gentis Anglorum, Historia Abbatum, Epistula ad Egbertum ed. C.Plummer, 2 vols. Oxford 1896	HE HA
	Old English Version of HE in EETS 95–96, 110–111 London 1890–1898	
	Chronica MGH AA 13 (Chronica Minora 3) 247 ff.	
Benedict of Nursia	*Regula* CSEL 75	
Beowulf	ed. R.W.Chambers and A.J.Wyatt, London 1914; also C.L.Wrenn, Oxford 1953; cf. II Chambers; see Finn's Burg Fragment, below	
Hector Boece	*History of Scotland* STS series 3, 1946–; Rolls 6	
Boniface	*Epistulae* ed. M.Tangl *Die Briefe des heiligen Bonifatius* MGH Epp. Selectae 1, Berlin 1916	
Book of Armagh	ed. J.Gwynn (diplomatic text) Dublin 1913; facsimile of Patrician documents, ed. E.Gwynn, Dublin 1937	
of Ballymote	in the RIA; Kenney 24; facsimile, Dublin 1887	
of Chad	see *Book of Teilo*	
of Deer	ed. J.Stuart, Spalding Club, Edinburgh 1869; Kenney 656; K. Jackson *The Gaelic Notes in the Book of Deer* Cambridge 1972	
of the Dun Cow	*Lebor na hUidre* ed. R.I.Best and O. Bergin, Dublin 1929; facsimile, Dublin 1870; Kenney 15; in the RIA	
Yellow Book of Lecan	in TCD; Kenney 24; 89; facsimile, Dublin 1896, 1933;	
Great Book of Lecan	in the RIA; Kenney 25	
Book of Leinster	in TCD; ed. R.I.Best and others, Dublin 1954–83; facsimile 1880; Kenney 15	
of Lismore	Kenney 308; facsimile, Dublin 1950; cf. Stokes *Lismore Lives* (*Vitae*, below)	
of Llancarfan	*vita Cadoci* ch. 55–68	
of Llandaff	see *Liber Landavensis*	
of Rights	*Lebor na Cert*; ITS 46, 1962, ed. M. Dillon	
Black Book of St. Augustine	ed. G.J.Turner and H.E.Salter, 2 vols. London and Oxford 1915–24	
Book of Sligo	lost; cited in BM Egerton MS 1782, SG 72; 76; cf. viii	
of Teilo	unpublished; in Lichfield Cathedral	

	since the 10th century, therefore also called the Book of Chad; the Courtauld Institute has photographs. Memoranda are reproduced in LL	
Books, Welsh	see Welsh Literature, below, BA, BBC, BT, RBH etc.	
Book	see also *Lebor, Liber*	
Bower	see *Scotichronicon*	
Bruts	see Welsh Literature, below	
Caedmon	cf. Plummer *Bede* 2, 251; OET 125 ff. (cf. p. 421 *Age*); etc.	
Caesar	*de Bello Gallico* ed. Teubner, Loeb etc.	
Cáin Adomnáin	(Law of Adomnán) ed. K. Meyer, Oxford 1905; cf. SEIL 269 ff.; Kenney 245	
Cartulaire de Landevennec	ed. Le Men and Ernault, 1882; ed. de la Borderie, Rennes 1888	
Cartulaire de Quimper	*Bulletin de la Commission diocésaine de Quimper* 1901	
Cartulaire de Quimperlé	ed. L. Le Maitre and P. de Berthou, Paris 1896 (ed. 1)	
Cartulaire de Redon	ed. A de Courson, Paris 1863	
Cartularium Sithiense	(Abbaye de S. Bertin) Guérard *Cartulaires de France*, 1840–1857, vol. 3; cf. Seebohm EVC 256, with map	
Cassiodorus	PL 69, 70	
Catalogus Ordinum Sanctorum in Hibernia	Sal. 161 (see *Vitae* below); AB 73, 1955, 206	
CHARTERS (see C)		
Cartularium Saxonicum	W. de G. Birch, 3 vols. London 1885–1893; Index of Persons 1899	BCS
Codex Diplomaticus Aevi Saxonici	J. M. Kemble, 6 vols. London EHS 1839–1848	KCD
Anglo-Saxon Charters	A. J. Robertson, Cambridge 1939 (ed. 1)	ASCh
The Latin Charters of the Anglo-Saxon Period	F. M. Stenton, Oxford 1955	LC
The Crawford Collection of Early Charters and Documents	ed. A. S. Napier and W. H. Stevenson, Oxford 1895	NS
The Early Charters of Devon and Cornwall	H. P. R. Finberg, Leicester 1953 (ed. 1), supplement in Hoskins WEW; cf. II below	
The Early Charters of Eastern England	C. Hart, Leicester 1966	ECEE
The Early Charters of Essex	C. Hart, Leicester 1957 (ed. 1)	ECE
The Early Charters of the West Midlands	H. P. R. Finberg, Leicester 1961 (ed. 1)	ECWM
The Early Charters of Wessex	H. P. R. Finberg, Leicester 1964	ECW

see also II Sawyer, below; cf. Cartulaire, Cartularium, Diplomatarium, Wills, Writs; Books of Llancarfan, Llandaff, Teilo.

WORKS CITED IN THE NOTES : I, SOURCES

Chronicles and Memorials of Great Britain and Ireland during the Middle Ages	under the direction of the Master of the Rolls, London 1858–	Rolls
Chronicle of 452	MGH AA 9 (*Chronica Minora* 1) 652 ff.	
Chronicles of the Picts and Scots	ed. W.F.Skene, Edinburgh 1867	CPS
CHRONICLES see ANNALS (A)		
Church Historians of England	J.Stevenson, 6 vols. London 1852–1856	CHE
Claudian	*Carmina* MGH AA 10; CSEL 11	
Codex Theodosianus	ed. T.Mommsen, Berlin 1905, reprint 1954	CTh
Columban	*Opera* ed. G.S.M.Walker (Scriptores Latini Hiberniae 2) Dublin 1957; PL 80; cf. Kenney 186. *Epistulae* MGH Epp. 3	
Consuetudo West Sexe	Liebermann *Gesetze* 1,588	
Corippus	MGH AA 3	
Cormac mac Cuilennáin	*Glossary* (*Sanas Chormaic*) ed. W. Stokes translated J.O'Donovan, Calcutta 1868; AIM 4, 1912	
Corpus Inscriptionum Insularum Celticarum	ed. R.A.S.MacAlister, 2 vols. Dublin 1945–1949	CIIC
Corpus Inscriptionum Latinarum	ed. T.Mommsen and others, Berlin 1863–	CIL
Corpus Scriptorum Ecclesiasticorum Latinorum	Vienna 1866–	CSEL
Corpus Scriptorum Historiae Byzantinae	Bonn etc. 1828–	CSHB
Cyfreithiau Hywel Dda (Blegywryd)	ed. S.J.Williams and J.E.Powell, Cardiff 1942, ed. 2, 1961; ed. M. Richards, Cardiff 1957 (ed. 1); transl. M.Richards, Liverpool 1954	
Cynewulf	C.W.Kennedy *The Poems of Cynewulf* London 1940; cf. II Bateson	
DEDICATIONS to Saints (see E, P)	see II: *Wales* LBS, SCSW; *Ireland* O'Hanlon; *England* Arnold-Forster, Doble; *Scotland* Forbes, MacKinlay, cf. I *Vitae* Reeves *Adamnan*	
F.C.Diack	*The Inscriptions of Pictland* Aberdeen 1944	
Dialogue of Egbert	HS 3,403	
Dícuil	*de Mensura Orbis* ed. G.Parthey, Berlin 1870, cf. Kenney 546	
Dio Cassius	*Roman History* ed. Boissevain, Berlin 1895, Loeb etc.	
Diodorus Siculus	ed. Teubner, Loeb etc.	
Diplomatarium Anglicum aevi Saxonici	ed. B.Thorpe, London 1865	DAS
de Divina Lege	Jerome *Ep.* 7, PL 30, 104	

Domesday Book	ed. Farley, London 1783; ed. with translation, Morris, Chichester 1975–86; facsimiles, Ordnance Survey, Southampton 1861–1864; many county translations in VCH; and others elsewhere	DB
Duan Albanach	Skene CPS 57	
The Early Christian Monuments of Scotland	ed. J.Romilly Allen and J.Anderson, Edinburgh 1903	ECMS
The Early Christian Monuments of Wales	ed. V.E.Nash-Williams, Cardiff 1950	ECMW
Early English Text Society	London 1870–	EETS
Early Sources of Scottish History	ed. A.O. Anderson 2 vols. Edinburgh 1922	ESSH
Einhard, see *Annales Laurissenses*		
English Historical Documents I	ed. D.Whitelock, London 1955 (ed. 1)	EHD
Select English Historical Documents	ed. F.E.Harmer, Cambridge 1914	EHDS
English Historical Society	Publications, London 1833–1856	EHS
ENGLISH LITERATURE	cf. Alfred, Beowulf, Caedmon, Cynewulf, Finn's Burg Fragment, Saxon Chronicle, Widsith, etc.; cf. II Bateson, Baugh, Greenfield, Wrenn	
Eugippius	see *Vitae* Severinus	
Eunapius	*Fragments* FHG 4	
Eusebius	*Chronicon* ed. A. Schoene, 2 vols. Berlin 1866, 1875; PG 19, 99 ff. ed. R.Helm GCS 24 and 34 = 47, 1913, 1926, 1956 (Jerome's Latin translation only) ed. J.Karst GCS 20, 1911 (Armenian translation only, translated into German) ed. C. Siegfried and H. Gelzer, Leipzig 1884 (Syriac epitome only, with Latin translation)	
Fastidius	*de Vita Christiana* PL 40, 1031; translated R.S.T.Haslehurst; cf. Sicilian Briton, below	
Faustus of Riez	CSEL 21; PL 53; 58	
Félire, see Martyrology		
Finn's Burg Fragment	ed. J.R.Clark Hall and C.L.Wrenn, London 1950	
Florence of Worcester	*Chronicon* ed. B.Thorpe EHS 2 vols. London 1848–1849; MHB 522	FW
Flores Historiarum	Rolls 95, 1890	
John of Fordun	*Chronica* ed. W.F.Skene, Edinburgh 1871–1872; SRA 2; cf. *Scotichronicon*	
Fragmenta Historicorum Graecorum	ed. C.Müller, 5 vols. 1841–1883	FHG
Fredegarius	*Chronica* MGH SRM 2	

WORKS CITED IN THE NOTES : 1, SOURCES

GENEALOGIES (see G)

Armorican	(Brittany) Texts are few; the main sources are notices in the Lives of the Saints, especially Iudoc and Winnoc, and the lists of *Comites Cornubiae* in the Cartularies; see G A.	
English	The principal texts are in Bede HE; SC: Nennius; OET pp. 170 ff.; FW; HH; and other chroniclers; cf. G E.	
Irish	M.A.O'Brien *Corpus Genealogiarum Hiberniae* vol. 1 Dublin 1962; *The O'Clery Book of Genealogies* Analecta Hibernica 18, Dublin 1951; Keating, vol. 4 (ITS vol. 15), and other texts, including the MacFirbis Genealogies, cf. Kenney 45; O'Curry 121; cf. also T.O'Raithbheartaigh *Genealogical Tracts* Dublin 1932; cf. G 1.	CGH
Welsh	The principal modern collections are Wade-Evans, cf. *Vitae* below, and P.C.Bartrum *Early Welsh Genealogical Tracts* Cardiff 1966. The principal texts are	VSBG EWGT
	Bonedd Gwyr y Gogledd EWGT 72; Skene FAB 2,454; TYP 238	BGG
	Bonedd y Saint EWGT 51; VSBG 320	ByS
	Brychan Documents EWGT 14–21; VSBG 313–320	BD
	Harley MS 3859 EWGT 9; YC 9, 1888, 169	H
	Jesus College, Oxford, MS 20 EWGT 41; YC 8, 1887, 83	J
	Pedigrees are also given in a number of Saints' Lives, in Nennius and other sources. The texts printed in EWGT 35–40; 68–71; 75 ff. are mostly derived from the main texts, but are corrupted by antiquaries, often under the influence of Geoffrey of Monmouth, though a few preserve some incidental echoes of lost medieval origins; see G B.	
Scottish	The pedigrees of the several regions form part of the appropriate Irish, Welsh and English dynastic records; and are supplemented by the texts and incidental notices collected in CPS.	
Gennadius	*de Viris Inlustribus* PL 58; ed. E.C. Richardson, Leipzig 1896	
Geoffrey of Monmouth	*Historia Regum Britanniae* ed. A. Griscom, New York 1929, and many other editions	
	Vita Merlini ed. and translated Basil Clarke, Cardiff 1973	VM
Gildas	MGH AA 13 (*Chronica Minora* 3) 25 ff.; ed. and translated M. Winterbottom, Chichester 1978; ed. and translated H.Williams, London 1899–1901	
Giraldus Cambrensis	Rolls 21, 7 vols. 1861–1891	
Gregory of Tours	*Historia Francorum* and other works MGH SRM 1	HF
Gregory the Great	*Dialogi* PL 77, 149 ff.; *Epistulae* MGH Epp. 1–2	
Die Griechischen Christlichen Schriftsteller der ersten drei Jahrhunderte	Berlin and Leipzig 1897–	GCS
ed. A.W.Haddan and W.Stubbs	*Councils and Ecclesiastical Documents relating to Great Britain and*	HS

	Ireland 3 vols. Oxford 1869–1878	
Henry of Huntingdon	*Historia Anglorum* Rolls 74, 1879; MHB 689; ARS	HH
Hermas	*Pastor* GCS 48; PG 2; ed. A. Hilgenfeld, Leipzig 1866	
Collectio Canonum Hibernensis	in H.Wasserschleben *Die Irische Kanonensammlung* Giessen 1874; ed. 2, Leipzig 1885; cf. Kenney 247	
Hieronymus: see Jerome		
Hilary of Poitiers	*de Synodis* PL 40, 157	
Hisperica Famina	PL 90. 1185; ed. F.J.H.Jenkinson, Cambridge 1908	
Historians of the Church of York	ed. J.Raine, Rolls 71, 1879–1894	HY
Pope Innocent I	*Epp.* PL 20, 463	
Inscriptiones Latinae Selectae	ed. H.Dessau, Berlin 1902–1915	ILS
INSCRIPTIONS	see CIIC, CIL, Diack, ECMS, ECMW, ILS, RIB; II *Feil-Sgribhinn* 184	
Irenaeus	*adversus Haereseos* PG 7; ed. W.W. Harvey, London 1857; ed. A. Harnack, Leipzig 1907–1910; ed. A.Rousseau and others, Paris 1952	

IRISH LITERATURE editions and translations include

ed. Bergin, Best and others	*Anecdota from Irish Manuscripts* 5 vols. Halle 1907–13	AIM
J. Carney	*Medieval Irish Lyrics* Dublin 1967	
T.P.Cross and C.H.Slover	*Ancient Irish Tales* New York 1936	
J.Fraser and others	*Irish Texts* London 1931–1934	
K.H.Jackson	*A Celtic Miscellany* London 1951 (ed. 1)	
P.W.Joyce	*Old Celtic Romances* Dublin 1879	
A.G.van Hamel	*Immrama* (Voyages) Dublin 1941	
K.Meyer	*The Voyage of Bran* 2 vols. London 1895–1897	
	Selections from Ancient Irish Poetry ed. 2 London 1913	
	The Death Tales of the Ulster Heroes Dublin 1906	
S.H.O'Grady	*Silva Gadelica* (vol. 1 Texts, vol. 2 Translations) London 1892	SG
The Cattle Raid of Cooley	*Táin Bó Cualnge* ed. and translated E.Windisch, Leipzig 1905; J. Dunn, London 1914; C.O'Rahilly Dublin 1967; and others	
Irish Texts Society	Publications, with English translation on facing pages, London 1899–	ITS

WORKS CITED IN THE NOTES: I, SOURCES

Isidore of Seville	PL 81–83; *Chronicon* MGH AA 11; *Etymologiae* also ed. W.M.Lindsay Oxford 1911 (2 vols.)	
Jerome (Hieronymus)	PL 22–30. *Epistulae* CSEL 54–56. *Eusebii Chronicon* also GCS 47 (= 24 and 34); cf. Eusebius, above; *de Viris Inlustribus* also Teubner 1879	
John Cassian	PL 49, 50; *Collationes* CSEL 13; *Institutiones* CSEL 17	
Jordanes	*Getica*; *Romana* MGH AA 5; PL 69, 1251	
G.Keating	*History of Ireland* 1634, MSS; 4 vols. ITS 4, 8, 9, 15 London 1902–1914	
LAWS (see T)	see ALE, ALI, ALW, CTh, Consuetudo West Sexe, Cyfreithiau, Dialogue of Egbert, Collectio Hibernensis, LEEK, Leges, Lex, Liebermann, Schmid	
The Laws of the Earliest English Kings	ed. F.L.Attenborough, Cambridge 1922, reprint New York 1963; cited under the names of the kings who issued the codes	LEEK
Lebor	see Book	
Lebor Bretnach	ed. J.H.Todd *The Irish Version of Nennius* Dublin 1848; *Nennius Interpretatus*, translated into Latin, MGH AA 13, 143 ff.; ed. A.G.van Hamel, Dublin 1932	LB
Lebor na Cert	see Book of Rights	
Lebor Gabála Érenn	ed. R.A.S.MacAlister, 5 vols. ITS 34, 35, 39, 41, 44 Dublin 1938–1956	LG
Leges Saxonum	ed. MGH Leges 5; MGH Fontes 5 (with *Lex Anglorum*)	
J.Leland	*Itinerary* (c. 1540) ed. L.Toulmin Smith, 5 vols. London 1906–10 *Commentarii de Scriptoribus Britanniae* ed. A.Hall, Oxford 1709	
Lex Anglorum et Werinorum, hoc est Thuringorum	see *Leges Saxonum*	
The Irish Liber Hymnorum	ed. J.H.Bernard and R.Atkinson, 2 vols. London, Henry Bradshaw Society 13, 14, 1898; ed. J.H. Todd *The Book of Hymns of the Ancient Church of Ireland* 2 vols. Dublin 1855–1869	LH
Liber Landavensis	J.G.Evans *The Text of the Book of Llan Dâv* Oxford 1893	LL
Liber Pontificalis	ed. L.Duchesne, 2 vols. Paris	

ed. F. Liebermann	1886–1891; ed. T. Mommsen (to 530) MGH GP 1898 *Die Gesetze der Angelsachsen* 3 vols. Halle 1898–1916	
LIVES of the Saints	see *Vitae*	
Loeb Classical Library	with English translation on facing pages, London and New York	
Sir T. Malory	*Le Morte d'Arthur* (completed 1469) Caxton, London 1485; many later editions, especially J. Rhys, reprinted in Everyman's Library 1906	
J. D. Mansi	*Sacrorum Conciliorum nova et amplissima Collectio* 1759; facsimile, Paris and Leipzig 1901	
Marcellinus Comes	*Chronicon* MGH AA 11, 60 ff.	
MARTYROLOGIES (see T) of		M
Donegal	ed. J. H. Todd and W. Reeves, Dublin 1864	
Gormán	ed. W. Stokes, London 1895	
Oengus the Culdee	ed. W. Stokes, London 1905 (often called the *Félire of Oengus*)	
Tallaght	ed. R. I. Best and H. J. Lawlor, London 1931	
Monumenta Historica Britannica	ed. H. Petrie and J. Sharpe, London 1848	MHB
Monumenta Germaniae Historica	ed. G. H. Pertz, T. Mommsen and others, Hannover, Berlin, 1826– AA: Auctores Antiquissimi Diplomata GP: Gesta Pontificum PLAC: Poetae Latini Aevi Carolini SS: Scriptores SRG: SS Rerum Germanicarum SRL: SS Rerum Langobardorum SRM: SS Rerum Merovingicarum	MGH
L. A. Muratori	*Rerum Italicarum Scriptores* Milan 1786; ed. R. Cessi, Città di Castello 1913	RIS
Nennius	*Historia Britonum* ed. T. Mommsen MGH AA 13 (*Chronica Minora* 3) 143 ff.; ed. E. Faral *La Légende Arthurienne* (Bibliothèque de l'Ecole des Hautes Etudes 237) 3 vols. Paris 1929, vol. 3; ed. and translated J. Morris, Chichester 1980; see also LB	
Notitia Dignitatum (see T)	ed. O. Seeck, Berlin 1876, reprint Frankfurt-am-Main 1962	Not. Dig.
The Oldest English Texts	ed. H. Sweet EETS 83 London 1885	OET

T*

WORKS CITED IN THE NOTES : 1, SOURCES

Olympiodorus	*Fragments* FHG 4
Ordericus Vitalis	*Historia Ecclesiastica* ed. A. le Prévost, Paris 1838–1855; PL 188; translated T.Forester, London 1853–1856; M. Chibnall 1969–80
Origen	PG 11–17; *Homilies on Luke and Ezekiel* (and others) Latin translation by Jerome, PL 25, 691; 26, 229; GCS 9; ed. H.Crouzel and R.Girod, Paris (Sources chrétiennes 87) 1962
Orosius	ed. Teubner, 1889; CSEL 5; PL 31
Pachomius	*Regula*, translated into Latin by Jerome PL 23, 275; cf. *Pachomiana Latina* ed. A.Boon, Louvain 1932
Panegyrici Latini	*Panégyriques latins* ed. and translated É.Galletier, 3 vols. Paris 1949–55
Patrick (see T)	*Confessio; Epistula ad Coroticum* VT 357–380; ed. N.J.D.White PRIA 25 C 7 1905; ed. L.Bieler, Dublin 1952; ed. and translated A.B.E. Hood, Chichester 1978
Patrologia Graeca	ed. J.Migne, Paris 1857–66 (161 vols.) PG
Patrologia Latina	ed. J.Migne, Paris 1844–64 (221 vols.) PL
Paul the Deacon	*Historia Langobardorum* MGH SRL 45; translated W.D.Foulke, Philadelphia 1907
Paulinus of Pella	*Eucharisticus* CSEL 16, 291; Ausonius, ed. Loeb, vol. 2
Pelagius	*Commentary on the Pauline Epistles* PL Sup. 1, 1110 ff.
Pennant	T.Pennant *A Tour in Wales MDLXX* 3 vols. London 1778–83 TW
Pliny	*Natural History* ed. Teubner, 1875–1906 NH
Priscus	*Fragments* FHG 4
Procopius	*de Bello Gothico; de Bello Vandalico* BG ed. Teubner, CSHB, Loeb etc. BV
Prosper of Aquitaine	*Contra Collatorem* PL 51, 213 *Chronica* MGH AA 9 (*Chronica Minora* 1)
Prudentius	*Peri Stephanon* PL 60, 275
Regesta Regum Scottorum	ed. G.W.S.Barrow, Edinburgh 1960–
The Roman Inscriptions of Britain	ed. R.G.Collingwood and R.P. Wright, Oxford 1965– RIB
Rufinus	*Historia Ecclesiastica* PL 21 HE
SAINTS' LIVES	see *Vitae*
Salvian	*de Gubernatione Dei* CSEL 8; MGH AA 1

Sanas Chormaic	see Cormac *Glossary*	
The Saxon Chronicle (see A)	Rolls, 23, 1861, ed. B.Thorpe; MHB 291; ed. J.Earle, Oxford 1865; revised C.Plummer, 2 vols. 1892–1899; D.Whitelock and others, translation 1961; translated G.N. Garmonsway, Everyman's Library 1953	SC
ed. R.Schmid	*Die Gesetze der Angelsachsen* Leipzig 1822, ed. 2, 1858	
Scotichronicon	(Walter Bower's revision (1437) of Fordun) ed. W.Goodall, Edinburgh 1759; T. Hearne, Oxford 1722	
Scottish Annals from English Chroniclers	transl. A.O.Anderson, London 1908	SAEC
SCOTTISH HISTORY	see Boece, CPS, ESSH, Fordun, Regesta Regum, Scotichronicon, SAEC, STS, Wyntoun	
Scottish Texts Society	Publications, Edinburgh 1883–	STS
Scriptores Rerum Anglicarum	ed. T.Gale and W.Fulman, 3 vols. Oxford 1689–1691	SRA
Senchus Fer nAlban	Skene CPS 308; *Celtica* 7, 1966, 154 ff.; cf. 8, 1967, 90 ff.; 9, 1968, 217 ff., etc.	
Sicilian Briton	ed. C.P.Caspari *Briefe, Abhandlungen und Predigten* Christiania 1890; PL Sup. I (*Ep*. 1, col. 1687; other works 1375 ff.; cf. JTS 16, 1965, 26 ff.); translated R.S.T. Haslehurst *The Works of Fastidius* Westminster, Society of SS Peter and Paul, 1927	
Sidonius Apollinaris	*Carmina*; *Epistulae* MGH AA 8; ed. Teubner, etc.	
Simeon of Durham	*Opera Omnia* 2 vols. Rolls 75, 1882–1885; MHB 645; CHE 5; AHS	SD
Solinus	*Collectanea* ed. Mommsen, Berlin 1864; ed. 2 1895; cf. II Walter	
Suetonius	*The Twelve Caesars* ed. Teubner, Loeb etc.	
Sulpicius Severus	*Chronica*; *Dialogi*; *vita Martini* CSEL I	
Symmachus	*Epistulae*; *Orationes*; *Relationes* MGH AA 6	
Tacitus	*Agricola*; *Annals* ed. Teubner, Loeb etc.	Tac. Ann.
Tertullian	*adversus Iudaeos* CSEL 20; PL 2; ed. A.L.Williams, Cambridge 1935; ed. F.Oehler, Leipzig 1854	
Teubner	*Bibliotheca Scriptorum Graecorum et Romanorum*, Leipzig	

WORKS CITED IN THE NOTES: I, SOURCES

The Tribal Hidage (see T)	BCS 297; Rolls 2 ii, 1861, 626; cf. vol. 5 below.	
Translatio Sancti Alexandri	MGH SS 2, 673	
Trioedd Ynys Prydein	ed. R.Bromwich, Cardiff 1961; cf. WHR Special Number 1963, 82	TYP
Victor of Aquitaine	MGH AA 9 (*Chronica Minora* 1) 686 ff.	
Victricius	*de Laude Sanctorum* PL 20, 443	
de Virginitate	Jerome Ep. 13 (PL 30, 162 = 18, 77 = 20, 227 = 103, 671)	

VITAE SANCTORUM (Saints' Lives)
see E for full references
see also II Dedications

COLLECTIONS OF LIVES

i General

Acta Sanctorum	Brussels 1643–	ASS
Analecta Bollandiana	Brussels 1882–	AB
Breviarium Aberdonense	Aberdeen 1509–1510; facsimile London 1854; *Pars Estivalis*, and *Pars Hyemalis*	Brev. Ab. PE, PH

See also BHL; CSEL; GCS; MGH; PG; PL

ii Ireland and Scotland
(a) Latin Lives

Acta Sanctorum Hiberniae 1	ed. J.Colgan, Louvain 1645, reprint Dublin 1948	ASH
Trias Thaumaturga	(Patrick, Brigit, Columba) ed. J. Colgan, Louvain 1647	TT
Vitae Sanctorum Hiberniae e codice Salmanticensi	ed. C.de Smedt and J.de Backer, Brussels 1887; ed. W.W.Heist, (*Subsidia Hagiographica* 28), Brussels 1965. (References are here given to the columns)	Sal.
Vitae Sanctorum Hiberniae	ed. C.Plummer, Oxford 1910 (2 vols.)	VSH
Lives of the Scottish Saints	ed. J.Pinkerton, London 1789, revised W.M.Metcalfe, 2 vols. Paisley 1889	Pinkerton
The Tripartite Life of Saint Patrick	ed. W.Stokes, Rolls 89, 2 vols. 1887 (*Vita Tripartita*); collection of principal Patrician texts	VT

(b) Irish Language Lives

Lives of the Saints from the Book of Lismore	ed. W.Stokes, Oxford 1890 (with translation)	Lismore Lives
Bethada Náem nÉrenn (Lives of Irish Saints; in Irish)	ed. C.Plummer, Oxford 1922 (2 vols. with translation)	BNE
Miscellanea Hagiographica Hibernica	ed. C.Plummer (*Subsidia Hagiographica* 15) Brussels 1925	MHH

See also LH; Martyrologies; O'Hanlon

iii Wales
Vitae Sanctorum Britanniae et Genealogiae   ed. A.W. Wade-Evans, Cardiff 1944   VSBG

    See also Doble, LBS

iv Brittany
Les Vies des Saints de Bretagne   ed. A. Le Grand, Morlaix 1636; revised edition, Rennes 1901   AG

    See also Cartulaires; Doble; LBS

v England
Nova Legenda Anglie   collected by John of Tynemouth, c.1340, and John Capgrave, c.1440, ed. Wynkyn de Worde, 1516; ed. C. Horstman, 2 vols. Oxford 1901   NLA

    See also individual Lives below, BHL and E

vi Gaul
Vitae Sanctorum   MGH SRM 3–7, 1896–1920
Vitae Patrum and *de Gloria Confessorum*   Gregory of Tours MGH SRM 1, 661
Vitae Sanctorum   in Venantius Fortunatus MGH AA 4

    See also Individual Lives below, BHL and E

INDIVIDUAL LIVES

Normally only the principal versions are given; page references are not normally given to collections arranged in alphabetical order. The symbol † indicates that the Life is translated in one of the Collections cited below: for full references see E.

ABBÁN	VSH
AILBE	VSH
ADOMNÁN	CPS 408; cf. MHH 179, 2; AIM 2, 10; CR 5, 1908, 97
ALBINUS of Angers	by Venantius MGH 4, 2, 27; PL 88, 479
AMBROSE of Milan	by Paulinus PL 14, 27†
BEUNO	VSBG; *Arch. Camb.* 1930, 315
BONIFACE	by Willibald PL 89, 603; MGH SS 2, 333; MGH SRG Schol., 1905, 1†
BRENDAN	VSH; cf. C. Selmer *Navigatio Sancti Brendani* Notre Dame, Indiana, 1959†
BRIGIT	TT
CADOC (CADOG)	by Lifris VSBG†; by Caradoc of Llancarfan AB 60, 1942, 45
CADROE	ASS Mart 1, 474; ASH 494; cf. CPS 106, MGH SS 4, 483
CAINNECH	VSH
CARANTOC (CARANNOG)	VSBG†
CIARÁN of Clonmacnoise	VSH
CIARÁN of Saigir	VSH; BNE; Sal. 805†
COLUMBA of Iona	by Adomnán, ed. W. Reeves, Dublin 1857; also

	A.O. and M.O.Anderson, Edinburgh 1961; J.T.Fowler, Oxford 1894
	by M.O'Donnell TT 389; ZCP 3–5 and 9–11, 1901–1905, 1913–1916; ed. A.O'Kelleher and G.Schoepperle, Urbana, Illinois, 1918
COLUMBA of Terryglass	Sal. 445; cf. AB 72, 1954, 343
COLUMBAN	by Jonas MGH SRM 4, 1
CUTHBERT	by Bede, ed. B.Colgrave *Two Lives of St. Cuthbert* Cambridge 1940†
DAGAEUS	Sal. 891
DAVID	VSBG; ed. J.W.James, Cardiff 1967
DECLAN	VSH; ITS 16
DOCCO	NLA 1, 248; cf. AB 42, 1942, 100; JTS 20, 1918/19, 97, cf. 23, 1921/22, 15
DUBRICIUS (DYFRIG)	LL 78
ÉNDA	ASH 704; VSH
FINGAR	AG 812; ASS March 3, 454; ASH 387, cf. PL 159, 325
FINNIAN of Clonard	Sal. 189; ASH 393
FINNIAN of Llancarfan	vita Finnian Clonard, ch. 4–11
FINNIAN of Moville	ASH 634; NLA 1, 444; cf. LH 1, 22; 2, 11
FLANNÁN	Sal. 643; AB 46, 1928, 122
FURSEY	Sal. ASH 75; cf. NLA 1, 461, Sal. 77 (Fursey's Vision)
GERALD of Mayo	VSH
GERMANUS of Auxerre	by Constantius MGH SRM 7, 259 (ch. 12–18, 25–27 transcribed by Bede HE 1, 17–21)†
	by Heiric MGH PLAC 3, 421
GILDAS	by Caradoc of Llancarfan, and by a monk of Rhuys MGH AA 13, 91; Williams *Gildas* 322 ff.
GUTHLAC	by Felix, ed. B.Colgrave, Cambridge 1956; ASS April 2, 38; ed. W.de G.Birch, Wisbech 1881
GWENAEL	ASS Nov. 1, 674; AG 670
GWYNLLYW	VSBG†
ÍBAR	AB 77, 1959, 439; cf. Abbán
ILLTUD	VSBG†
ÍTA	VSH
IUDICAEL	AG 819; cf. Meven
IUDOC	AG 806; Ordericus 3, 13
JOHN THE ALMSGIVER	AB 45, 1927, 19; PG 93, 1614; PL 73, 337; translation E.Dawes and N.Baynes, London, 1948
KEBI (CYBI)	VSBG†
KENTIGERN	by Jocelyn of Furness, Pinkerton 2, 1
LASRIAN (Mo-Laisse) of Devenish	VSH
LEBUINUS	by Hucbald, MGH SS 2, 361; PL 132, 627 ff., 875 ff.†
LEONORUS	ASS July 1, 121 (107)
MARTIN of Tours	by Sulpicius Severus CSEL 1†
MELOR	AB 5, 1886, 166; NLA 2, 183
MEVEN	AB 3, 1884, 142
MOCTEUS	Sal. 903
NINIAN	by Ailred, Pinkerton 1, 9; NLA 2, 218; AHS
OUDOCEUS (EUDDOGWY)	LL 130
PATERNUS (PADARN)	VSBG†

PATRICK (see also T)	by Muirchú, VT 269; AB 1, 1882, 545; PRIA 52 C 1948/50, 179; *Patrick*, ed. Hood, Chichester, 1978 by Tírechán, VT 302; AB 2, 1883, 35 *Bethu Phátraic*, VT 2; ed. K.Mulchrone, Dublin 1939 by Probus, TT 51 other Lives, TT 1 ff. see Kenney 319 ff.; Bieler CPL 16 ff.
PAUL AURELIAN	RC 5, 1881–1883, 417; AB 1, 1882, 209; cf. ASS March 2, 111 (probably by Vitalis of Fleury).
PETROC	AB 74, 1956, 145; NLA 2, 317
RUADÁN	VSH
SAMSON	I: ASS July 6, 573; ed. R. Fawtier *La Vie de S. Samson*, Paris (Bibliothèque de l'Ecole des Hautes Etudes 197) 1912; translation T.Taylor, London 1925 II: AB 6, 1887, 79, cf. 12, 1893, 56 III, by Baldric: cited in II above IV: AG 409 V: LL 6 VI: NLA 2, 350
SENÁN	Sal.
SEVERINUS	by Eugippius MGH AA 1, 1; SRG 1898; CSEL 9, 2; PL 62, 1167: translation G.W.Robinson, Harvard 1914
TATHEUS	VSBG†
TEILO	LL 97
WENEFRED	VSBG†
WILFRED	by Eddius Stephanus MGH SRM 6; HY 1; ed. B.Colgrave, Cambridge 1927†
WINNOC	(with Audomar) MGH SRM 5, 753; MGH SS 15, 775; cf. PL 147, 1179 ff.
WINWALOE	AB 7, 1888, 172

NAMED AUTHORS OF SAINTS' LIVES

Adomnán	COLUMBA of Iona	Muirchú	PATRICK
Ailred	NINIAN	O'Donell	COLUMBA
Animosus	BRIGIT	Paulinus	AMBROSE
Bede	CUTHBERT	Probus	PATRICK
Caradoc of Llancarfan	CADOC, GILDAS	Ricemarchus	DAVID
Cogitosus	BRIGIT	Stephanus	WILFRED
Constantius	GERMANUS	Sulpicius Severus	MARTIN
Eddius: see Stephanus		Tírechán	PATRICK
Eugippius	SEVERINUS	Ultán	BRIGIT
Felix	GUTHLAC	Vitalis	PAUL AURELIAN
Heiric	GERMANUS	Willebald	BONIFACE
Jocelyn of Furness	KENTIGERN	Wrdesten	WINWALOE
Jonas	COLUMBAN	Wrmonoc	PAUL AURELIAN
Lifris	CADOC		

WORKS CITED IN THE NOTES : 1, SOURCES

COLLECTIONS IN TRANSLATION include VSBG; BNE: Lismore; C.W.Jones *Saints' Lives and Chronicles in Early England* Cornell 1947; J.F.Webb *Lives of the Saints* (Brendan, Cuthbert, Wilfred) Penguin, 1965; F.R.Hoare *The Western Fathers* (Martin, Ambrose, Augustine of Hippo, Honoratus, Germanus) London 1954; C.H.Talbot *Anglo-Saxon Missionaries in Germany* (Willibrord, Boniface, Sturm, Leoba, Lebuin) London 1954.

WELSH LITERATURE

ANCIENT POEMS (see **T**)

J.G.Evans	*The Book of Aneirin* Pwllheli 1908	BA
	The Black Book of Carmarthen Pwllheli 1906	BBC
	The Text of the Book of Taliesin Llanbedrog 1910	BT
	Poetry from the Red Book of Hergest Llanbedrog 1911	RBH
K.H.Jackson	*Early Welsh Gnomic Poems* Cardiff 1935; ed. 2, 1961	
A.O.H.Jarman	*Ymddiddan Myrddin a Thaliesin* Cardiff 1951	
W.F.Skene	*Four Ancient Books of Wales* 2 vols. Edinburgh 1868	FAB
Ifor Williams	*Canu Aneirin* Cardiff 1938	CA
	Canu Llywarch Hen Cardiff 1935	CLH
	Canu Taliesin Cardiff 1960	CT
	Armes Prydein Cardiff 1955	AP
	Chwedl Taliesin Cardiff 1957	

BRUTIAU

J.G.Evans	*Bruts from the Red Book of Hergest* Oxford 1890
	cf. *Brut y Tywysogion* Myv. Arch. 685; MHB 841; Rolls 17, 1860

MABINOGION

J.G.Evans	*The White Book Mabinogion* Pwllheli 1907
	Pedeir Keinc y Mabinogi Wrexham 1897
J.G.Evans and J.Rhys	*The Text of the Mabinogion from the Red Book of Hergest* Oxford 1887
Ifor Williams	*Pedeir Keinc y Mabinogi* (The Four Branches of the Mabinogion, from the White Book of Rhydderch) Cardiff 1930; cf. THS Cymm 1970, 263

TRANSLATIONS include		
Lady Charlotte Guest	*The Mabinogion* text and translation, London 1849, translation reprinted 1877 and Everyman's Library where replaced by	
Gwyn Jones and Thomas Jones	*The Mabinogion* London 1949 (ed. 2), reprinted in Everyman's library	
K.H.Jackson	*The Gododdin* Edinburgh 1969 (translation of CA)	
ANTHOLOGIES include		
E.Williams (Iolo Morgannwg) and others	*The Myvyrian Archaeology of Wales* London 1801; reprint Denbigh 1870 (based on medieval MSS)	Myv. Arch.
T.Williams (Taliesin ab Iolo)	*Iolo Manuscripts* Liverpool 1848, reprint 1888 (almost entirely forged)	Iolo MSS
H.I. and C.I.Bell	*Poems from the Welsh* Caernarfon 1913	
	Welsh Poems of the Twentieth Century in English Verse Wrexham 1925	
A. Conran	*The Penguin Book of Welsh Verse* London 1967	
A.P.Graves	*Welsh Poetry Old and New in English Verse* London 1912	
E.A.Jones	*Welsh Lyrics of the Nineteenth Century* Newport 1907	
ed. T.Parry	*The Oxford Book of Welsh Verse* Oxford 1962	
Gwyn Williams	*The Burning Tree* London 1956	WBT
	Presenting Welsh Poetry London 1959	PWP

Widsith	ed. K.Malone, London 1936, etc.	
William of Malmesbury	PL 179; *de Gestis Regum* Rolls 90, 1887–1889; *de Gestis Pontificum* Rolls 52, 1870	
Anglo-Saxon Wills	ed. D.Whitelock, Cambridge 1930	ASWi
Anglo-Saxon Writs	ed. F.E.Harmer, Manchester 1952	ASWr
Andrew of Wyntoun	*Original Chronicle of Scotland* ed. F.J.Amours, 6 vols. STS 63, 50, 53, 54, 56, 57, Edinburgh 1903–1914	
Zonaras	*Epitome Historiarum* ed. Teubner; PL 134	
Zosimus	*Historia Nova* ed. L.Mendelsohn, Leipzig, 1887; CSHB ed. B.G. Niebuhr, Bonn 1837 etc.	

11 Modern Works

* Lists of further books and articles are contained in several of the works cited, especially in those marked with a star (*).

* Nils Åberg *The Anglo-Saxons in England* Uppsala 1926   ASE
  L.Alcock *Dinas Powys* Cardiff 1963
  L.Alcock *Arthur's Britain* London 1971 (ed. 1)
  A.O.Anderson, see 1 ESSH
  Angles and Britons (O'Donnell Lectures) Cardiff 1963
  F.Arnold Forster *Studies in Church Dedications* 3 vols. London 1899   SCD

  A.Bach *Deutsche Namenkunde: II, die deutschen Ortsnamen* 2 vols. Heidelberg 1953–1954
* G.Baldwin Brown *The Arts in Early England*, especially vol. 3, London 1915   BB
  S.Baring-Gould *A Book of Brittany* London 1901
  S.Baring-Gould and J.Fisher *The Lives of the British Saints* 4 vols. London, 1907–1913   LBS
* F.W. Bateson *The Cambridge Bibliography of English Literature* Vol. 1 Cambridge 1940
* A.C.Baugh *A History of the English Language* London 1935, ed. 2, 1951
* A.C.Baugh *A Literary History of England* New York and London 1940, reprint 1950
* H.I.Bell *The Development of Welsh Poetry* Oxford 1936
  Bibliotheca Hagiographica Latina 2 vols. Brussels 1898–1901; supplement Brussels 1986 (*Subsidia Hagiographica* 70)   BHL
  L.Bieler *Codices Patriciani Latini* Dublin 1942   CPL
  E.G.Bowen *The Settlements of the Celtic Saints in Wales* Cardiff 1954 (ed. 1)   SCSW
  J.Brøndsted *Danmarks Oldtid: II, Jernalderen* Copenhagen 1940
  J.B.Bury *The Life of Saint Patrick* London 1905

  W.Camden *Britannia* London 1586; ed. Gibson 1772; ed. R.Gough 1789; also ed. Holland 1610
* J.Carney *The Problem of St. Patrick* Dublin 1961
  J.Carney *Studies in Irish Literature and History* Dublin 1955 (ed. 1)   SILH
  C.P.Caspari *Briefe*: see 1 Sicilian Briton
  Celt and Saxon ed. N.K.Chadwick 1963; rev. imp. 1964
  H.M.Chadwick *Early Scotland* Cambridge 1949
  H.M.Chadwick *Origin of the English Nation* Cambridge 1924 (ed. 2)   OEN
  H.M.Chadwick *Studies in Anglo-Saxon Institutions* Cambridge 1905   SASI
  H.M. and N.K.Chadwick *The Growth of Literature* Cambridge 1932–1940
  N.K.Chadwick *The Druids* Cardiff 1966
  N.K.Chadwick *Poetry and Letters in Early Christian Gaul* London 1955   PLECG
  N.K.Chadwick, ed. see *Celt and Saxon*; *Studies*
* R.W.Chambers *Beowulf* Cambridge 1932
  Christianity in Britain 300–700 ed. M.W.Barley and R.P.C.Hanson, Leicester 1968
  The Civitas Capitals of Roman Britain ed. J.S.Wacher, Leicester 1966
* R.R.Clarke *East Anglia* London 1960
  R.Collingwood and J.N.L.Myres *Roman Britain and the English Settlements* Oxford 1937 (ed. 2)
  Fustel de Coulanges *La Monarchuie Franque* Paris 1888

S.E.Cruden *The Early Christian and Pictish Monuments of Scotland* (HMSO)   ECPMS
    Edinburgh 1957, ed. 2, 1964
A.O.Curle *The Treasure of Traprain* Glasgow 1923

Dark Age Britain (Studies presented to E.T.Leeds) ed. D.B.Harden, London   DAB
    1956
Dark Age Dates John Morris, see Jarrett and Dobson pp. 145 ff.
P.David *Etudes historiques sur la Galice et le Portugal* Lisbon 1947
E.Davies, ed. *Celtic Studies in Wales* Cardiff 1963   CSW
P.Delamain *La cimetière barbare d'Herpes* Angoulême 1892
Dictionary of English Place-Names ed. E.Ekwall, Oxford 1936; ed. 4, 1960   DEPN
Dictionary of Christian Biography ed. W.Smith and H.Wace, 4 vols. London   DCB
    1877–1887
* M.Dillon and N.K.Chadwick *The Celtic Realms* London 1967, ed. 2, 1972
G.H.Doble *Dedications to Celtic Saints in Normandy* in *Old Cornwall* Summer
    1940, 1 ff.
G.H.Doble *The Saints of Cornwall*, 48 booklets, 1923–1944, republished in
    5 vols. Truro 1960–70 (incomplete)
C.Du Cange *Glossarium Mediae et Infimae Latinitatis* Paris, Niort etc. 1772,
    1844, 1886, etc.
L.Duchesne *Fastes Episcopaux de l'ancienne Gaule* 3 vols. Paris 1907–1915
W.Dugdale *Monasticon Anglicanum* 3 vols. London 1655–1673; ed. 2, 6 vols.
    London 1817–1830
F.Duine *Saint Samson* Rennes 1909
F.Duine *Notes sur les saints bretons* Rennes 1902

M.Ebert (ed.) *Reallexikon der Vorgeschichte* 15 vols. Berlin 1924–32   RV
H.J.Eggers *Der römische Import im freien Germanien* (Atlas der Urgeschichte 1)
    Hamburg 1951
E.Ekwall *English River-names* Oxford 1928   ERN
T.P.Ellis *Welsh Tribal Law and Custom in the Middle Ages* 2 vols. Oxford 1926
English Place-Name Elements A.H.Smith EPNS 25–26 Cambridge 1956   EPNE
English Place-Name Society Survey by counties, Cambridge 1924 –   EPNS
  The counties published are Beds., Bucks., Cambs., Cheshire, Cumberland,
  Derby, Devon, Essex, Gloucester, Hertfordshire, Hunts., Middlesex,
  Northants., Notts., Oxon., Surrey, Sussex, Warwick, Westmorland,
  Wiltshire, Worcestershire, Yorkshire. (More published since 1973.)
  Other studies of counties not yet published in the Survey include *Berkshire*
    W.W.Skeat, Oxford 1911; *Dorset* A Fägersten, Uppsala 1933; *Durham* see
    Northumberland; *Herefordshire* A.J.Bannister, Cambridge 1916; *Isle of
    Wight* H.Kökeritz, Uppsala 1940; *Kent* J.K.Wallenberg, Uppsala 1931,   PNK
    1934; *Lancashire* E.Ekwall, Manchester 1922; *Northumberland and Durham*
    A.Mawer, Cambridge 1920; *Shropshire* E.W.Bowcock, Shrewsbury 1923;
    Staffordshire H.Duignan, London 1902; *Suffolk* W.W.Skeat, Cambridge
    1913.
  Most of these studies are less comprehensive than the Survey volumes.
  The counties for which no considerable published survey is available are
    Cornwall, Hampshire, Leicestershire (cf. Philological Society Transactions
    1917–1920, 57–78), Lincolnshire, Norfolk, Rutland and Somerset.
  For place-names in France, see Gröhler; in Germany, see Bach; Scandina-
    vian names have been extensively studied, but virtually no work has
    been done on Slavonic place-names, save for a few isolated regions of Germany.

Excavations at Richborough 5, SAL Report 23, Oxford 1968

E.Faral *La Légende Arthurienne* 3 vols. (Bibliothèque de l'Ecole des Hautes Etudes 257) Paris 1929
Feil-Sgribhinn Eoin mhic Néill (MacNeill Essays) Dublin 1940 (ed. J. Ryan)
H.P.R.Finberg *The Agrarian History of England* Vol. 1, pt 2, 1972
H.P.R.Finberg *Lucerna* London 1964; see also 1 Charters
A.P.Forbes *Kalendars of the Scottish Saints* Edinburgh 1872
Sir Cyril Fox *The Personality of Britain* Cardiff 1932; ed. 4, 1943
Sir Cyril Fox *The Archaeology of the Cambridge Region* Cambridge 1923, revised 1948   ACR
* S.S.Frere *Britannia* London 1967 (ed. 1)

* A. Genrich *Formenkreise und Stammesgruppen in Schleswig-Holstein* Neumünster 1954
R.L.Green *King Arthur* Puffin Story Books 1955
S.B.Greenfield *A Critical History of Old English Literature* New York 1965, London 1966 (reprint 1968)
H.Gröhler *Ursprung und Bedeutung der französischen Ortsnamen* Heidelberg 1913–1937

* Isabel Henderson *The Picts* London 1967
T.Hodgkin *Italy and her Invaders* 8 vols. Oxford 1880–1899
E.Hogan *Onomasticon Goedelicum* Dublin 1910
W.G.Hoskins *The Westward Expansion of Wessex* Leicester 1960   WEW
V.Hruby *Staré Mesto* (Monumenta Archaeologica 14) Prague 1965
* K.Hughes *The Church in Early Irish Society* London 1966   CEIS
M.R.Hull *Roman Colchester* SAL Report 20, Colchester 1957

K.H.Jackson *Language and History in Early Britain* Edinburgh 1953   LHEB
K.H.Jackson *The Oldest Irish Tradition; a Window on the Iron Age* (Rede Lecture) Cambridge 1964   OIT
K.H.Jackson *The International Popular Tale* (Gregynog Lecture) Cardiff 1961
H.Jankuhn *Geschichte Schleswig-Holsteins* 3 vols. Hamburg 1957
M.G.Jarrett and B.Dobson (ed.) *Britain and Rome* (Essays Presented to Eric Birley) Kendal 1966
H.Jedin and others *Atlas zur Kirchengeschichte* Freiburg-im-Breisgau 1970
E.John *Land Tenure in Early England* Leicester 1960
J.E.A.Jolliffe *Pre-Feudal England* Oxford 1933, reprint 1962   PFE
* A.H.M.Jones *The Later Roman Empire* 4 vols. Oxford 1964   LRE
P.W.Joyce *A Social History of Ancient Ireland* 3 vols. Dublin 1913

J.M.Kemble *The Saxons in England* London 1848, revised edition ed. W.de G. Birch 1876 (2 vols.)   SE
T.Kendrick *The Druids* London 1928
J.F.Kenney *The Sources for the Early History of Ireland* 1, Ecclesiastical (all published), New York 1929, revised reprint New York 1966
W.P.Ker *The Dark Ages* London 1904, reprint New York 1958
D.Knowles *Great Historical Enterprises* London 1963
* M.L.W. Laistner *Thought and Letters in Western Europe* London 1931 (ed. 1)
E.T.Leeds *The Archaeology of the Anglo-Saxon Settlements* Oxford 1913   AASS
E.T.Leeds *A Corpus of Anglo-Saxon Great Squareheaded Brooches* Oxford 1949

E.T.Leeds *The Distribution of Anglo-Saxon Saucer Brooches* in *Arch.* 63   DSB
    1911/12, 159 ff.
Lefebvre des Noëttes *L'Attelage et le Cheval* Paris 1931
* J.E.Lloyd *History of Wales* 2 vols. London 1912 (ed. 2)   HW
* H.R.Loyn *Anglo-Saxon England and the Norman Conquest* London 1962
* E.Löfstedt *Philologische Kommentar zur Peregrinatio Aetheriae* Darmstadt 1962

* J.M.MacKinlay *Ancient Church Dedications in Scotland* 2 vols. Edinburgh   ACDS
    1910–1914
Eoin MacNeill *Celtic Ireland* Dublin 1921 (ed. 1)
Eoin MacNeill *Phases of Irish History* Dublin 1919
MacNeill Essays see *Feil-Sgribhinn*
* *Magna Moravia* University of Brno, Faculty of Philosophy Publications 102,
    Prague 1965
F.W. Maitland *Domesday Book and Beyond* Cambridge 1897, reprint (Fontana)   DBB
    London 1960
* M.Manitius *Geschichte der lateinischen Literatur des Mittelalters* 3 vols. Munich
    1911–1931
H.I.Marrou *A History of Education in Antiquity* London 1956
H.I.Marrou *St. Augustin et la fin de la culture antique*, ed. 2 Paris 1958
C.L.Matthews *Ancient Dunstable* Dunstable 1963
* A.Meaney *Gazetteer of Early Anglo-Saxon Burial Sites* London 1964
* R.Merrifield *The Roman City of London* London 1965
K.Meyer *Learning in Ireland in the Fifth Century* Dublin 1913
C.de Montalembert *Les Moines d'Occident* 7 vols. Paris 1860; English edition,
    The Monks of the West London 1861
J.Morris *The Age of Arthur* London 1973   Age
* L. Musset *Les Invasions, les Vagues germaniques* (Nouvelle Cleo 12) Paris 1965
J.N.L.Myres *Romano-Saxon Pottery* DAB 66 ff.
* J.N.L.Myres *Anglo-Saxon Pottery* Oxford 1969   ASP

Eugene O'Curry *Lectures on the Manuscript Materials of Ancient Irish History*
    2 vols. Dublin 1861
J.O'Hanlon *Lives of the Irish Saints* 10 vols. Dublin 1875–1903
T.F.O'Rahilly *The Two Patricks* Dublin 1942
T.F.O'Rahilly *Early Irish History and Mythology* Dublin 1946   EIHM
Ordnance Survey *Map of Dark Age Britain* ed. 1, Southampton 1936; ed. 2,
    Chessington 1966
Ordnance Survey *Map of Roman Britain* ed. 3, Chessington 1956
* A.Ll.Owen *The Famous Druids* Oxford 1962

* T.Parry (translated H.I.Bell) *A History of Welsh Literature* Oxford 1962   HWL
S.Pender *Essays and Studies presented to Tadhg Ua Donnchadha* Cork 1947
G.de Plinval *Pélage* Lausanne 1943
* A.Plettke *Ursprung und Ausbreitung der Angeln und Sachsen* Hildesheim 1921
* F.Pollock and F.W. Maitland *History of English Law* Cambridge 1895; ed. 2
    1898, revised 1968
H.Preidel *Slawische Altertumskunde des Ostlaender Mitteleuropas in den 9ten
    und 10ten Jahrhunderten* Munich 1961
* *The Prosopography of the Later Roman Empire* ed. A.H.M.Jones, J.R.Martindale,   PLRE
    J.Morris, Cambridge, 3 vols.

Recueil de Travaux offerts à M. Clovis Brunel Paris 1955
* A.L.F. Rivet (ed.) *The Iron Age in Northern Britain* Edinburgh 1966 — IANB
J.H. Round *Studies in Peerage and Family History* London 1901
Royal Commission on Historical Monuments, County Series — RCHM

* B. Salin *Die altgermanische Tierornamentik* Stockholm and Berlin 1904
* E. Salin *La Civilisation Mérovingienne* 4 vols. Paris 1949–1959
* P.H. Sawyer *Anglo-Saxon Charters* London 1968 (RHS Handbook 8)
L. Schmidt *Allgemeine Geschichte der germanischen Völker* Munich and Berlin 1909
G. Schoepperle *Tristan and Isolt* Frankfurt and London 1913
F. Seebohm *The English Village Community* London 1883 (ed. 1) — EVC
F. Seebohm *The Tribal System in Wales* London 1904 (ed. 2) — TSW
F. Seebohm *Tribal Custom in Anglo-Saxon Law* London 1911 (ed. 2) — TCASL
R.C. Shaw *Post-Roman Carlisle* Preston 1964
W.D. Simpson *The Celtic Church in Scotland* Aberdeen 1935
W.F. Skene *Celtic Scotland* 3 vols. Edinburgh 1876–1880 (ed. 1) — CS
W.F. Skene, cf. 1 CPS above
T.C. Smout *A History of the Scottish People 1560–1830* London 1969
* F.M. Stenton *Anglo-Saxon England* Oxford 1943 (ed. 1) — ASE
C.E. Stevens *Sidonius Apollinaris and his Age* Oxford 1933
Studies in the Early British Church ed. N.K. Chadwick, Cambridge 1958 — SEBC
Studies in Early British History ed. N.K. Chadwick, Cambridge 1959 (ed. 2) — SEBH
* B. Svoboda *Čechy v Době Stehování Národů* (Bohemia in the Migration Period) (Monumenta Archaeologica 13) Prague 1965

R.J. Thomas et al. *Geiriadur Prifysgol Cymru* Cardiff 1950– — GPC
E.A. Thompson *The Early Germans* Oxford 1965
R. Thurneysen and others *Studies in Early Irish Law* Dublin 1936 — SEIL
F. Tischler *Der Stand der Sachsenforschung* (35 Bericht der Römisch-Germanischen Kommission) 1956, 21 ff.
J.H. Todd *St. Patrick, Apostle of Ireland* Dublin 1864
Torna Festschrift see Pender

Victoria County History of the Counties of England, County Volumes — VCH
P. Vinogradoff *The Growth of the Manor* London 1911 (ed. 2) — GM

* F.T. Wainwright (ed.) *The Problem of the Picts* Edinburgh 1955 (ed. 1) — PP
H. Walter *Die Collectanea.. des.. Solinus* (Hermes Einzelschrift 22) Wiesbaden 1969
W.J. Watson *The History of the Celtic Place-Names of Scotland* Edinburgh 1926 — CPNS
J. Werner *Münzdatierte Austrasische Grabfunde* Berlin 1935
G.K. Whitehead *The Ancient White Cattle of Britain* London 1953
G.K. Whitehead *Ancient White Cattle* London 1963
H. Willers *Die roemischen Bronzeeimer von Hemmoor* Hamburg 1900
* Gwyn Williams *An Introduction to Welsh Poetry* London 1953 — IWP
M. Winterbottom *Gildas* Chichester 1978
C.L. Wrenn *A Study of Old English Literature* London 1967

III Periodicals

Alt Thüringen	1953/4	
Analecta Bollandiana	1882 –	AB
Annales de Normandie	1951 –	
Année épigraphique	1962 –	
Antiquaries Journal	1921 –	Ant. Jl.
Antiquity	1927 –	Ant.
Archaeologia	1773 –	Arch.
Archaeologia Aeliana	1822 –	Arch. Ael.
Archaeologia Cambrensis	1846 –	Arch. Camb.
Archaeological Journal	1845 –	Arch. Jl
Archiv für celtische Lexicographie	1898–1907	ACL
Ausgrabungen und Funde	1956 –	
Bedfordshire Archaeological Journal	1962 –	Beds. Arch. Jl.
Beiträge zur Namenforschung, n.f.	1966 –	
Berkshire Archaeological Journal	1895 –	Berks. Arch. Jl.
Bericht über die Fortschritte der Römisch-Germanischen Kommission des Deutschen archäologischen Instituts	1908 –	RGKB
Britannia	1970 –	
Bulletin of the Institute of Classical Studies	1954 –	BICS
Bulletin of the Board of Celtic Studies	1921–93	BBCS
Cambridge Antiquarian Society Proceedings	1840 –	CASP
Celtica	1946 –	
Celtic Review	1904–16	CR
Current Archaeology	1967 –	CArch
Economic History Review	1922 –	ECHR
English Historical Review	1886 –	EHR
Ériu	1904 –	
Hertfordshire Archaeology	1968 –	
Journal of the British Archaeological Association	1846 –	JBAA
Journal of Celtic Studies	1949 –	JCS
Journal of the English Place-Name Society	1969 –	JEPN
Journal of Roman Studies	1911 –	JRS
Journal of the Royal Institution of Cornwall, n.s.	1951 –	JRIC
Journal of the Royal Society of Antiquaries of Ireland	1870 –	JRSAI
Journal of Theological Studies	1899 –	JTS
Lochlann	1961–74	
Medieval Archaeology	1957 –	MA
Miscellany of the Irish Archaeological Society 1846 (only)		MIAS
Norfolk Archaeology	1847 –	
Northern History	1966 –	
Notes and Queries	1849 –	
Numismatic Chronicle	1881 –	NC
Past and Present	1952 –	P and P
Proceedings of the Prehistoric Society	1934 –	PPS
Proceedings of the Royal Irish Academy	1837 –	PRIA
Proceedings of the Society of Antiquaries of London	1843 –1920	PSA
Proceedings of the Society of Antiquaries of Scotland	1852 –	PSAS
Revue Celtique	1870–1934	RC
Rheinisches Museum für Philologie	1827 –	
Somersetshire Archaeological and Natural History Society Proceedings	1851 –	SANHS
Speculum	1926 –	
Studia Hibernica	1961 –	
Surrey Archaeological Collections	1854 –	SyAC
Traditio	1943 –	
Transactions of the Honourable Society of Cymmrodorion 1892/3 –		THSCymm
Transactions of the Royal Historical Society	1868 –	TRHS
Transactions of the Royal Irish Academy	1787–1907	TRIA
Welsh History Review	1960 –	WHR
Y Cymmrodor	1877–1951	YC
Zeitschrift für celtische Philologie	1896 –	ZCP

NOTES TO
THE AGE OF ARTHUR

The initial references (e.g., xv.2 or 12.1) are to page and paragraph of *The Age of Arthur*.

The notes aim to indicate the main sources relevant to each subject discussed. Space prevents discussion of many of the possible alternative interpretations which could be based upon them. *Age* following a page-number refers to *The Age of Arthur*.

Proper names are themselves references, since they are discussed and indexed in *Arthurian Sources* whose relevant sections, listed on p. 1 above, are here cited for many of the more important persons, places, and subjects.

References to places
Italic figures and letters give National Grid map-references:
    two letters and four figures, as *TL 01 23*, refer to Great Britain;
    one letter and two figures, as *N 58*, refer to Ireland;
    one letter and one figure, as *H 2*, refer to Brittany.
The National Grid for Great Britain is explained on Ordnance Survey maps, in the Automobile Association Handbook, and elsewhere.
The Irish National Grid is shown on Maps 9 and 27.
The Grid devised for Brittany is shown on Map 14 and explained in the notes thereto.

Introduction

xv.2   BIELER: *Irish Ecclesiastical Record* 1967, 2.
xv.3   GILDAS, NENNIUS, PATRICK: text and translation, ed. M.Winterbottom; J.Morris; A.B.E.Hood, published by Phillimore, 1978–80.
xv.3   ARTHURIAN SOURCES: Phillimore 1995 (6 vols.).
xvii.2   CHADWICK: *Growth of Literature* 1, xix.

1 Britain in 350 (pp. 1–9)

2.1   CLAUDIAN: *de Laudibus Stilichonis* 3, 150–153.
4.1   AUSONIUS: his estate, *de Herediolo* 29 ff.; his uncle, *Professores Burdigalenses* 17, cf. *Parentalia* 5; his father, *Parentalia* 3, *Epicedion*, etc.
4.3   PHILO: Ausonius *Ep.* 22.
5.1   IUGUM: the evidence is summarised by Jones LRE 62 ff.; the assessment varied from province to province, and was sometimes by area. In Syria, a *iugum* was reckoned at 40 *iugera* (about 25 acres) of average land, 20 of good land, 60 of poor land. The calculation of the British *iugum* is not known.
5.3   GEOGRAPHY: see Fox *Personality of Britain*.
6.2   PEASANTRY: see especially Jones LRE 774 ff.
8.1   BACAUDA: see especially E.A.Thompson in *P and P* 2, 1952, 11 ff.
9.3   AUSONIUS: *Mosella* 389 ff.

2 Ending of the Western Empire (pp. 10-28)

10.1 MAGNENTIUS: see PLRE 1.
10.1 ALAMANNI: Ammian 16, 12, 4; cf. Zosimus 2, 53.
10.1 MURSA: casualties rated at 54,000, Zonaras 13, 8.
10.2 CONSTANTIUS AT MURSA: Sulpicius Severus *Chron.* 2, 38, 5-7.
11.1 CONSTANTIUS' INQUISITION: Ammian 14, 5. 2-9.
12.1 TOIL AND SWEAT: Barnabas 10.
12.1 BARREN ELM: Hermas 3, 2.
12.1 IRENAEUS: *adversus Haereseos* 4, 46.
12.3 CHRISTIAN COMMUNITIES: see Duchesne *Fastes Episcopaux* 1, 31-32; Lyon, Paris, Sens, Rouen, Reims, Metz, Bordeaux, Bourges and Toulouse, with Arles and Vienne in Provence, Trier and Cologne in the Rhineland, are the known pre-Constantinian bishoprics; cf. Greg. Tur. HF 10, 31, and p. 335 *Age*.
13.2 ARIAN CONTROVERSY: the clearest concise account, here cited, is that of Sulpicius Severus *Chron.* 2, 38 ff.
14.1 AUGURIUS: see E.
15.2 RAIDS: in 360 and 364, Ammian 20, 1 and 26, 4, 5; in 367, Ammian 27, 8 and 28, 3, 7-8.
15.3 COUNTRY HOUSES: notably Park Street near St. Albans, and Norton Disney on the borders of Lincolnshire and Nottinghamshire.
15.3 LONDON: see P.
16.2 NIALL: see p. 157 *Age*.
16.3 AREANI: variant *Arcani*.
16.3 YORKSHIRE SIGNAL TOWERS: see p. 51.2 below.
16.3 ANTICIPATORS: *Not. Dig.* Occ. 40, 31 *Praefectus numeri Supervenientium*
17.2 *Petueriensium, Derventione.*
17.2 CRIMTHANN: see p. 157 *Age*.
17.2 BRITAIN, channel: see P Alba, Icht.
17.2 VALENTIA: see P.
17.3 PATROL UNITS: *Exploratores* at Risingham and Rochester, *Raeti Gaesati* at Risingham and Cappuck, RIB 1235, 1243-4, 1262, 1270, 1217, 2117. Neither the forts nor troops of north-eastern Northumberland have yet been identified.
18.1 THEODOSIUS ... AFRICA: Ammian 29, 5, 35.
18.1 AUGUSTINE: *Ep.* 199, 46: cf. Jones LRE 652 and note.
18.2 FRAOMAR: Ammian 29, 4, 7, *potestate tribuni Alamannorum praefecit numero.* He was doubtless *tribunus gentis Alamannorum,* analogous to the *tribunus gentis Marcomannorum* in Pannonia Prima, *Not. Dig.* Occ. 34, 24. The *vir tribunitiae potestatis* whom Germanus met in 429 (Constantius ch. 15) was perhaps a similar *Tribunus gentis*.
18.3 PATRICK: *Ep.*, 2.
19.2 SYMMACHUS: *Oratio* 4, 6.
20.2 GRATIAN: Rufinus HE 11, 13; Ausonius *Gratiarum Actio* 14. Ammian 31, 10, 18 compares him with Commodus.
20.2 MAXIMUS: see PLRE 1 Maximus 39.
20.2 BRITTANY: see p. 250 *Age*.
21.5 UNITS: Claudian *de bello Getico* 414 ff.
21.5 LEGION: the *Notitia Dignitatum* omits the 20th, but names the other legions of Britain.
23.2 JEROME: *Commentary on Ezekiel,* Prologue, and preface to book 3.

23.2 YOUNG BRITON: Sicilian Briton (see E and pp. 340 ff. *Age*) *Ep.* 1, 1 (PL Sup. 1, 1687 ff.).
23.5 AMMIAN: 27, 3, 14.
24.3 EFFICIENT HEAD: e.g., Ambrose *Ep.* 11, 4 *totius orbis Romani caput Romana ecclesia*.
25.2 EUSEBIUS: Ambrose *Ep.* 63, 66.
25.3 MATTERS OF FINANCE: Ambrose *Ep.* 40, 27.
25.3 OLD TESTAMENT: Ambrose *Ep.* 20, 23.
25.3 MILAN: Ambrose *Ep.* 20, cf. 21 (*contra Auxentium*); Augustine *Confessio* 9, 7; Paulinus *vita Ambrosii* 13.
26.1 THESSALONICA: see especially Ambrose *Ep.* 51, 6 ff.
26.2 MARTIN: Sulpicius Severus; ELECTION *vita Martini* 9, cf. *Dialogi* 1, 26, 3; SCHOOL *vita* 10; AMATOR *Dialogi* 3, 1, 4; VICTRICIUS *Dial.* 3, 2, 4; CLERGY ALONE *Dial.* 1, 26, 3; VALENTINIAN *Dial.* 2, 5, 5; LAY JUDGE *Chron.* 2, 50, 5; BANQUET *vita* 20, 2; 20, 5–7.
27.3 SAME MOUTH: Gregory the Great *Ep.* 11, 34.
28.1 MARCELLINUS: *Chronicle* AD 454, on the assassination of Aëtius.

3 Independent Britain: The Evidence (pp. 29–43)

29.1 HONORIUS' LETTER: Zosimus 6, 10; cf. T.
29.2 PROVINCIAL COUNCIL: see T.
32.2 PAGAN ENGLISH: see also S.
32.2 PLETTKE: *Ursprung* 65 dates the migrations to Britain to some time before 441/442, citing L. Schmidt *Allgemeine Geschichte* 159 ff., who rightly based his conclusions on the Chronicle of 452 (p. 38 *Age*). Plettke uses this date as a main criterion for the dating of German pottery and brooches; cf. e.g. pp. 44–45 where the latest forms of vessels of Type A 6 are prolonged 'perhaps into the early 5th century' because they are occasionally found in England, and type A 7 is centred on the early 5th century both because it derives from A 6 and because 'diese Form besonders häufig in England gefunden ist und die Hauptüberwanderung der Angelsachsen doch wohl mit Sicherheit in die erste Hälfte des 5. Jahrhunderts zu setzen ist.' In general, Plettke's dating, and the reasoning behind it, remain the basis of modern German archaeological dates; so Tischler *Sachsenforschung* 41 'Unsere Chronologie ... weicht letzten Endes nur wenig von der Anschauung Plettkes ab.' German estimates of Anglian and Saxon burial dates about the Elbe still ultimately derive from the Chronicler of 452; the notion that there exist independent 'German dates', which can be used to guide dates in Britain, is an illusion. See below, vol. 4, pp. 73–9.
33.1 CRUCIFORM BROOCHES: cf. p. 269 *Age*. The most useful study is still that of Åberg ASE 28 ff. The principal corrections are that Åberg's starting date is a generation too late; his groups III and IV are contemporary; and the border lines between groups need adjustment by closer attention to the foot of the brooch. The term 'cruciform' is restricted to the series of brooches that begin with Åberg's group I; it excludes the prototype brooches found at Dorchester, Beetgum and elsewhere, and also 'small long' brooches, sometimes miscalled cruciform.
33.1 SAUCER BROOCHES: see especially Åberg ASE 16 ff.; Leeds DSB; SyAC 56, 1959, 80 ff.; cf. p. 269 *Age*.

33.2 AFTER 400: until recently unnecessary uncertainty has bedevilled modern English, but not German discussions of the date when the first pagan cemeteries came into use. Bede's date of '450' (p. 39 *Age*) was long repeated without examination; an equally untenable date of about 360 has been advanced by Myres ASP 71 ff. The argument stresses some vessels that 'on the Continent are dated in the fourth or at latest the early years of the fifth century', i.e. about 400, not 360. Such relatively small numbers do not date cemeteries. Most migrating or conquering peoples bring with them a small proportion of objects that are at least a generation old; the Roman conquest of AD 43 brought with it a number of Arretine and other pots that were then 20 or 30 years old, but these vessels do not alter the date of the Roman invasion; and early English graves in Britain also contained a few brooches, as well as pots, that were fashionable in Germany about 400. A proportion of objects about 30 or 40 years old forms a necessary part of the furniture of cemeteries first used about 430. The extreme date of 360 appears to rest chiefly on a single vessel, typologically intermediate between one dated in continental English territory to the 3rd century and another of the early 5th century, and is for that reason placed halfway between, 'no later than the second half of the fourth century'. A vessel with so frail a date is not enough to alter the date of a national migration by two generations.

Equally important is the evidence of what is not found in Britain. Brooches that in Germany are normally dated to the later fourth century, notably the prototypes of the cruciform brooch, of the Beetgum or Dorchester-on-Thames pattern, and the latest Germanic 'crossbow' forms, have not yet been discovered in pagan Saxon cemeteries in England; and those that date to 'about 400', notably the 'equal arm, series 2' and the 'tutulus', are very rare; two of the former and one of the latter are known. The essence of the matter however is that the ultimate criterion that persuades German scholars to date a pot or brooch to the fourth century or to the early fifth is whether or not its parallel has been found in England. In general, the continental dates fit the rest of the evidence because they rest on the assumption that the pagan cemeteries of England began in the early fifth century; that assumption is securely grounded because it is based on the contemporary statement of the Chronicler of 452, reported by Schmidt, and adopted from him by Plettke. The dating based upon it has stood the test of time. See below, vol. 4, pp. 73–9.

33.3 CHIP CARVED: or *Kerbschnitt*, cf. p. 51 *Age*.

33.3 SCANDINAVIA ... DATING: the chief independent means of dating are gold bracteates (medallions) and coin hoards, from the late 5th century; but as yet they give few dates to other objects.

34.1 HALF A DOZEN PERIODS: based chiefly on cruciform brooches, the periods are A, 430/470: B, 460/500: C, 490/530: D, 510/590, subdivided into D 1, 510/540; D 2, 530/560; D 3, 550/590; E 570/610; F, 7th century. Maps 3, 6, 18, 21, 22 (*Age* pp. 59, 107, 285, 297, 305) show the sites and areas where burials began in these periods. A number of sites on the margins of periods might alternatively be shown on the succeeding or preceding maps.

34.1 COINS: e.g. J. Werner *Münzdatierte Austrasische Grabfunde*.

34.1 WEAPONS: e.g. the axe termed 'francisca' is found in dated Frankish graves from the early 5th century, and might in theory be as early in Kent. Though it has not yet been reported in dated English graves before the later 6th century, it has sometimes been treated as though it were by

NOTES TO *THE AGE OF ARTHUR* (pp. 33–40) 39

  itself evidence of a 5th-century date in Britain. In general, dates assigned to weapons as yet inspire little confidence.

34.1 PURE TYPOLOGY: e.g. Harden's important study of glass vessels paid 'little or no attention to the evidence of associated objects. The omission is deliberate' (DAB 139). The neglect of evidence is in some particulars troublesome; the largest class of vessels (Cone beakers III a i and Claw beakers II a) are assigned by typology to the 5th and early 6th centuries, but have not yet been found in dated graves earlier than the mid or late 6th century; cf. MA 2, 1958, 37; SyAC 59, 1959, 115.

34.1 ANIMAL ORNAMENT: the fundamental work is Salin *Tierornamentik*. Animals clearly represented, mostly in the late 4th and earlier 5th centuries, present fewer problems; abstract motifs, part animal and part otherwise, tread upon uncertainties.

34.2 RECENT STUDIES: notably Meaney *Gazetteer*, that for the first time pulls together all known sites, though the information, dates and grid reference locations require close examination; Myres ASP is an important preliminary to a full corpus of the pottery, though the starting date of c. 360 is not tenable (p. 33.2 above). Hawkes and Dunning *Soldiers and Settlers* MA 5, 1961, 1 ff. have made a new and important class of object available for study, though it is still over easy for the unwary to treat late Roman metal as 'Germanic'.

35.2 BRITISH AUTHORS: especially Pelagius, Fastidius, the Sicilian Briton and his colleagues, with Patrick and Faustus of Riez; see E, and pp. 338 ff. *Age*. See also below, vol. 6, pp. 17–51.

35.5 GILDAS: see E. See also below, vol. 6, pp. 179–86.

36.2 ROMANS: Gildas 18, 1.

36.3 WHIPS: Gildas 7, 1.

37.1 ARMED FORCES: Gildas 14, 1.

37.2 NO EARLIER AGE: Gildas 21, 2; cf. p. 70 *Age*.

37.2 COUNCILLORS: Gildas 23, 1.

37.2 AMBROSIUS: Gildas 25, 2 ff.; cf. pp. 48 and 95 *Age*.

37.3 NENNIUS: see E. The Kentish Chronicle, ch. 31, 36–38 and 43–46; the Chronographer, ch. 66. See the edition in *Arthurian Period Sources*, vol. 8.

38.2 ANOTHER ... ALLUSION: in asserting his suzerainty over the Germanic peoples of Europe, in 448, Attila the Hun claimed to rule the 'Ocean Islands', evidently Britain (Priscus, FHG 4, 90, Fragment 8); his claim implies that he then regarded the island as under German control; cf. C.E.Stevens EHR 56, 1941, 263.

38.3 BRITISH VICTORIES: Zosimus 6, 5, cited p. 70 *Age*; cf. T Honorius's Letter.

38.4 MIGRATION: Sidonius *Ep*. 3, 9; Jordanes *Getica* 45; Greg. Tur. HF 2, 18; Mansi 7, 941; see E Mansuetus, and p. 90.5 below.

39.1 WHEN THEY DIED: Gildas 26, 3.

39.1 BADON: see P and p. 112 *Age*.

39.2 AETIUS: Gildas 20.

39.3 BEDE: see E. See also A.

40.1 BEDE ... AETIUS ... DATE: see A. Bede also corrected the error in the manuscripts of the Chronicle. He inserted the year date, '23rd year of Theodosius', into the middle of the entry, though it is placed at about Theodosius' 10th year. The correction was emphasised by the insertion of a correct date, the '8th year of Theodosius' at the end of the preceding entry. Elsewhere in Bede's Chronicle year-dates are very rare, and are placed after the opening words of the entry, and at the right place in the sequence of events. The evidence is discussed in vol. 6, pp. 60–5, below.

40.2	SAXON CHRONICLE: see **A**.
41.2	BRITISH: some confusion arises from the use of 'Breton'. In English, its meaning is restricted to the British who have retained their national name in France, in Brittany. It is a valid modern geographical term, for the British of Brittany have long been sundered from Britain, save in their language. But when the word is applied to their 5th- and 6th-century ancestors, it implies a separation that had not yet occurred. The British who settled in Roman Armorica and gave it the modern name of Brittany were as fully British as their relatives at home; and were numerous elsewhere in northern France, not yet confined to Brittany.
41.2	COMBROGI, CYMRY: see p. 98 *Age*, and P Combrogi.
41.3	ANGLES, SAXONS: see P; cf. p. 311 *Age*.
41.3	WEST SAXONS: Jutish and Saxon ornament is prominent in the early graves of the West and South Saxons, but not of the East Saxons. The earliest name of the West Saxons was however *Gewissae*, or Confederates, and the term Middle Saxons is not known before the late 7th century. The name did not arise from a belief that the southern English were descended from the Saxons of Germany rather than the 'Angles'; its use created that belief; cf. p. 294 *Age*.
42.1	CONTINENTAL ORIGIN: cf. p. 269 *Age*.
42.2	ANGLO-SAXON: see P; in 1865 Earle published *Two Saxon Chronicles Parallel*, not 'Anglo-Saxon', and Kemble published *The Saxons in England* in 1848. The titles were retained in revised editions in 1896 and 1876. The hybrid term was used earlier, but plain 'Saxon' lingered long.
42.3	SCOT: the origin of the Latin word is not known. It was not used in the Irish language.
42.3	PICT, CRUITHNI: see P Picts and pp. 186 ff. *Age*.
43.2	PERIODS: outlined in vol. 6, pp. 53–93, below; summarised Frere *Britannia* 1967, 381 ff.; cf. 'phases' Myres ASP 1969, 63 ff.

4 Independent Britain: Vortigern (pp. 44–70)

44.1	THE BRITISH: Zosimus 6, 5, probably citing Olympiodorus and other contemporaries, cf. T Honorius's Letter.
44.2	HORDES: Gildas 19, 1–4.
44.2	NATH–Í: Yellow Book of Lecan 192 b 25, cited Watson CPNS 192, cf. Book of Leinster 190 a 27 (4,836); cf. O'Curry 591. All that remains is the title of a lost tale.
45.1	IRISH SETTLEMENT: see P Dál Riada, Maps 7 and 25; and p. 158 *Age*.
45.2	HOMILY: *de vita Christiana*, PL 4, 1031 ff., ascribed to Fastidius in one MS; Augustine quotes a copy that had reached Sicily by 412 (vol. 6, pp. 23–7, below); see E Fastidius.
45.2	FASTIDIUS: Gennadius *de Viris Inlustribus* 56; see E.
45.2	FASTIDIUS: *de Vita Christiana* 11 and 14.
48.2	PROCOPIUS: BV 1, 2.
48.2	KINGS ANOINTED: Gildas 21, 4.
48.2	AMBROSIUS: see p. 95 *Age*.
48.3	SICILIAN BRITON: *Ep.* 2 *opto te semper Deo vivere et perpetui consulatus honore gaudere.* For the imagery, cf. Prudentius *Peri Stephanon* 2, 559–560 *quem Roma caelestis sibi Legit perennem consulem*, on St. Lawrence. The Saint earned office in heaven by martyrdom; the unchristian British

NOTES TO *THE AGE OF ARTHUR* (pp. 40–52)

48.3   magistrate's only qualification was earthly office, that reformed conduct might perpetuate in heaven. The metaphor is pointless unless he were a consul.

48.3   CONSUL: the elder Ambrosius is also called *unus de consulibus Romanicae gentis* in the fable of the dragons on Snowdon, Nennius 42. The fable is older than medieval usage of the word, and the title therefore may derive from early tradition.

49.3   NOTITIA DIGNITATUM: see T.

49.4   COMMANDS: *Comes Britanniarum* listed in *Not. Dig.* Occ. 7, 154–156, 200–205; *Comes Litoris Saxonici* Occ. 28; *Dux Britanniarum* Occ. 40.

49.4   SAXON SHORE FORCES: The *Anderetiani*, listed in the *Notitia* in the field army of Gaul, on the Rhine, and at Paris (Occ. 7, 100; 41, 17; 42, 22), probably came from Anderida, Pevensey; the units of the three southern forts of Portchester, Pevensey and Richborough, *Exploratores, Abulci*, and *Secundani* also appear in the field army of Gaul (Occ. 7, 109; 110; 84; cf. 5, 241). The duplicate names, as elsewhere in the *Notitia*, suggest that detachments, and occasionally whole units, were posted from the coastal forts to Gaul by Constantine and earlier emperors, from Pevensey on two separate occasions.

50.2   VALENTIA: see P, and p. 17 *Age*.

50.4   OUT OF DATE: S.S.Frere, *Britannia* 230 ff., 354 ff., discards earlier views that the Wall list was more than a hundred years out of date, but deems it 'inconceivable' that 'old regiments survived' after the raid of 367. The frontier was then reorganised and reconstructed. But reconstruction does not imply that any units other than those named by Ammian were annihilated, disbanded or replaced. Valentinian had no new troops to spare, and on other frontiers retained the remnants of similar old units of the lesser schedule who had survived worse disasters.

51.1   REBUILDING: e.g. the Commandant's House at Housesteads, *Arch. Ael.*[4] 39, 1961, 279 ff.; cf. 38, 1960, 61 ff.

51.1   BURIALS: e.g. Saxon: Cumberland, Birdoswald; Durham, Hurbuck (Lanchester); Lancashire, Ribchester and Manchester; Northumberland, Benwell and Corbridge; Westmorland, Brough-by-Stainmore and perhaps Low Borrow Bridge. British, Chesterholm, Brigomaglus, RIB 1722 = CIIC 498, late 5th century (Jackson LHEB 192 note 2) or later, probably also Old Carlisle, Tancorix, RIB 908.

51.2   YORKSHIRE TOWERS: p. 16 *Age*; see especially *Arch. Jl.* 89, 1932, 203 ff.

51.2   FARMING SITE: Yorkshire: Scarborough, Crossgates.

51.3   IRISH: see p. 158 *Age*.

52.1   TWO UNITS: Fraomar, under Valentinian, probably *tribunus gentis Alamannorum*, cf. p. 18.2 above; *numerus Hnaudifridi*, 3rd or 4th century, at Housesteads, RIB 1576, cf. 1593–4; the commander of the mid-third-century *numerus Maurorum* at Burgh-by-Sands RIB 2042, cf. *Not. Dig.* Occ. 40, 47, was Roman; and so doubtless was the commander of the early third-century *cuneus Frisiorum* at Housesteads RIB 1594, cf. 1593.

52.2   GENTILES: *Not. Dig.* Occ. 42, 33 ff.

52.2   COMMERCIAL POTTERIES: 'Romano-Saxon' ware; cf. J.N.L.Myres in DAB 16 ff. Though some of the vessels there discussed are now held to be earlier, the majority are not.

52.2   PAGAN ENGLISH GRAVES: a very few contain an occasional sherd of 'Romano-Saxon' ware, for surface Roman sherds of all kinds are not uncommon; unbroken Roman, and perhaps Romano-Saxon, vessels are found, but very rarely.

52.2 SERVICE WITH ROME: for example, Silvanus the Frank, impeached before Constantius, dared not seek refuge with the barbarian Franks, since they would certainly either kill him or sell him; Ammian 15, 5.
53.1 AEGIDIUS, SYAGRIUS: see especially Greg. Tur. HF 2, 11, 18, 27.
53.2 ROMAN EMPIRE: Eugippius *vita Severini* 20.
53.2 BATAVIANS: *Not. Dig.* Occ. 35, 24; the MS reads *novae* for *nonae*.
53.2 MAMERTINUS: Eugippius *vita Severini* 4.
53.2 BARBARIAN GARRISON: Eugippius *vita Severini* 2.
53.2 REFUGEES: Eugippius *vita Severini* 30.
53.3 EGYPT: papyri, cited Jones LRE 662–3, with note 128.
54.4 THE ISLAND: Gildas 21, 2–3.
55.2 VORTIGERN: see L.
55.2 AMBROSIUS: see L.
56.2 THE FEATHERED FLIGHT: Gildas 22, 1–2.
56.2 TRANSMARINI: Gildas 14; coracles, *curucae,* modern Welsh cwrwg, Gildas 19, 1; booty carried *trans maria,* in the plural, by Picts, as well as Scots and Saxons, Gildas 17, 3.
57.2 NORFOLK: an inscribed Pictish knife-handle found on the surface at a Roman farming site at Weeting in Norfolk, near the Devil's Dyke (*Ant. Jl.* 32, 1952, 71; *Norfolk Archaeology* 31, 1955, 184; cf. R.R.Clarke *East Anglia* pl. 44) might have been lost by a Saxon or Roman who took it from a Pict; or by a raiding Pict. There is no evidence to show how early the Picts adapted Ogam script to wood and bone; see p. 191 *Age*.
57.3 TIME DREW NIGH: Gildas 22–23; 'keels', *cyulae*.
57.3 THREE KEELS: *ciulae* Nennius 31.
60.3 EXCAVATED EVIDENCE: There is no evidence for the settlement of federates in Gaul before 418, or in Britain before the 420s (cf. p. 33.2 above). *Gentiles* are attested by texts in Gaul and Italy, perhaps by pottery in Britain, but not by cemeteries. Cemeteries in Gaul that contained both German and Roman grave goods were probably used by newly raised barbarian units of the Roman army, perhaps *Auxilia Palatina.*
61.2 HENGEST: Nennius 38.
61.2 ORKNEYS: a Saxon urn in Edinburgh Museum, said to have been 'found in Buchan', may be mislabelled; or may be a relic of this expedition, a freak counterpart to the Pictish knife in Norfolk, p. 57.2 above.
61.2 FRENESSICAN SEA: probably the Forth.
62.1 DUMFRIES: Watson CPNS 422 demonstrated that the name means 'Fort of the Frisians' linguistically, but proposed a fanciful alternative, solely because he did not think that Frisians settled in Scotland; Glensaxon (CPNS 356) and similar names might concern English settlement at this, or any other date.
62.4 GERMANUS ... ARMIES: Constantius *vita Germani* 17, cf. Bede HE 1, 20.
63.1 LLANGOLLEN: see p. 64 *Age*. The traditional site, marked by an obelisk, north of Maes Garmon, at Rhual (*SJ 223 647*), near Mold in Flintshire, is probably no more than an antiquarian guess from the place-name.
63.2 NENNIUS: 32–35, placed at the beginning of Vortigern's reign; the second visit, Nennius 47, is placed at the end of the reign.
63.2 ELISEG: ECMW 182.

NOTES TO *THE AGE OF ARTHUR* (pp. 52–71) 43

63.2 BRITTU: It is possible that the names derive from a single individual, Catellius Brutus.
63.3 PAGENSES: Jackson LHEB 443; cf. 91.
63.3 CORNOVII: see P Cornovia.
64.1 WELSH POEM: *Angar Kyvyndawt* BT 21, 14 (FAB 529–530; 134) '*py dydwc garthan Gereint ar Arman*', 'why Geraint committed (?) the camp to Germanus'; the work is a late hotch-potch of allusions to earlier, lost poems.
64.2 PICT SAXON ... ALLIES: late Welsh legend called the Powys foreigners *Gwyddyl Ffichti*, 'Irish Picts'; the earliest reference is in the 13th-century Jesus Genealogy 23 (see vol. 5, p. 60); the phrase may originate from a misunderstood 'Scotti (et) Picti' in a version of the Germanus tradition.
64.3 MOEL FENLI: *SJ* 163 601, see P.
64.3 MOEL-Y-GERAINT: *SJ* 202 419, otherwise called Barber's Hill, see P.
64.3 GERMANUS CHURCHES: see E.
64.4 UNWARY CRITIC: e.g. PLECG 259 ff.; cf. E 'German mac Cuill'.
64.5 PALLADIUS, PATRICK: see E and p. 345 *Age*.
65.1 SAXON RAID: see A 434; the texts do not support the translation 'raid from Ireland'.
65.2 MARRIAGE: see E Foirtchern and L Vortigern; cf. p. 166 *Age*.
65.2 IRISHMEN ... CHRISTIANITY: e.g. E Coelestius, Corcodemus, Michomerus.
66.2 NENNIUS: 62, reproducing the 7th-century spelling, Cunedag; cf. LHEB 458; *atavus* means ancestor in general, not only great-grandfather.
66.2 KIDWELLY: Nennius 14.
67.1 VOTADINI: Gododdin; see P Votadini.
67.1 TRAPRAIN LAW: in East Lothian, *NT* 58 74; see P.
67.1 YEAVERING BELL: *NT* 928 924; see P.
67.2 INSCRIPTIONS: see p. 124 *Age*.
68.1 SPLENDID IN BATTLE: BT 69, 11–12; 24; 70, 5–6; 11–12; cf. FAB 257, 200. Durham and Carlisle, *Kaer Weir a Chaer Liwelyd*; Caer Weir, Durham, did not exist before the Norse invasions, and is an anachronism, comparable with a modern statement that a Roman fort is 'in Yorkshire'.
68.2 OCTHA: see p. 61 *Age*.
68.2 GERMANIANUS: The dynasty of Decianus (see p. 17 *Age*), probably Lothian, may also have originated at this time, but is more likely to have been established somewhat earlier.
68.3 CORNWALL: Cornovia, etc. The name does not come into use in any form until after the English conquest of Devon; see P Cornovia. It means the land of the Cornovian Welsh.
69.3 COHORS: *Not. Dig.* Occ. 40, 34.
70.1 THE BRITISH: Zosimus 6, 5; cf. p. 38 *Age*.
70.1 AFFLUENT: Gildas 21, 1; cf. p. 37 *Age*.

5 The Overthrow of Britain (pp. 71–86)

71.1 THE PICTS: Nennius 31.
71.1 AMBROSIUS: see L, and p. 95 *Age*.
71.2 AUGUSTINE, PELAGIUS: see pp. 339 ff. *Age*.

72.4	THE KING:	Nennius 36.
73.1	RANSOMS:	Alaric demanded 4000 lb. of gold in 407, rather more in 409; some senators are said to have received 4000 lb. of gold in rent annually; cf. texts cited in Jones LRE 185–6, 554.
73.4	CHRONOGRAPHER:	Nennius 66.
73.4	WALLOP:	see P.
74.2	HENGEST:	Nennius 37. Chartres MS 19 keels; other MSS 16, 17 or 18.
74.2	HENGEST'S DAUGHTER:	Nennius 37.
74.4	HENGEST:	Nennius 37.
75.1	CANTERBURY:	see P.
75.2	OCTHA:	see p. 61 *Age*.
75.2	EBISSA:	the name is perhaps Celtic, and, if so, implies a joint command by a Roman officer and a German Captain.
75.3	COMPLAINED:	Gildas 23, 5.
75.4	BARBARIANS:	Gildas 23–24.
75.4	GREATER TOWNS:	*coloniae*.
76.1	CAISTOR-BY-NORWICH:	JRS 21, 1931, 232 and plate xxi. The excavator's interpretation has been challenged, but without good reason.
76.1	COLCHESTER:	Hull *Roman Colchester* 41. The north-east gate was twice stormed; the most likely occasions are the first and second Saxon revolts, about the 440s and the 570s.
76.1	LINCOLN:	the burnt stones are preserved in place for public view.
78.1	AETIUS:	Gildas 20, 1.
78.1	FIRE OF VENGEANCE:	Gildas 24, 1.
78.1	WENT HOME:	25, 2.
78.1	THE EAST:	Gildas 24, 1; cf. 23,3; cf. p. 57 *Age*.
78.2	UNEXPECTED RAID:	Eugippius *vita Severini* 4.
78.2	THE CITIZENS:	Eugippius *vita Severini* 30.
79.2	VERULAMIUM OVEN:	*Ant. Jl.* 40. 1960, 19–21; *Ant.* 38, 1964, 110–111; *Civitas Capitals* 97.
80.2	ELAFIUS:	Constantius *vita Germani* 26–27. The name is Roman and needs no emendation, see PLRE Aelafius.
80.3	SOUTHAMPTON:	cf. the Gallic tradition that on one of his visits Germanus sailed from near Cherbourg, de Plinval *St. Germain* 46.
80.4	VORTIGERN'S SON:	Nennius 43.
81.1	SECOND ACCOUNT:	Nennius 44 assigns four battles to Vortimer, but names only three. If the figure 4 is not a scribal error, it may derive from a tradition that included the battle of the mid-450s (SC 473; cf. p. 86 *Age*).
81.1	ARCH:	*Excavations at Richborough* 5, 1968, 40 ff.; cf. RIB 46 ff.
82.1	STRATEGY:	cf. Map 3, p. 59 *Age*.
82.5	VORTIMER'S PROPHECY:	Nennius 44.
83.2	BARBARIANS RETURNED:	Nennius 45.
83.2	BARBARIANS SENT ENVOYS:	Nennius 45.
84.2	HENGEST ... TOLD HIS MEN:	Nennius 46. Most MSS read *Eu Saxones, eniminit saxas,* with minor variants; two read *nimed Eure* (or *hlore*) *saxes*.
84.3	FAUSTUS OF RIEZ:	see E and p. 338 *Age*.
84.3	VORTIGERN HATED:	Nennius 48.
85.1	WRETCHED SURVIVORS:	Gildas 25, 1.
86.1	FOUGHT AGAINST THE WELSH:	SC 473.

NOTES TO *THE AGE OF ARTHUR* (pp. 72–95) 45

6 The War (pp. 87–115)

88.1 WESTERN EMPIRE: cf. p. 28 *Age*.
90.3 NORTH OF THE LOIRE: Sidonius *Ep.* 1, 7, 5 *supra Ligerim*; cf. p. 91 *Age*; to Sidonius in the Auvergne 'beyond the Loire' meant to the north (and east) of the river.
90.3 BRETTEVILLE: *Annales de Normandie* 10, 1960, 312, based on M.H.Chanteux in *Recueil ... Clovis Brunel*, 248 ff. A large number of churches and places named in honour of 6th-century British monks, extending eastward into Belgium, also suggest a substantial British element in the population; see Map 4 and notes thereto. The place-name Breteuil, near Evreux, 40 miles south of Rouen, and near Beauvais, 60 miles south of Amiens, probably has the same origin.
90.4 RIOTHAMUS: Sidonius *Ep.* 3, 9.
90.5 NEWLANDS: Mansuetus (see E) is termed 'Bishop of the British' in 461, Mansi 7, 941, cf. p. 38 *Age*. His name is also inserted, at much the same date, in the episcopal lists (cf. p. 12.3 above) of Toul, on the borders of Burgundian territory, and of Meaux and Senlis, in Syagrius' dominions; both Senlis and Toul list subsequent bishops with British names; cf. E Conotigirnus. The reason may be that substantial numbers of Mansuetus' British congregation settled in these towns. The place-names and dedications of these regions have not yet been examined in the manner of those of Normandy.
90.5 BACAUDAE: cf. p. 8 *Age*.
91.1 FREQUENT CHANGES: Jordanes *Getica* 45.
91.1 PREFECT: Sidonius *Ep.* 1, 7, 5.
91.2 LOWER LOIRE: Greg. Tur. HF 2, 18.
91.2 ODOVACER: see L and p. 93 *Age*.
92.3 FRISIANS: *vita Meloris* 1; cf. E Melorius.
92.3 GRADLON: see Wrdesten *vita Winwaloe* (cf. E) 2, 15.
93.1 GOTHIC ADMIRAL: Sidonius *Ep.* 8, 6, 13–15.
93.2 SOUTH COAST HARBOURS: Sidonius' words *de continenti in patriam vela laxantes* imply that their home was not on the European mainland; and was therefore in Britain.
93.2 ALAMANNI: see p. 130 *Age*.
94.1 AELLE: SC 477 (= c. 456); see L.
94.2 ARUN: cf. Map 6, p. 107 *Age*.
94.3 ESSEX: the sites by Tilbury appear to belong to the first settlement of the 420s, and are exceptional, remote from inland Essex.
95.1 SEALS: PSA 22, 1863, 235 cf. 87; cf. *Arch. Jl.* 16, 38; the objects, probably seals, contain about 75% tin and 25% lead.
95.2 SURVIVORS: Gildas 25–26.
95.2 LAST DEFEAT: Gildas 2 *postrema patriae victoria*; cf. 26, 1 *novissimaeque ferme de furciferis non minimae stragis*.
95.2 NENNIUS: 43, conclusion of the first account, after Vortimer's victories; cf. 56.
95.3 AMBROSIUS: see L.
95.3 ARTHUR: see L.
95.3 COMMANDER: *tunc Arthur pugnabat ... cum regibus Brittonum, sed ipse dux erat bellorum* Nennius 56.

96.2   WELSH POEMS: see T.
96.2   GERMAN CAVALRY: see E.A.Thompson *The Early Germans,* especially pp. 127–130, with texts there cited; cf. *P and P* 14, 1958, 2 ff.
96.2   ENGLISH ... HORSES: Procopius BG 8, 20, 28.
96.3   ARMORICAN CAVALRY: see p. 258 *Age.*
96.3   ONE POEM: *Marwnad Gereint,* cited p. 104 *Age.*
96.3   ECDICIUS: Sidonius *Ep.* 3, 3, 3–8. Sidonius was Ecidicius' brother-in-law, and was therefore well informed. The story is reproduced by Greg. Tur. HF 2, 24, where the words *et octo* have fallen from the text. See PLRE 2; for the date, cf. C.E.Stevens *Sidonius Apollinaris* 202.
98.2   COMBROGI: not *Combroges* Jackson WHR Special Number 1963, 85; cf. p. 41 *Age.*
99.2   CADBURY CASTLE: see P and p. 137 *Age.*
100.2   AMBROSIUS ... NAME: see L. Discordant explanations advanced by various editors of older EPNS volumes include several types of plants and birds and the alleged personal name of an 'archaic Vandal'.
102.1   EXCAVATION ... GROUPS: see Map 5.
102.1   DUNSTABLE: see below, vol. 4, pp. 124–5; C.L.Matthews *Ancient Dunstable* 71.
103.2   PEVENSEY: SC 491 (=c. 470).
103.3   WEST SAXON ENTRIES: see A; cf. p. 323 *Age.*
104.3   PORT: SC 501 (=c. 480).
104.4   GERAINT: BBC 71–72 (folios xxxvi a–b), RBH 1042 ff., cf. FAB 1, 266 ff.; 2, 37 and 274; translated WBT 43.
106.3   OESC: see P Badon.
106.3   THE SAXONS: Nennius 56.
106.3   THE KINGS: cf. p. 272 *Age.*
106.3   ANGEL EMPTY: Bede HE 1, 15; Nennius 38.
109.1   SURREY: see S.
109.3   DYKES: cf. Fox ACR ed. 1948 Appendix iv, p. 123.
110.1   HASLINGFIELD: EPNS Cambridgeshire 77, where the inferred name **Haesela* is a variant of Esla. Other Eslingas settled at Essendon near Hertford (EPNS 233) and at Eslington near Alnwick, in Bernicia, (DEPN 169), both probably in or after the late 6th century.
111.5   NENNIUS ... POEM: Nennius 56; see E. The sites are 1, the river Glen; 2–5, the river Douglas in Lindsey; 6, the river Bassas; 7, Celidon Forest; 8, Fort Guinnion; 9, the City of the Legion; 10, the river Tribruit; 11, Agned Hill, or Bregion; 12, Badon Hill.
112.5   BADON: see P.
114.3   RICH GOTH: Theodoric the Great, cited in *Anonymus Valesianus* 61 (12).

7 The Peace of Arthur (pp. 116–141)

116.1   ARTHUR: see L.
116.2   POET: Aneirin *Gododdin* 1241–2.
116.2   HEIRS OF ... ARTHUR: cf. p. 242 *Age.*
116.2   NAME OF ARTHUR: the name of Arthur was given to their sons by Aedán of Dál Riada and his son Conang; Peter of Demetia; Pabo of the Pennines; by Coscrach of Leinster (CGH 78 R 125 a 41); and by Bicoir the Briton, probably of the Clyde, Annals 626. All these children were born and named in the

NOTES TO *THE AGE OF ARTHUR* (pp. 96–124) 47

mid or late 6th century; no other child is known to have been named Arthur for 500 years, until after the diffusion of the Norman romances.

The name of Arthur, father of Ascelin, whose land at Caen William the Conqueror appropriated about 1070 (Ordericus Vitalis 7, 13), suggests that tales were told of Arthur in Normandy at least a hundred years before the composition of the oldest known Norman romances of the Arthurian Cycle. There are also three or four Arthurs in DB.

The letters ARTR, inscribed on ECMW 287, probably about AD 700, Jackson LHEB 668 note 1, are however not likely to represent the name Arthur.

117.2 RULERS: Gildas 26, 2.
117.3 ARTHUR LEGEND: see L.
118.1 TRISTAN: see below, vol. 6, p. 14(-15), n. 13.
118.2 PRINCE CONSORT: Tennyson *Idylls of the King*, dedication.
119.2 GREAT JEOPARDY: Malory *Morte d'Arthur* 1, 5.
119.2 IN THIS REALM: Malory *Morte d'Arthur* 20, 17.
119.2 SIR BORS: Tennyson *Holy Grail* 702 ff.
119.2 ARTHUR'S KINGDOM: R.L.Green *King Arthur* p. 11.
120.2 CERTAIN TYRANT: *vita Paterni* 21.
120.2 BUT LO: *vita Cadoci*, prologue. The hill 'Bochriu Carn' is Fochriw *SO 10 05*, cf. Map 7 and notes thereto.
120.3 GREAT GENERAL: *vita Cadoci* 22. The place is named 'Tref Redinauc', now Tredunnock, *ST 37 94*, cf. Map 7 and notes thereto.
121.2 CATO AND ARTHUR: *vita prima Carantoci* 4.
121.2 CUILL: *vita Gildae* (Caradoc) 5, Hueil; cf. *vita Gildae* (Rhuys) 2, Cuillus.
121.2 ILLTUD: *vita Iltuti* 2.
122.3 GILDAS ... SIXTH CENTURY SPELLING: *Beatus Gildas Arecluta ... oriundus, patre Cauuo* (misread as *Cauno* MGH) *vita Gildae* (Rhuys) 1; the names are 'clearly ... sixth century ... from contemporary manuscripts' LHEB 42; cf. 306, 307.
123.3 DUMNONIAN POEM: see p. 104 *Age*.
123.3 NENNIUS POEM: Nennius 56; see E and p. 111 *Age*. See also the edition in *Arthurian Period Sources*, vol. 8.
124.2 INSCRIPTIONS: see L Cauus. The relevant stones are
1 ECMW 282 Llanfor *SH 94 36*, near the Roman fort of Caer Gai. CIIC 417.
   Cavo[s] Seniargii [filius] (hic iacit)
   Possible variant readings *Cavoseni Argii* or *Cavos Eniargii*.
   Date: 5th to early 6th ECMW; early to mid 6th LHEB 521. The stone is extant.
2 ECMW 283 Caer Gai *SH 87 31*. CIIC 418.
   Hic iacet Salvianus Burgo Cavi, filius Cupetian[i]
   Possible variant readings: *hec* for *hic*; *Burso* for *Burgo*.
   Date: 5th to early 6th ECMW; not noticed LHEB. The stone is lost; the reading derives from a 17th-century copy.
3 ECMW 284 Llan-y-mawddwy *SH 90 19*, seven miles south of Caer Gai. CIIC 419.
   Filiae Salvia[n]- hic iacit Ve ... maie uxsor Tigirnici et filie eius Onerat-[uxsor ia]cit Rigohene [mater? ...]ocet- [et? ...]ac-
   Possible variant readings: *Verimate, Vetti[a] Maie; [hic iac] Rigohene.*
   Date: 6th-century ECMW; not noticed LHEB. The stone is lost; 18th-century reading reproduced ECMW.

4 ECMW 285 Tomen-y-mur *SH 70 38*, the next Roman fort on the road from Caer Gai to Caernarvon. CIIC p. 397.

D M Barrect- Carantei

Date: 5th ECMW, apparently solely on the basis of the formula DM; not noticed LHEB. The stone is lost; the reading is 19th-century.

5 CIIC 514 Liddel Water, Roxburgh, between Newcastleton *NY 48 87* and Hawick *NY 56 96*. PSAS 70, 1935–6, 33.

Hic iacit Caranti fili Cupitiani

Date: late 5th to early 6th LHEB 290. The stone is extant.

6 CIIC 510 Kirkliston *NT 12 74*, 8 miles west of Edinburgh.

In [h]oc tumulo iacit Vett[i]a f[ilia] Victr[ici?]

Possible variant reading: *Vict[o]r[is]*.

Date: early 6th LHEB 407. The stone is extant; it was found in a long cist cemetery.

Notes

1 and 2. *Burgo Cavi,* placed between the name of Salvianus and of his father, is not a personal name; it should indicate the place to which he belonged. *Burgus* is the normal late western Latin for a small fort, in this case 'the fort of Cavos'. Since Cavos is buried nearby, he is likely to have been the person who named the fort.

2 and 5; 4 and 5. The personal names Carant(e)us and Cupetianus are both otherwise unrecorded in these centuries in Britain; it is therefore improbable that two pairs of different people bore the names in the same context.

3 and 6. Vettius is a Roman family, not otherwise known in Britain in these centuries; the restoration is uncertain, but if it was inscribed on both stones, it suggests the likelihood that the persons were related.

The Persons

If the three pairs of people who have the same name were identical, as seems probable, the relations between them are

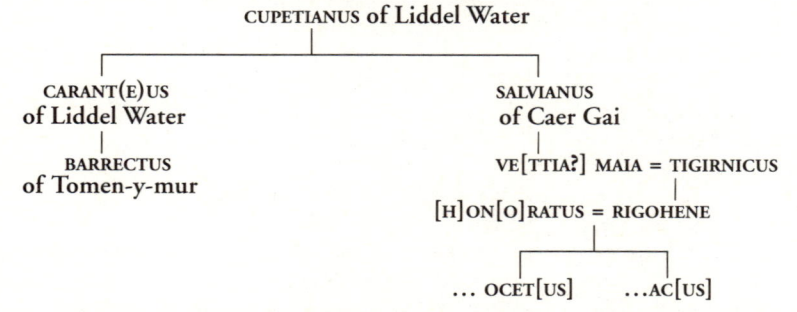

```
                    CUPETIANUS of Liddel Water
                              |
         ┌────────────────────┴────────────────────┐
   CARANT(E)US                               SALVIANUS
   of Liddel Water                           of Caer Gai
        |                                         |
   BARRECTUS                         VE[TTIA?] MAIA = TIGIRNICUS
   of Tomen-y-mur                                 |
                                      [H]ON[O]RATUS = RIGOHENE
                                                 |
                                    ┌────────────┴────────────┐
                                 ... OCET[US]            ...AC[US]
```

All dates suggested for British inscriptions of the 5th and following centuries rest upon somewhat fragile assumptions; but those advanced for these stones are consistent with the relationships that the stones report, except for the date given to the lost Barrectus stone, on the basis of a formula not otherwise known. The deaths of both sons of Cupetianus are placed '5th to early 6th'; Salvianus' descendants are allotted to the

6th century. Cupetianus' lifetime should therefore be mid to late 5th century. The stones suggest that Salvianus moved from his father's homeland, on the borders of the Selgovae and the Votadini, to central Wales, about the end of the fifth century; and that his nephew accompanied or followed him, while his daughter may have used the same family-name as a native of the Edinburgh region.

Salvianus was an approximate, perhaps a younger contemporary of Cavos, who named the fort where he lived and died in Merioneth. A text in 6th-century spelling names a Cauuus, father of Gildas; his home was north of the Clyde, but his son was in Wales, in infancy, by about the year 500 (see p. 205.3). A late, but quite independent genealogical tradition lists half a dozen relatives of Gildas, two of them in or near Roman forts within ten miles of Caer Gai, the rest elsewhere in mid-Wales, at Caersws, Clyro and near Abergavenny.

Each separate strand of evidence bristles with uncertainties. They combine to suggest a migration from the lands of the Votadini and their neighbours to Merioneth and mid-Wales at about the time when Cunedda's nephew Marianus is said to have moved from Votadinian territory to name Merioneth; and at a time when the lands by and south of Forth and Clyde are said to have obeyed Dyfnwal, apparently a firm ally of Arthur. The context suggests that the movement was Arthur's answer to renewed Irish attacks, matching the Demetian campaign in the south (p. 126 *Age*).

124.3   FERGUS: see p. 180 *Age*.
125.1   CUNORIX, EBICATOS: see L Cunorix and p. 137 *Age*.
125.1   SILCHESTER: Ebicatos may have had a neighbour or successor, noteworthy in his own day. Berkshire is the shire of Barruc or Berroc, and until the 12th century the woodland in the south-east of the county, north of Hungerford and including the early English area about East Shefford, bore the same name; Asser (ch. 1) in the 9th century supposed that the county was named from the woodland. 'Barruc' is a pre-English regional name, and is commonly derived from British *barr* (top), with locative suffix -*aco*-. But, since elsewhere in Britain 'Barrock' names normally refer to single hilltops, and since British regional names that are not of Roman origin often derive from 5th- or 6th-century rulers, an alternative possibility is that Barruc was the personal name of a local lord, either of Silchester or of a small territory on its north-eastern border. If so, the name is probably Irish. See P Silchester.
125.1   CYNRIC: see p. 225 *Age*.
125.2   CATWALLAUN: see p. 168 *Age*.
125.2   ILLAN: see p. 168 *Age*.
125.3   KIDWELLY: see Nennius 14; cf. p. 158 *Age*.
125.3   DEMETIA: the dynasty were of the Uí Liatháin, not of the Déssi: see p. 158 *Age*.
126.2   BRYCHAN: see texts in VSBG and EWGT.
126.4   THEODORIC: see L. The significance of the name is easily overlooked because the Welsh form, Tewdrig, superficially resembles Tewdwr, which transliterates Theodore and is Englished as Tudor. There is no direct relationship between Germanic Theude-ric and Greek Theo-dorus. Tewdrig's Germanic ancestry is confirmed by the name of his father, Theudebald, transcribed in the Brychan documents as 'Teithfallt', or in similar spellings.
127.1   NAMED PLACES: see note to Map 7. The distances are Brecon (Llan Maes) to

Lan Semin 24 miles; thence to Methrum 28 miles; thence to Caer Farchell 31 miles (to Porth Mawr 35 miles).

127.1 LLAN MARCHELL: the name should normally denote the monastery of a monk named Marcellus, but might mean a monastery established at a place already named after Marcellus. In North Wales a Marcellus or Marcella named Llanmarchell, the old name of Denbigh; Ystrad Marchell near Welshpool; and Capel Marchell in Llanrwst, LBS 3, 438, but there is no trace of a monastic Marcellus in south Wales.

129.1 BOIA: see L and E David.

130.2 BROCAGNUS: CIIC 478.

130.2 FINGAR: see E Fingar, Guiner and L Theodoric.

130.2 CORNISH PARISHES: see Map 25, p. 362 *Age*.

130.3 BUDIC ... MAXENTIUS: see p. 93 *Age*.

132.3 RECTORES: Gildas 1, 14; for *speculator* in the meaning of bishop, not here relevant, see AB 76, 1958, 379.

133.2 MASUNA: Dessau ILS 859.

133.2 ARMORICA: Greg. Tur. HF 4, 4; cf. p. 251.3 below.

133.3 AMERAUDUR: e.g. BBC 72, 9 cited p. 104 *Age*.

133.4 IUDICES: see p. 201 *Age*.

133.4 MAGISTRATUS: ECMW 103.

135.2 RECTORES: Gildas 1, 14; cf. p. 132 *Age*.

136.1 DIVORTIO: Gildas 10, 2.

136.1 KEMPSTON: see S Beds. and Map 18. These sites will be better understood when 'small long' brooches have been more closely studied.

137.1 CITIES: Gildas 26, 2 *sed ne nunc quidem, ut antea, civitates patriae inhabitantur; sed desertae dirutaeque hactenus squalent.*

137.1 JEROME: *Ep.* 1, 3; the city of Vercellae in northern Italy was in 370 *raro habitatore semiruta*; but its decay did not prevent a consular governor from holding his court in the city.

137.1 WROXETER: *Ant. Jl.* 48, 1968, 296; cf. L Cunorix; cf. p. 125 *Age*.

137.1 SILCHESTER: P; CIIC 496; cf. p. 125 *Age*. Local tradition also named a former supposed ruler whose name may possibly have been British. Camden's *Britannia* 1, 222 (Gough) reported that local people gave the name 'Onion's pennies' to Silchester Roman coins, 'fancying this Onion a great giant who formerly lived in this city'. I am grateful to Mr K.R.Davis, who drew my attention to this statement and to the possibility that 'Onion' might derive from the Welsh name En(n)iaun.

137.2 MAGIOVINIUM: unpublished; see P.

137.2 LONDON: see P.

137.3 CADBURY CASTLE: *ST 62 26* in South Cadbury parish, to be distinguished from nearby North Cadbury, and also from Cadbury, near Congresbury, *ST 43 64*, south-west of Bristol. The site has been dubbed 'Camelot' by antiquaries from the 16th century to the 20th; though not Camelot, it was an important fortress of the Arthurian period; cf. *Ant. Jl.* 47, 1967, 70; 48, 1968, 6; 49, 1969, 30; 50, 1970, 14; 51, 1971, 1; *Ant.* 41, 1967, 50; 42, 1968, 47; 43, 1969, 52; 44, 1970, 46.

139.2 WALES ... TRIBUTE: see p. 220.3.

139.2 NO NEW EMPEROR: later traditions name two sons of Arthur, but do not regard either of them as rulers of any territory; cf. L Arthur.

140.3 MEDRAUT: The only other record of the name Medraut is BYS 51, Dyfnauc Sant m. Medraut; Dyfnauc (Domnoc) is a common name, but the only

6th or 7th century Domnoc known in Britain named Dunwich in Suffolk, Bede HE 2, 15.

141.2   WILLIAM OF MALMESBURY: *de Gestis Regum* 1, 8.

8 Pagan Ireland (pp. 142–163)

142.1   PATRICK: *Confessio* 46.

142.1   TOLD SEPARATELY: in the following narrative it has proved necessary to repeat the accounts of many events, and sometimes the comments made upon them, since they are viewed from a different standpoint in the context of the history of the Irish or the British, the English or the Northerners.

143.4   GENEALOGIES: see G Introduction, and G 1.

144.2   ANNALS: see A Introduction. The main European source seems to have been a Latin translation, no longer extant, of Eusebius' Chronicle, with continuations, fuller than the translation by Jerome which has been preserved (see vol. 2, pp. 19-32). This text was also a main source of Bede's Chronicle, since he and the Annals quote from it independently, and occasionally reproduce passages that are otherwise preserved only in the Armenian translation of Eusebius. Irish notices are said to have been collected from the 6th century onward. Most of the apparent inconsistencies are due to comments incorporated from corrupt genealogies or to mistakes, usually identifiable, in the European sources. Except for the Inisfallen Annals, most printed texts are faulty, and fail to distinguish the body of the MSS they reproduce from glosses added thereto.

145.3   MAELGWN ... IDA: Nennius 62, cf. 61; 63.

146.1   SAINTS' LIVES: see p. 164 *Age*.

146.1   EVIDENCE OF ... DEDICATIONS: outlined by Bowen SCSW 6 ff.

146.1   ARGUMENTS: cf. e.g. Simpson *Celtic Church* and Owen Chadwick SEBH 173 ff.

146.1   CHURCH OF MARTIN: Gregory of Tours, sensitive to the conventions of his own day, is careful to describe the church as 'the church which Briccius built over Martin'.

146.1   NINIAN: see p. 337 *Age*. Bede's statements are explicit; it is most improbable that Ninian, devoted to Martin's then rare advocacy of monastic discipline and preaching to peasants and barbarians, could have avoided visiting Tours on his return from Rome in the 390s, and spending some time with Martin.

146.2   LOCAL ... TRADITION: a clear instance is St. Asaph, formerly Llanelwy, the monastery on the river Elwy. The conventions of the medieval founders of the see did not permit a cathedral to be dedicated to a river; it was therefore given the name of a saint who was already widely honoured locally, but who was not, like others, the national saint of a Welsh kingdom.

146.2   NATIONAL TRADITION: Irish Norse brought Columba to Iceland, and Patrick and Brigit to Cumberland, and sometimes elsewhere in England; for the few dedications in England to Welsh and Armorican saints, see p. 370 *Age* and map 28, p. 393 *Age*. It is noteworthy that dedications to the numerous major or local saints of Normandy, Brittany and Flanders are not found in lands settled by lords from these territories after the Norman conquest.

147.3   PREHISTORY: the main sources are *Lebor Gabála Érenn* (The Book of the Invasion of Ireland), the substance of whose tradition was known to Nennius, and to Cormac mac Cuilennáin in the 9th century; Keating's

	History of Ireland 1635; and the annals. LG incorporates some 136 poems older than itself, varying in length up to about 150 lines. The synchronists supply dates, which the annals repeat.
147.3	ANTIQUARIES: cited Keating 1, 5, 4 (ITS 1, 149). The 'Just Canon' is the Old Testament.
147.3	I LIKE NOT: CS p. 9.
147.3	NOT GENUINE HISTORY: Keating 1, 5, 4 (ITS 1, 147), cf. AT (Tigernach) 307 BC (RC 16, 1895, 394) *omnia monimenta Scottorum usque Cimbaed incerta erant.* Cimbaed, whose reign is dated 307–279 BC in the annals, was the legendary founder of the Ulaid dynasty of Emain; recent excavation has shown that the great ceremonial mound of Navan (Emain, near Armagh), was constructed at a radio-carbon date of 245 BC, + or – 50 years; cf. CArch. 22, 1970, 304 ff., where the date given needs slight adjustment. Tigernach accepts the historical reality of the Ulaid heroes, but rejects their mythological predecessors; recent discovery tends to confirm rather than to challenge his judgment.
148.2	BRONZE AGE ... ROUTES: e.g. JRSAI 75, 1945, 94, fig. 6, cauldrons with conical rivets, a dozen by the Tyrrhene Sea, 4 about the headwaters of the Rhine and Danube, 10 in Denmark and Sweden, 7 in Ireland and 1 in Wales.
149.2	PTOLEMY: his account of Ireland is conveniently set forth in the Ordnance Survey's Map of Roman Britain, p. 20; cf. O'Rahilly EIHM, 1 ff.
149.3	CRUITHNE: held to have been powerful in the distant past (cf. e.g. AI, AT AD 172) 'Seven kings of the Cruithne ruled Ireland before Conn'; Tuathal's predecessor Elim was regarded both as king of Ireland and as king 'of the Domnann' LG 9, 95 (para. 593a) (ITS 5, 311), etc.
149.3	CRUITHNE ... IDENTITY ... LANGUAGE: change of language need not imply change of national identity; a modern Jones or Williams does not cease to be Welsh because he speaks English and bears a name of English origin.
150.1	JACKSON: OIT 44–45 note.
151.3	TUATHAL: extensively treated in AC 50–54, Keating 1, 39 (ITS 2, 243), LG 9, 95 (para. 593 ff.) (ITS 5, 309).
151.5	AGRICOLA: Tacitus *Agricola* 24, in 81 or 82 AD.
155.2	CAERNARVON: RIB 430; the repair of a ruined aqueduct implies rebuilding after disuse.
155.2	BENNE BRIT: see A 217; cf. also CGH 403 LL 328f II, 14; Keating 1, 41 (ITS 2, 272), etc. The name is a corruption rather than an invention; invented foreigners were normally given Irish names, as 'Fergus the king of Spain's son', AC 59 etc.
155.3	CORMAC: see A 217–257; cf. also especially AC 60 ff., Keating 1, 43 ff. (ITS 2, 298 ff.) etc.
155.3	OBSOLUTELY: AC 60.
155.3	ALBA: see P.
156.1	REACHTAIRE: Keating 1, 43 (ITS 2, 306).
156.1	FINN: see especially A 257.
156.1	WISE, LEARNED: AC 60.
156.3	INSCRIPTIONS 244–264; of Philip (244–249) RIB 327 (Caerleon), 882–883 (Papcastle), 915 (Old Penrith); of Gallus (251–253) 2057–8 (Bowness-on-

NOTES TO *THE AGE OF ARTHUR* (pp. 147–162) 53

        Solway); of Valerian (253–258, in Britain) 316, 334 (Caerleon), 913 (near Carlisle), 2042 (Burgh-by-Sands); of Postumus (258–268) 605 (Lancaster, dated 262/266).

157.2 AMARGEIN: e.g. Keating 1, 43 (ITS 2, 304); cf. Plummer VSH clxiii 6.
157.3 EMAIN: the ceremonial mount at Navan, p. 151 *Age*, remained important for several centuries after 300 BC. The hill-top of Armagh, 2 miles away, was fortified at a radio-carbon date of AD 310, + or − 80 years; cf. CArch. 22, 1970, 308, where '5th century' is mistaken. Cf. 147.3 above.
157.5 CRIMTHANN: The Southern Irish texts do not refer to the Picts of north Britain.
158.1 DERGIND: CGH 196 R 148a 31; see P. Inscriptions, CIIC 488, 489, 492, 493, 494.
158.2 UI LIATHAIN: see especially CGH 228 R 151b 37 Lec.
158.2 NENNIUS 14: *filii autem Liethan obtinuerunt in regione Demetorum et in aliis regionibus, id est Guir Cetgueli, donec explusi sunt a Cuneda et a filiis eius ab omnibus Brittannicis regionibus.*
158.2 MUNSTER: see L Builc.
158.2 LEINSTER: the peninsula of Lleyn, by Caernarvon, may take its name from the Laigin of Leinster; cf. also the later campaigns of Illán of Leinster (see E Brigit and p. 168 *Age*), possibly fought in support of compatriots who had settled earlier in Britain.
159.2 NIALL: King of Alba, king of the western world, CGH 122 R 136 b 27, b 23; king of the western world, invaded the kingdom of Letha (Letavia, Llydaw, see P), meaning the Continent in general, or specifically Gaul, as here, and especially Brittany, LG 9, 114 (para. 612; ITS 5, 348).
160.1 CORCC: see A 439 Senchus Mór, FM etc.; Keating 1, 3 (ITS 1, 122–124), etc. Eoganacht genealogists legitimised his sovereignty by marrying him to Crimthann's sister Mongfind, whose other connections place her generations earlier, and make her the wife of Eochaid.
160.2 NIALL'S SONS: see *Ériu* 13, 1942, 92; Hogan *Onomasticon* Cenél, Tír, Uí etc.
160.3 NAMES: the fundamental discussion remains MacNeill's *Early Irish Population Groups* (PRIA 29 C, 1911/12, 59 ff.); cf. *Ériu* 3, 1907, 42 ff.
160.3 PATRICK: *Confessio* 41, cf. 52; *Ep. ad Coroticum* 12.
161.2 MUIRCHU 9: *imperator barbarorum regnans in Temoria, quae erat caput Scotorum, Loiguire nomine, filius Neill, origo stirpis regiae huius pene insolae.*
161.2 ADOMNAN: 1, 36, adding *deo auctore ordinatus.*
161.2 BRIAN BORU: Book of Armagh 16v *ego scripsi id est Calvus Perennis, in conspectu Briain imperatoris Scotorum*. Brian plainly authorised and accepted a title written under his eyes. The scribe's name translates Mael Suthain.
161.3 ADOMNAN: Comgall, Cormac 3, 17; Columbanus 3, 12.
161.4 GLOSSES: e.g. *Cenél Conaill Cernaig*, Great Book of Lecan 190, Book of Leinster 312, cited Hogan 218; *Clann Cathair Máir* CGH 78 R 125 a 50, in contrast with the normal usage of e.g. CGH 358 LL 318 b 60 *Ic Cathair Mór condrecat Hui Falgi 7 Hui Enechglais ... 7 Hui Crimthaind 7 clanda Cathair archena*; cf. e.g. CGH 44 R 121 a 19 ff., where Cathair is made ancestor of families named from persons elsewhere dated to the early 5th century; *Cenél Rochada* CGH 139 R 140 b 46. Such associations are not made in the main pedigrees or their headings.
162.1 BEC: AC 550.
162.1 ALL SUBJECTS: Ultán 66 (TT 534). The Life is early.

9 Christian Ireland (164–176)

164.1   COULANGES: *La Monarquie Franque* 9–12, cited Stokes *Lismore Lives* xci-xcii; cf. also below, vol. 6, pp. 100–3, 165–8.

164.2   SUPPRESSED ... DOCTRINE: e.g. Jocelyn of Furness complained, *vita Kentigerni* prologue, that his sources were full of 'solecisms' and also *relatu perverso et a fide averso*; he took pride in his attempt, in rewriting them, *barbarice exarata Romano sale condire*, and tried to restore *sana doctrina*. Serious study cannot rest content with poking fun at Jocelyn's pretentious style and boundless ignorance of the times he described; the need is to get rid of the 'Roman salt' and 'sound doctrine', and to seek out the 'barbarisms' and 'perversity' that Jocelyn was unable to suppress.

164.2   GARRULITY: *Britannica garrulitate,* Vitalis of Fleury *vita Pauli Aureliani* ASS prologue; cf. RC 5, 1881/3, 415.

164.2   UNCOUTH ... NAMES: *absona ... barbara Britonum nomina,* Vitalis of Fleury; cf. note above; cf. AB 1, 1882, 209. The nature and extent of the omissions and alterations may be observed, since a version of the original which Vitalis abbreviated is extant.

165.1   HISTORICAL CRITICISM: the starting point of criticism is the comparison between those Lives that survive both in their original form, or in an early version that reproduces much of its names and content, and in 12th-century or later recensions. The Lives of Samson, p. 357 *Age*, and of Paul Aurelian, cf. note 164.2 above, are among the most important of those so preserved. Such comparison demonstrates how medieval editors actually altered their originals and disperses subjective speculation about what was or was not 'forged' or invented. No such comparison has yet been systematically undertaken.

166.1   ENDA: see E and p. 352 *Age*.

166.2   CIARAN SAIGIR: *vita* (VSH) 18. See E.

166.2   CIVIL VIOLENCE: Prisoners freed, e.g. *vitae*: Ciarán Clonmacnoise 19; Colmán Elo 24; Adomnán 1, 11. Cruelties, e.g. the tossing of a murderer's child, which survived to Viking times as *gall-cherd*, Macnissi (Sal.) 9; Cainnech 34, etc. Execution, e.g. Fintan 17; cf. Ruadán p. 170 *Age*. Opposition to war e.g. Tigernach (VSH) 10, where the glory of the saint's deception was that 'the enemy army was put to flight without hurting anyone and without being harmed itself'. Comgall startled contemporary notions of justice by sentencing a slave girl, convicted of trying to poison her mistress, to be freed both of her slave status and of her prison, to spend the rest of her life in perpetual penance. Other saints, however, became patrons of their people, whose military victory their prayers ensured.

166.2   VORTIGERN'S DAUGHTER: see E Foirtchern, and p. 65 *Age*. The surviving notices report that Foirtchern, whose name is an Irish transliteration of the British Vortigern, was the son of Fedlimid, son of Loegaire, and of the daughter of an unnamed British king. Since she gave her son the alien name of Vortigern, it is probable that in the original version of the tale he was her unnamed royal father; for the surviving fragments are unaware that there was a British king so named. Foirtchern became a notable ecclesiastic, particularly active in South Leinster, and his name subsequently passed into common use for a short period, especially in the south, since he was the principal teacher of Finnian of Clonard, the father of Irish monasticism. The name is not recorded in Ireland before his time, and soon after disappeared. Cf. L Vortigern.

NOTES TO *THE AGE OF ARTHUR* (pp. 164–174)

166.3   PATRICK ... POPE ... BISHOP: see pp. 64 and 348 *Age*.
167.4   OCHA: cf. MacNeill *Phases* 190 ff., 231 ff. Though the annals and genealogies do not support the view that *derbfine* succession already obtained generally in the 5th century, the battle secured Uí Néill kingship.
168.2   DAL RIADA: see p. 180 *Age*, also P.
168.3   ILLAN: *Novemque certamina in Britannia prospere egit* Ultán *vita* Brigit 90 (TT 538); variant *octosque* Animosus 2, 12 (TT 551).
168.3   SERIGI: (Triad 62, etc.) see L Serygei.
168.4   DEMETIA, CORNWALL: see L Theodoric, and pp. 125 ff. *Age*.
168.5   MAC ERCA ... LIVED AT PEACE: the numerous featureless battles entered in A 530, 531, appear to derive from a saga, whose date should be 6th or 7th century, since the source is given as Cennfaelad, and are entered for convenience in the annals at Mac Erca's death. The only other wars noted by the annals are dated before his accession.
169.2   REIGN OF TUATHAL: *Secundus vero ordo ... ab extremis Tuthayl Maylgairb temporibus* Catalogus 2, confirmed by very many individual accounts.
169.3   DIARMAIT ... BRIGIT: Ultán 64 (TT 534).
169.3   CIARAN: *vita Columbae* (O'Donnell), 44 (TT 396; ZCP 74).
169.4   DERRY: the traditions are summarised in Reeves' *Adamnan* 160. The annals' date agrees with the tradition that Derry was founded immediately after the death of Mobhí Cláirainech (E).
170.2   RUADAN: *vita* 15–18; AC 85–88.
170.2   PEACEFUL KING: *vita Ruadán* 17, *Rex enim defensor patrie pacificus erat, adiutor ecclesiarum et pauperum, verax in sermone, equus in iudicio, et firmus in fide.*
170.2   ULAID POET: Beccán, M. Oengus, prefaces, pp. 6 and 14.
170.2   HIS OWN SON: Book of Leinster 358, Book of Lismore 94 b, cited Stokes *Lismore Lives* xxvii; M. Donegal April 5.
170.3   BRITISH KING: perhaps Peter or Arthur of Demetia; the powerful Rhun of Gwynedd is less likely to have feared Irish threats.
171.1   COUNTRY SECURE: *vita Ruadán* 17, *Ego firmavi regiones, et pactum firmum feci in omni loco, ut pax firma ecclesiis et plebibus esset ubique. Ego bonum defendo secundum legem Christi; vos autem malum operamini, defendentes reum mortis. De parva enim multa surgent.*
171.1   PRICE: the author of the Life understood an ordinary compensation, and resumes his own jejune narrative, and inferior Latinity, with a story of miraculous horses who acquitted the payment.
172.1   COLUMBAN HOUSES: Reeves *Adamnan* 276 ff. lists 37 Irish and over 50 Scottish houses. The list is not exhaustive, but is likely to include some later offshoots which claimed personal foundation; see Map 26, p. 371 *Age*.
172.2   FINNIAN'S BOOK: the story is told many times, and is here cited from *vita Columbae* (O'Donnell) 2, 1 (TT 408 (misnumbered 402)–409), ZCP 168; see also E Columba, Finnian of Moville.
172.4   CURNAN: A 560; *vita Columbae* (O'Donnell) 2, 2 (TT 409), ZCP 168; the lost Book of Sligo, cited Egerton MS 1782, *Silva Gadelica* 1, 79, translation 2, 84; cf. Stokes *Lismore Lives* xxviii; and other versions.
173.1   CUIL DREMHNI: *vita Columbae* (O'Donnell) 2, 3 (TT 409), ZCP 170 ff., cf. A 561, etc. The essential facts are reported by Adomnán, see E Columba, and p. 377 *Age*.
173.2   BRENDAN OF CLONFERT: see p. 384 *Age*.
174.2   COLUMBA ... CROWN: cf. p. 169 *Age* and *Betha Coluim Chille* (Stokes *Lismore Lives* 749), 'By inheritance his was the natural right to the kingship of Ireland, and it would have been offered him if he had not put it from him for the sake of God.'

174.2 THRONE OFFERED: *vita Columbae* (O'Donnell) 1, 44 (TT 396) *sceptrum antequam offeretur abrenunciavit*; 'it was offered many a time but he refused it' ZCP 74.
174.3 SYNOD ... EXCOMMUNICATED: Adomnán *vita Columbae* 3, 3 etc.
174.3 LASRIAN: *vita* 31 (VSH) *Sanctus vero Columba visitavit sanctum Lasrianum, confessorem suum, post bellum de Cul Dremni, petens ab eo salubre consilium, quomodo post necem multorum ibi occisorum benevolenciam Dei ... mereretur accipere. Beatus igitur Lasrianus ... imperavit illi ut tot animas a penis liberaret quot animarum causa perdicionis extiterat; et cum hoc ei precepit ut perpetuo moraretur extra Hiberniam exilio.* Exile did not of course preclude frequent visits to Ireland; it forbade permanent residence.
174.4 GILDAS: see p. 379 *Age*.
175.1 CAIN ADOMNAN: ed. Meyer; cf. Kenney 245; SEIL 269 ff.
175.4 MONASTIC UPSURGE: see p. 357 *Age*.
176.2 KING ... BORN IRISH: Aldfrith; cf. p. 196 *Age*.

10 The Dál Riada Scots (177–185)

177.1 SCOTLAND: see Maps 2, 10–12, 26 (pp. 47, 179, 187, 189, 371), and P Atecotti, Caledonii, Circinn, Fortrenn, Miathi, Picts, Scotland. The principal collection of the sources is still the work of W.F.Skene, more than a hundred years ago, especially in CPS and CS; selections thereof are translated, with some supplementation, by Anderson ESSH. Much of Skene's interpretation is coloured by the assumptions of his day; but since no comparable comprehensive history of early Scotland has since appeared, any discussion of the formation of the Scottish nation must admit a considerable debt, directly or indirectly, to the body of evidence which Skene assembled and used.
177.2 ATECOTTI: the official 4th-century spelling of the *Notitia Dignitatum* means 'the very ancient peoples'; see P.
180.2 IRISH LEGEND: Watson CPNS 213 ff. summarises a number of the main stories.
180.2 BEDE: HE 1, 1, *Brittania ... Scottorum nationem in Pictorum parte recepit, qui duce Reuda de Hibernia progressi ... a quo ... hodie Dal Reudini vocantur, nam lingua eorum 'daal' partem significat.*
180.2 FERGUS ... DAL RIADA: see p. 168 *Age*.
180.3 TWO TEXTS: *Senchus Fer nAlban*, History of the Men of Alba (Skene CPS 308): *Cethri prím ceneoil*, The Four Chief Dynasties (Skene CPS 316), see p. 451 *Age*.
180.3 COWALL, GOWRIE: see P Dál Riada.
180.4 PICT RECORDS: see p. 191 *Age*.
181.1 IONA: granted by Conall, A 574; by Bridei and the Picts, Bede HE 3, 4.
181.2 IONA ... BURIAL PLACE: *Bethu Adomnán*, cited CPS 408; cf. MHH 179, 2 (AIM 2, 10 ff.; *Celtic Review* 5, 1908, 97 ff.).
181.2 NINIAN, KENTIGERN, COLUMBA: see Map 26, p. 371 *Age*.
181.4 SEPARATE PORTIONS: *rí Aodhán na n-iol-rann* (Duan Albanach, CPS 60); the verses single out the particular distinction of each king, and therefore imply their author's view that Aedán was the first to unite the portions, to master Cenél Loairn and Cenél nOengusso.
182.1 CONSECRATE AEDAN: Adomnán 3, 5.
182.3 DRUM CEAT: see P.

182.4	PEACE ... BRITISH:	Aedán may have attacked the Clyde after Columba's death.
183.3	FIFE:	Skene CPS 315–316, variant note 7.
183.3	CUMMENE:	Adomnán 3, 5.
183.4	GLEN MURESON:	cf. Skene CS 1, 249.
184.2	CUMMENE:	Adomnán 3, 5.

11 The Picts (pp. 186–199)

186.1	PICTS:	see P; cf. especially Chadwick *Early Scotland* 1 ff. and Isabel Henderson *The Picts*.
186.3	INSCRIPTION:	RIB 191 *Lossio Veda ... nepos Vepogeni, Caledo*; cf. Vepoguenech, placed about the first half of the third century in the king-lists.
188.2	PLACE NAMES:	Map 11; Watson CPNS surveys Celtic, but not English or Norse names. 'Scotland north of the Forth' (206 ff.) is treated as a single unit, but the survey is almost entirely confined to districts east of the Great Glen. Four isolated Pictish place names opposite Skye suggest a garrison whose names endured; a few stones in Caithness, the islands and southern Scotland are probably memorials of lords and colonists in the years of Pictish supremacy.
188.3	DUNS AND BROCHS:	see Map 12. Many contained Roman objects of the early Empire but, unlike other native sites in Scotland, none has any of the late Empire; cf. *Britannia* 1, 1970, 202, cf. 210, 212. See especially IANB 111 ff.; *Ant.* 39, 1965, 266; PPS 31,1965, 93; *C.Arch.* 2, 1967, 27; 12, 1969, 5.
188.3	ORKNEYS:	not part of Pictland, but situated 'beyond the Picts' (*ultra Pictos*), Nennius 8; their king was a subject foreign tributary of the Pict king Bridei, p.193 *Age*.
190.4	OTHER INDICATIONS:	e.g. various confused Irish traditions, backed by Tacitus (*Agricola* 11) 'the red hair and huge limbs of the Caledonians proclaim their German origin; the dark complexions and the frequency of curly hair among the Silures (of Monmouthshire) ... justify the belief that their ancestors crossed from Spain and settled there'. Excavation has confirmed the tradition of migration from Spain to South Wales, some two thousand years before Tacitus' time, and thereby adds weight to his comment on the more recently arrived Caledonians. Tacitus uses 'Caledonia' as a general term for all north Britain; the dated evidence of the brochs and their situation suggests that in his time their builders were the dominant power in most of northern Britain. At the time of their arrival in Britain it is probable that the larger part of the Germanic peoples still dwelt in Scandinavia. See P Caledonii.
190.4	SOME OTHER CONQUERORS:	e.g. the Normans, in England, France and Italy, and the Bulgarians, among the Slavs of the eastern Balkans, etc.
190.5	ATECOTTI:	see P and p. 177 *Age*.
190.5	ABORIGINES:	they are unlikely to have been concentrated in a single area. Communities who cling to a dying language are often isolated from each other by considerable distances, as, for example, the pockets of Slavonic speaking peoples who survived into modern times in widely separated regions of Germany.
191.1	OGAM:	see p. 422 *Age*.
191.1	STONES INSCRIBED IN OGAM:	ed. MacAlister *MacNeill Essays* 184 ff.; cf. Diack

Inscriptions. Of 17 such Ogam stones, 7 are in the Orkneys and Shetlands, where brochs are numerous, but only 3 in Caithness and Sutherland, and none at all in Skye and the Hebridean area, where brochs are equally numerous. There are 3 in the Northern Pictish lands and 4 in the southern; none in the regions where duns are frequent. In addition, there are three similar inscriptions on knife handles, in Orkney, in the Hebrides, and in Norfolk (p. 57 *Age*); but portable knives are not evidence of settlement. One stone from the Isle of Man may or may not belong to the same series.

Three of the inscriptions were added to Christian crosses, five to Pictish memorial stones, and can therefore hardly be earlier than the 7th or 8th centuries, if so early. But these stones cannot date the others, for date depends upon the origin of the script. The chief consideration is that its authors were familiar with Irish Ogam characters; but no Irish Ogams are known in the countries whence these inscriptions came, and only two are known anywhere in Scotland, both in Dál Riada, in Argyll. The most likely of the several possible origins of the script is therefore Irish Ogams inscribed on wood, by the earlier Irish population of north-western Scotland. The inscriptions appear on stone only in those regions where stone memorials were familiar.

If the symbols represent Irish letters, if the modern transcripts are secure, and if they represent a language at all, it is possible to detect Irish and Norse words for son and daughter, and some Pictish and Latin personal names; but it is also possible that all are an illiterate ornamental borrowing by persons who had seen Irish Ogams, but could not read or understand them. If the symbols do represent a language, the language is unknown, and attempts to 'translate' it have not succeeded.

191.3	BEDE:	HE 3, 4.
191.3	NINIAN:	see E, and p. 337 *Age*; cf. Map 26, p. 371 *Age*.
192.2	INHERITANCE:	see P, Picts; land and property inherited through the woman, CPS 328; 126; 319; sovereignty through the woman, CPS 40; 45; 329. The Picts perpetuated customs that had been more widespread in pre-Roman Britain, and which also survived in other parts of northern Britain. Sovereignty through or of the woman is reported of the Iceni and Brigantes in Britain in the 1st century AD. In the 7th century the queen of Eigg exercised wide authority among the *Iardomnan,* M.Oeng. April 17; in the 6th century or earlier the Hebrides maintained a king who was denied marriage, children and personal property, Solinus (Irish version), ed. Mommsen p. 219; cf. Walter *Solinus,* especially p. 38, and Chadwick ES 92. Matrilinear inheritance still survives in parts of Asia, especially south-western India.
192.2	BRIDEI:	see L.
193.1	BRIDEI'S ROYAL FORTRESS:	Adomnán 2, 35.
193.1	BEDE:	HE 3, 4 *venit ... Columba ... praedicaturus verbum Dei provinciis septentrionalium Pictorum ... gentemque illam verbo et exemplo ad fidem Christi convertit.*
193.1	ADOMNAN:	3, 3 *populorum ducem ad vitam*; cf. 3, 1 *animarum dux ad caelestem*; but Picts are one among several peoples in Adomnán's narrative, and are not the most prominent.
193.1	MAGI:	Adomnán 2, 33–34.
193.1	WINDS:	Adomnán 2, 34.
193.1	LOCH NESS MONSTER:	Adomnán 2, 27 *aquatilis bestia, bilua,* that bit and killed swimmers in the river Ness, below the Loch.

NOTES TO *THE AGE OF ARTHUR* (pp. 191–200)

193.2 LORDS: e.g. at Urquhart, Adomnán 3, 14. Emchath was local, since his son Uirolec was baptised *cum tota domu*.
193.3 ORKNEY KING: Adomnán 2, 42.
194.1 MEMORIAL STONES: Map 11; see P Picts; cf. J.Romilly Allen and J.Anderson ECMS; Isabel Henderson *The Picts* 104 ff.; *Arch. Jl.* 120, 1963, 31, cf. 118, 1961, 14; PSAS 91, 1957/8, 44; Wainwright PP 97; Cruden ECPMS.
194.1 STONES ... DATE: a few of the earliest, e.g. Dunnichen, imitate 6th-century Saxon saucer-brooches too closely for coincidence.
195.1 PENTLAND ... PEHTLAND: so Skene CS 1,238, without citation of evidence; cf. *Pettaland* (Pictland) for the Pentland Firth, between Caithness and Orkney, Watson CPNS 30.
195.2 AETHELFERTH'S SONS: his heir Osric was killed in an Irish battle shortly before Edwin's death A 631.
195.2 EANFRITH: Bede HE 3, 1.
195.3 ENGLISH KING: Talorcan filius Enfreth. It is likely that foreign-born Pictish kings who used Pictish names assumed them on their accession. Talorcan's English name is not recorded.
195.3 BEDE: HE 2, 5.
195.3 ENGLISH UNDER-KING: Beornhaeth (Eddius 19), apparently already in office on the outbreak of the revolt at the beginning of Egferth's reign.
196.1 BESTIAL NATIONS: Eddius 19.
196.1 WASTE ... THE PICTS: Bede HE 4, 26.
196.1 ALDFRITH: see p. 176 *Age*.
196.3 SCOTLAND: The most useful brief survey of Scottish history from the 7th to the 11th century remains that of Skene CS 1,240 ff., though much detail has since been corrected.
197.3 ALBAN: at the Battle of the Standard in 1138, the Scots from beyond the Forth *exclamant Albani! Albani!* HH 8, 9; cf. GESTA STEPHANI *Scotia quae et Albania dicitur*; Richard of Hexham *in fronte belli erant* Picti, Rolls 82, 3, 35 and 163.
197.4 EDINBURGH 960: CPS 365.
197.4 LOTHIANS 1018: Simeon of Durham *de Obsessione Dunelmi* 6.
198.1 DUNCAN KILLED: AT (AD 1040) *Donncadh m. Crinán, aird rí Alban, immatura etate a suis occisus est* ('Duncan mac Crinan, High King of Albany, was killed in youth by his own people'). Tigernach wrote within fifty years of the event.
198.3 WALTER OF OSWESTRY: cf. e.g. G.W.S.Barrow *Regesta Regum Scottorum* 1; for the genealogy see e.g. *Complete Peerage* 5, 391–2, Round *Peerage and Family History* 115 ff.; 129. Walter's grandfather was Flaald, brother of abbot Rhiwallon and son of Alan, steward of Dol; hence the later spread of the name Alan in England and Scotland.

12 British Supremacy (pp. 200–224)

200.1 SOURCES: see pp. 143 and 164 *Age*.
200.2 ARCHAEOLOGICAL EVIDENCE: is still much less in the midlands and the south than in the west and north; and little of it can yet be dated with confidence. 'Grass tempered' pottery, recently recognised, and provisionally dated to the Arthurian centuries, cannot yet be clearly

interpreted; Celtic metalwork, listed by E.Fowler in *Arch. Jl.* 120, 1963, 135 ff., with an extensive bibliography, is reported from a number of southern and midland sites; but the import of British or Irish ornaments and craftsmen does not always imply a British or Irish population. Hanging-bowl escutcheons with unequivocally Irish ornament, mostly of the 7th century, are known almost entirely from English graves, since they survive only in burials; in living use they are likely to have been at least as common among the Irish and British, and among the English they argue only the purchase of objects manufactured by Irishmen, who are as likely to have worked in Britain as in Ireland. Major British sites of the 5th and 6th centuries, outside the north and west, are few, and are at present most numerous in the Home Counties; cf. London, Colchester, Verulamium etc.

What is now known is surveyed in Alcock *Arthur's Britain* 142 ff. As yet the material is disjointed and of uncertain date, and there is not much of it. But since it has only recently begun to be recognised, it is likely that twenty years hence much more will be known, its dates more surely estimated, and that recognisable sites and objects will be more evenly distributed throughout Britain. They may well provide the most useful means of resolving many present uncertainties.

201.1 GILDAS' KINGS: 27 ff.
202.2 EMESA: *Novella Theodosii* 15, 2 (CTh. vol. 2, p. 36).
203.3 PERHAPS OF GLOUCESTER: see L (Aurelius) Caninus.
203.3 VIOLATED HIS DAUGHTER: the offence was no more startling than many other dynastic marriages, e.g. Radiger's with his step-mother (p. 287 *Age*) or the suggestion of marriage between Henry VII and his widowed daughter-in-law; but papal dispensation was less familiar in Gildas' time than a thousand years later.
206.4 ILL-STARRED GENERALS: *infausti duces* Gildas 50, 1.
207.5 CAERWENT: see especially E Tatheus.
208.1 PENYCHEN: see E Cadoc.
208.1 DEMETIA ... BORDER: *Venta provincia proxima eiusdem Demetiae* vita 1 Samsonis 1; *ultra Sabrinae fluminis fretum Demetarum sacerdotes* Aldhelm *Ep.* 4 (MGH p. 484), written from Malmesbury.
208.1 DUBRICIUS, TEILO: see E. David is freely called 'bishop' and 'archbishop' in the Lives; but no episcopal acts, comparable with those ascribed to Dubricius and Teilo, are related of him.
208.3 POMPEIUS, TURPILIUS: ECMW 198; 43. Cf. p. 251 *Age*.
208.3 ILLTUD: see E.
208.3 CHEPSTOW: *vita Tathei* 4; see E Tatheus; the place is probably Portskewett.
208.3 CARRIAGE AND PAIR: Gildas *Ep.* 4 *habent pecora et vehicula vel pro consuetudine patriae vel sua infirmitate*; cf. *Ep.* 2. *vehiculis equisque vehuntur*.
210.1 DECANGI: Tac. *Ann.* 12, 32; Decanti ACM 822, cf. 812; cf. Degannwy by Llandudno, traditionally a royal centre of Maelgwn; Decangli, inscribed on lead pigs CIL VII 204–206; JRS 12, 1922, 283 15; cf. Tegeingl (Flintshire). It is possible but not probable that these spellings relate to two distinct adjacent peoples; cf. P Decangi.
210.2 WANSDYKE: see P. The frontier work included stretches evidently wooded in the 5th and 6th centuries, where it was not necessary to dig a dyke.

NOTES TO *THE AGE OF ARTHUR* (pp. 201–219)

210.3   GREAT KINGS: e.g. Amlaut, Kassanauth.
211.1   SILCHESTER: see p. 137 *Age*.
211.1   SILCHESTER DYKES: *Ant*. 18, 1944, 113, cf. 17, 1943, 188; cf. *Berks. Arch. Jl.* 54, 1954, 50.
211.2   ENGLISH TEXTS: SC.
211.3   CALCHVYNYDD: see P.
211.3   VERULAMIUM: cf. p. 137 *Age*.
211.4   LONDON, COLCHESTER: see p. 137 *Age*. The latest relics of British London are an *amphora* (wine or oil jar) imported from the eastern mediterranean, probably in or about the 6th century *Britannia* 1, 1970, 292 (where note 127 corrects the text), and several others excavated earlier, but first recognised after this discovery. The exact dating of these vessels is still uncertain.
211.4   ARTHUR'S CAMPAIGN: Nennius 56; see p. 111 *Age*.
211.4   LINDSEY: one of its early 7th-century rulers is said to have borne the British name of Caedbad.
211.4   POETS: see T and p. 241 *Age*.
212.1   WROXETER: see p. 241 *Age*.
213.3   DEIRANS: see p. 77 *Age*.
214.3   YEAVERING: see p. 320 *Age*.
214.4   REGED: see P.
214.4   DENT: *regio Dunotinga* is one of four districts of north-western Yorkshire overrun by the English in or before the 670s, Eddius 17. The passage is overlooked in EPNS WRY 6, 252, where the early spellings Denet(h) are rightly related to a British *Dinned* or the like, and Ekwall's derivation from a non-existent British equivalent of the Old Irish *dind*, hill, is properly dismissed. EPNS does not observe that Dent was, and still is, the name of a considerable region, and that the village is still locally known as Dent Town, in contrast with the surrounding district of Dent. The physical appearance of the village is still strikingly unlike that of any other in the Yorkshire Dales, and it has been aptly described as a 'Cornish village stranded in the Dales.' *Regio Dunotinga* plainly takes its name from a person named Dunawt, Latin Donatus, as does the district of Dunoding in Merioneth, named from another Dunawt, son of Cunedda. See P Dent.
214.4   SAMUEL: see E Cadoc.
215.2   GUALLAUC: his memory caused later parents in the area to name their children Wallace.
215.3   KENTIGERN: see E. Cambria, Jocelyn 11; Morken, Cathen, Jocelyn 22.
215.3   MANAU: see P.
216.3   RHUN: see p. 192 *Age*.
216.3   BRIDEI: see p. 193 *Age*.
216.4   LLYWARCH ... PASSIVE: Triad 8.
217.2   CYNDDELW: references assembled in TYP 502.
219.1   CELIDON: Nennius 56 (cf. E); see P.
219.2   URIEN: see p. 232 *Age*.
219.2   ROYAL RESIDENCE: Llwyfenydd, near the Roman fort of Kirkby Thore, by Penrith.

219.3 CERETIC: Muirchú 28 cited p. 416.4 below.
219.3 MAELGWN: Gildas 34 *auscultantur ... laudes ... propriae ... praeconum ore ritu Bacchantium concrepante*; cf. p. 416.4.
220.1 DINAS POWYS: Coed Clwydgwyn see p. 431 *Age*.
220.3 MAELGWN ... TRIBUTE: e.g. Maelgwn imposed a tribute of a hundred cows and a hundred calves on each pagus; his *exactores* collected them in Glevissig, with a force of three hundred men, *vita Cadoci* 69.
220.4 LAWS ... OF WALES: see T and p. 445 *Age*.
220.4 ROMAN: see Jones LRE, especially 672 ff.; cf. 258–259 and 449 ff., and the texts there cited.
220.4 EROGATOR MILITARIS ANNONAE: cf. e.g. the texts cited in Du Cange, *Erogator*.
221.2 CAIS etc.: see p. 460 *Age*. The evidence is briefly surveyed by W.Rees in *Angles and Britons* 148; cf. G.W.S.Barrow *Northern History* 4, 1969, 1 ff. It will be better understood when the texts, including the Yorkshire documentation, have been more fully studied. Random observation suggests that survivals of British administration were not confined to the north. *Gwestva,* tribute of food to the king, was reported in Flintshire in the 11th century, as *hestha* (DB 269 b (Cheshire FM 7); in the East Riding, as *hestcorne* oats, and as *hestra(st)la* or *hest(e)rasda*, horse fodder (Mon. Ang. 2,367; 1,170; HY 1,298); and, in the 13th century, as *ghestum*, loaves, in Northamptonshire (Northants. RS 5,793) and in Somerset (Archaeological Institute, Salisbury volume, 1851, 208; Somerset RS 5,83; cf. 89.90.93; cf. HMC Report 12, 1, 288, 329; SANHS 20, Supplement 67). I owe the references to *ghestum* to the kindness of Mr R.E.Latham. The obligation survived elsewhere without the name; cf. e.g. BCS 612 (Taunton, AD 904) 'one night's supplies *(pastus)* for the king and his kenneler and eight dogs, and nine nights' supplies for his falconers, and whatever the king may desire to convey thereof with waggons and horses to Curig (?) or Wilton'.
221.5 GILDAS: 1, 2 ff., quoting *Ecclesiastes* 3, 7.
222.1 MONKS: cf. chapters 18–20 *Age*.
222.3 TRADE: see p. 441 *Age*.
223.1 EGYPTIAN SAINT: cf. p. 441 *Age*.
223.2 PARTITION: see p. 134 *Age*.
223.2 IRISHMEN: see E Abbán, Columba of Terryglass and p. 386 *Age*.
223.2 BRITISH ... AMONG ... ENGLISH: see E Gwenael, Winwaloe, and p. 314 *Age*.
223.2 GIDEON: Gildas 70, 3; cf. 72, 3.
223.3 AFRICA: Corippus *Iohannidos* 3, 388–389 (p. 36; cf. xvi), *Gentes non laesit amaras Martis amica lues.*

13 British Collapse (pp. 225–248)

225.1 SAXON REVOLT: cf. p. 293 *Age*.
226.2 CIVIL WARS: the most likely cause of conflict between Winchester and Salisbury is a division of the *civitas* of the Belgae between the heirs of a former ruler, possibly Caradauc Vreichvras; cf. pp. 211, 293 and 324 *Age*.
226.2 CEAWLIN, CUTHA: see p. 293 *Age*.

NOTES TO *THE AGE OF ARTHUR* (pp. 219–236)

227.1   GLOUCESTER ... POPULATION: BCS 60; cf. Finberg ECWM 158 ff.; p. 497 *Age*.

227.2   FETHANLEA: see P; the name might be a misreading of *Feranlea*, any of the several places now called Fernley or the like, which include the old name of Hereford HW 282.

227.3   MAEDOC: *vita* (VSH) 17 see E.

227.3   FINNIAN: *vita* (Sal.) 8 see E.

228.1   BOULDERS: the story might suggest to the unwary that it was borrowed from Bede's account of Germanus' Alleluia victory (p. 62 *Age*). But Irish tradition knew Germanus only as Patrick's teacher; the point of the story is not borrowed, and battles in Wales are commonly fought among hills; it is not therefore prudent to assume the influence of Bede.

228.2   CADOC ... PRAYED THE LORD: *vita Cadoci* 25; cf. E.

228.2   LLANCARFAN, LLANDAFF: see T Gospel Books.

228.2   THEODORIC: see pp. 126 ff. *Age*.

228.3   KING THEODORIC: LL 141–142.

229.1   BROCKWEIR: see P.

229.1   SIGBERT: Bede HE 3, 18.

229.2   AXMINSTER: *Beandun*, Bindon SC 614, see P Beandun and p. 307 *Age*.

229.2   IDON: LL 123.

229.3   DUMNONIA: cf. p. 302 *Age*.

230.1   BADON ... MORCANT: see p. 309 *Age*.

230.2   UNTIL 775: The reigns of a father and son for 110 years, from 665 to 775, are unusually long; but not unduly longer than those of Louis XIII and XIV of France, 105 years, or of Attalus I and II of Pergamon, 104 years. Queen Victoria's last surviving child died 107 years after her mother's accession to the throne.

231.2   RECORD OF THE ENGLISH: see A; cf. p. 317 *Age*.

231.2   WELSH POEMS: see T.

231.5   NENNIUS: 62.

232.2   TALHEARN: Nennius 62.

232.3   URIEN OF ECHWYD: CT 3, 1–4; 7–11; 27–30; translated IWP 28.

232.3   ECHWYD: possibly Solway; see P Echwyd.

233.4   TERRITORIES ... SPLIT: see p. 234 *Age*.

233.4   CAER GREU: ACm 580.

234.2   ULPH: CT 7, 11–12; 29.

234.2   FOUR ARMIES: CT 6, 10; the Bernician forces were still organised in four armies at Catraeth, *Gorchan Tudfwlch* CA 1296 ff.

234.2   ARGOED LLWYFEIN: CT 6, translated WBT 29, PWP 18; see P.

234.3   URIEN'S ELEGY: CLH 3 (FAB 359, 259).

234.3   PILLAR OF BRITAIN: *Post Prydein* CLH 3, 16; cf. T 5, bracketed with Pabo, father of Dunaut, and Cynvelyn Drysgl of Edinburgh.

234.3   HUSSA: Nennius 63. The text is early, using the 7th-century spelling Urbgen for Urien.

234.3   METCAUD: Lindisfarne, A 635 (Metgoit); cf. P.

235.1   FIACHNA: Fiachna Lurgan.

235.3   WHEN OWAIN: CT 10, 11 ff., translated Parry HWL 3; cf. IWP 27.

236.2   THE HEAD I CARRY: CLH 3, 8; 30–31; cf. 46; 51; 53; 56; 59.

237.2 CATRAETH: see P and A 598.
237.2 DEIRAN TREACHERY: CA 198–201 'The treacherous Deirans asked "Is there a Briton truer than Cynan?" ' Jackson *Ant.* 13, 1939, 27; *Gododdin* A 18.
237.3 MEN WENT TO CATRAETH: CA 33 (372–375); 31 (361–2); 58 (670–674); 60 (689–694); Jackson *Gododdin* A 33; 31; 56; 59.
238.1 BEDE: HE I, 34.
238.2 DEIRA: the statement of SC that Aelle died in 588 is formally denied by Bede and other earlier texts.
238.2 CHESTER: Bede HE 2, 2; cf. A 614.
239.1 CONTEMPLATED CONQUEST OF NORTHUMBRIA: see p. 301 *Age*.
240.2 VESTIGES OF POEMS: BBCS 7, 1933, 24; cf. TYP 294.
240.2 MEVANIAN ISLANDS: Bede HE 2, 5, cf. 2.9; see P.
240.3 PENDA: see pp. 302 ff. *Age*; one tradition held that he was first attacked and subdued by Catwallaun, another that Catwallaun married his sister or niece.
240.3 EDWIN KILLED: the campaign apparently involved two battles, near Welshpool and Doncaster.
240.4 MERIONETH: Idris, see A 627 x 636.
241.2 OSWALD IN WESSEX: SC 635.
241.2 MAES COGWY: see P.
241.2 GAIUS CAMPUS, WINWAED: see P Winwaed.
241.3 CYNDRWYN: Triad 60, his son Gwiawn at 'Bangor Orchard'.
241.3 CYNDDYLAN: CLH II, 3 and 4.
241.3 WROXETER: CArch. 4, 1969, 84; 23, 1970, 336; 25, 1971, 45; where however the word Germanic is misleading.
242.2 MAES COGWY: CLH II, III.
242.2 OAKEN COFFIN: CLH 13, 1; 25 ff.
242.3 MY HEART IS AFLAME: CLH 13, 42 ff.
243.1 LUITCOET: see P.
243.1 MORFAEL: see p. 308 *Age*.
243.2 OSWY … RAIDED: ACm 656.
243.2 TRIBAL HIDAGE: see T and p. 492 *Age*.
243.2 WULFHERE'S FORD: DB f. 259 d, Shropshire IV, last entry, cf. HW 195.
244.1 CYNDDYLAN: CLH II, 6 (Tren); 15–16; 18; 27; 29; 31; 66; 69; 71–72; 85; 87.
245.2 WREKIN: CLH II, 81, 'Once I looked from Dinlle Wrecon, Down upon the land of Freuer'. Freuer is represented as the sister of Cynddylan.
246.1 BROKEN SHIELD: CLH II, 55–56.

14 Brittany (pp. 249–260)

249.1 ARMORICAN BRITISH: see P.
249.1 SAINTS' LIVES: see p. 164 *Age*.
249.2 MANUSCRIPTS: many of the published texts were discovered by a deliberate search conducted by French scholars in the Bibliothèque Nationale, the libraries of Fleury, St.-Germain-des-Prés, and other houses, chiefly between 1880 and 1914; further search in such libraries offers the most likely chance of finding unpublished texts that concern Britain and Brittany.
249.2 PERTINACIOUS ENQUIRY: *Cartulary of Quimperlé*, preface, pp. vi–ix.

NOTES TO *THE AGE OF ARTHUR* (pp. 237–257)   65

249.2   LE GRAND ... TEXTS: including Breviaries and *Propria*, service books, in manuscript, or printed in the 16th and 17th centuries for the use of particular houses, which were also extensively consulted by Baring-Gould LBS; full publication is likely to add to knowledge.

249.2   CHARTERS: editions listed above, p. 14, s.v. *Cartulaire*.

250.1   GREGORY OF TOURS: see E.

250.1   PILGRIM: see p. 383 *Age*.

250.2   MANY REGIONS: Nennius 27.

251.2   SECOND MIGRATION: cf. pp. 38 and 90 *Age*.

251.3   BRITISH COUNTS: Greg. Tur. HF 4, 4 *nam semper Brittani sub Francorum potestatem post obitum regis Chlodovechi (511) fuerent, et comites non reges appellati sunt*. The language of the Lives is normally precise, using *rex* for 5th-century rulers, *comes* for 6th-century rulers.

251.3   THIRD MIGRATION: for its date and nature see especially p. 364 *Age*.

251.4   CONOMORUS, RIWAL: the most important of the 6th-century emigrant leaders was probably Arthmael (see E), but little is known of him.

251.4   RIWAL ... FROM OVERSEAS: *vita Winnoci*; cf. LBS 1, 297 note 3; cf. also *vitae Leonori, Tudwali*.

251.4   FRACAN: *vita Winwaloe* 1, 2.

252.2   HORSE RACE: *vita Winwaloe* 1, 18; cf. E.

252.4   PAUL TRAVELLED: *vita Pauli Aureliani* 15; cf. E.

253.2   ROSCOFF ... POTTERY: discovered by the late Professor J.B.S. Haldane.

253.3   BACAUDAE: see pp. 8 and 90 *Age*.

253.4   VICTOR: *vita Pauli Aureliani* 15, cf. 19 *rex Philibertus istam mihi regionem sub suae potestatis conditione ad regendam tradidit*.

256.1   DANIEL, BUDIC, THEODORIC etc.: see p. 130 *Age*.

256.2   MACLIAVUS: Greg. Tur. HF 5, 16.

256.3   MACLIAVUS, CONOMORUS: Greg. Tur. HF 4, 4.

256.3   CONOMORUS: *iudex externus* in Armorican tradition, *vita I Samsonis* 1, 53; *vita Leonori*, a foreign ruler, in contrast with the immigrants who had forsaken their homes in Britain; to those in Britain, Armorica was also *externae gentis regio* (vita Pauli Aureliani 9). His kingdom is approximately located by the Life of Paul Aurelian, whose father took service in Glevissig, but whose ancestral estates lay on the Channel coasts and within the dominion of Conomorus. Conomorus' royal centre is explicitly located at Castle Dore by the Norman poets; see references in vol. 6 below, p. 14(-15) n. 13. No evidence locates him in South Wales, as THS Cymm. 1953, 47 ff.; cf. TYP 446.

257.1   BANHEDOS ... MARCUS: *vita Pauli Aureliani* 8; variant reading *Bannhedos*.

257.1   DRUSTANUS: CIIC 487, corrected JRIC n.s.1, 1951, 117, *His iacit Drustanus Cunomori filius*; the name *Drustanus*, no longer legible, is restored, chiefly from earlier readings. It recalls Pictish Drust, but is rare; cf. Columba's pupil Drostanus, abbot of Deer, *Book of Deer* p. 91, who is however said to have been son of an Irish Coscrach, *Brev. Ab.* PH 19 d. The Tristan of the legends is transformed into a nephew of Mark and given alternative fathers, Rivalen in Brittany, Tallwch in Wales; both names are late additions, not related to the realities from which the legend originated.

257.3   CHRAMN: Greg. Tur. HF 4, 20; cf. 21, death of Clothair; cf. *vita Samsonis* (AG) 14–15; the AG Life of Samson concentrates upon events in Brittany; the early *vita prima* and its derivatives deal chiefly with events in Britain.

258.2   BURIED AT CASTLE DORE: *vita Pauli Aureliani* 8.
258.4   THEODORIC: Greg. Tur. HF 5, 16; cf. p. 228 *Age*.
259.2   MALO: see E; the principal life is a 9th-century text, using 7th-century sources.
259.3   IUDICAEL, IUDOC, WINNOC: see E.
259.3   MEVEN: see E.
259.4   FITZALANS, STUARTS: see p. 198 *Age*.

15 English Immigrants (pp. 261–292)

261.2   GERMANIC LEGEND: especially the poem *Widsith,* notably lines 18 ff. and 57, and *Beowulf.*
261.4   MIGRATION: the fundamental survey of the texts is Thomas Hodgkin *Italy and her Invaders.* Lucien Musset *Les Invasions: les Vagues Germaniques* summarises more recent thinking. The viewpoint is Roman. From the barbarian standpoint the fullest study is L.Schmidt *Allgemeine Geschichte der Germanischen Völker.* There is no comprehensive survey of the archaeological evidence.
262.2   CHAMAVI: Eunapius, fragment 12.
264.3   SCANDINAVIA: *vagina nationum* Jordanes *Getica* 4.
264.3   OTHERS: e.g. the Burgundians, whose name is preserved in Bornholm and elsewhere.
264.3   GERMANIC NATIONS: the nearest equivalent to a comprehensive map of barbarian Europe is the *Grosse Gesamtkarte* in Eggers *Römische Import*; though it excludes sites that have no import, few areas had none, and the blanks on the map are usually devoid of native as well as of imported finds.
264.4   LANGOBARDI: Cassius Dio 71, 3, 1a; see P.
265.2   EORMENRIC: see PLRE 1, Ermanaricus.
266.3   HENGEST: Hengest and Hors mean 'Stallion' and 'Mare', evidently the nicknames, and perhaps the ensigns of the two leaders. One genealogy suggests that Hengest's name may have been Aethelbert. Bede HE 1, 15 says that the name of Hors was to be seen on a monument in East Kent. What was seen was doubtless the remnant of a Roman inscription erected by a [CO]HORS; if so, the place was probably Reculver, the only place in Kent or in southern Britain where a cohort was stationed in the period when such inscriptions were commonly erected.
266.3   BEOWULF: for Hengest, see lines 1068 ff.
266.3   FINN'S BURG: see P.
267.5   GRAVE GOODS: see p. 32 *Age*.
268.2   ROUTES: they were a particularly unhappy handicap to the sensitive and perceptive studies of E.T.Leeds; in other hands the concept often verged upon the absurd.
269.3   CRUCIFORM AND SAUCER BROOCHES: cf. p. 32 *Age*.
270.2   THE NATION: Bede HE 1, 15.
270.2   HE KNEW: Bede HE 5, 9.
272.1   ENGLISH: Nennius 56; cf. p. 106 *Age*.
272.1   PROCOPIUS: BG 4, 20.
272.3   NAME OF ICEL: in Sussex a few Icel names, together with Cutha names and

great squareheaded brooches, suggest some East Anglian settlement in the later 6th century; cf. Map 20. Personal names in Cutha are numerous at all periods, but, on the evidence so far published by EPNS, are relatively infrequent in place names outside the districts overrun by the Eslingas; the most noticeable other Cutha region is in northern Mercia.

273.2 ESLINGAS: see p. 110 *Age*.
273.4 ENGLISH IN EUROPE: Map 16.
274.1 EVERY OARSMAN: Sidonius *Ep*. 8, 6, 13 *Saxones ... archpiratas ... ita ut simul omnes imparent parent, docent discunt latrocinari*.
274.2 CORSOLDUS: see p. 92 *Age*.
274.2 ODOVACER: see L and p. 91 *Age*.
276.1 PRESSURES: exactly defined and keenly remembered in the native tradition of the continental Saxons, e.g. *Translatio S. Alexandri* 1, reporting that their ancestors had been continually obliged to defend their living space (*spacia*) against four named enemies who pressed upon them, *a meridie Francos ..., a septentrione vero Nordmannos ..., ab ortu Obroditos ..., ab occasu Frisos*. The *Obroditi* were Slavs, the *Nordmanni* Danes.
278.1 DANISH INVASION: Greg. Tur. HF 3, 3; cf. the Latin sources printed in Chambers *Beowulf* 3-4, cf. pp. 381 ff. Frisian territory, though not settled by Franks, seems to have been a subject *pagus* of the Frank kingdom before 520; see P Frisians.
278.3 SLAVS: see P. The main difficulty in the interpretation of the evidence is that the same grave-goods are often given quite different dates by modern German and modern central European scholars. Identical pots are sometimes assigned to the 7th or 8th centuries if they are excavated in Baltic lands and published in Germany, to the 5th and 6th centuries if they are excavated by the Danube and there published. Until a thorough comparative study is available, it is only possible to observe that the Danubian dates are based on the evidence of associated Roman objects, while the north German graves have no such evidence. The Danubian material justifies the conclusion of, e.g. Preidel (*Slawische Altertumskunde* 2, 14 ff.) that Slav graves begin in the 4th century, and that the 'Prague Type', and related pottery vessels, were 'dominant' during the 5th and 6th centuries, rare thereafter. They are markedly absent from 7th-century southern Slav sites. Such vessels are quite common in north Germany; though it is theoretically possible that their manufacture might have begun later and continued longer in the north, such a hypothesis cannot be maintained until decisive evidence is clearly demonstrated.
278.4 HAMBURG CEMETERY: Tischler *Sachsenforschung*, plate 29, p. 85; cf. H. Jankuhn *Geschichte Schleswig-Holsteins* 3, 1957, 100, citing local publications. The view that the large vessel there illustrated seems to be a normal Slavonic Prague Type, and that the smaller vessels are imitations of late Roman provincial wares, is endorsed by Czech scholars conversant with these vessels, who have been kind enough to look at the illustration. Present conditions preclude a more precise pursuit of the opinions expressed.
279.1 PROCOPIUS: especially BG 2, 15, 1 ff.; 3, 55.
279.3 AGRICULTURAL TECHNOLOGY: it is sometimes schematically pretended that a 'slash and burn economy' is necessarily more 'primitive' than the cultivation of lands already cleared. But the opening up of virginal lands

commonly requires greater application and a technology as 'advanced' as inherited cultivation, or more so; 'slashing and burning' is the most suitable technique for the clearance of lightly wooded lands. It may only be dismissed as 'primitive' when it is not followed by continuing cultivation. The nature of Slavonic agriculture in Bohemia and the Baltic lands will be better understood when adequate comprehensive and comparative study has been directed to excavated Slavonic objects; to old Slavonic words for tools; and to Slavonic place-names. Circumstances have tended to inhibit such study.

280.1 STIRRUP ... HORSE COLLAR: cf. p. 437 *Age*.
280.3 MAP 8: Partition, p. 134 *Age*.
281.2 PROCOPIUS: BG 4, 20.
281.3 SMALL PEOPLES: most are mapped on the Ordnance Survey's *Map of Dark Age Britain*.
282.1 BERNICIANS ... FOUR PEOPLES: cf. pp. 233–234 *Age*.
283.2 ANGLIAN CHRONICLE: cf. Liebermann MGH SS 28, 11. Differently excerpted by Henry of Huntingdon and *Flores Historiarum*, both under the year 527. In the reconstructed text below, the words common to both are printed in capitals; those excerpted by Henry only are in italics, and those excerpted by the *Flores* only are in Roman type.

> VENERUNT *multi et saepe* pagani DE GERMANIA ET OCCUPAVERUNT EST ANGLIAM (id est regionem illam quae Orientalium Anglorum regio dicitur) *et* quorum quidam MERCIAM invadentes bella cum Brittonibus plurima peregerunt SED *necdum sub uno rege redacta erant. Plures autem proceres certatim regiones occupabant, unde innumerabilia bella fiebant,* quoniam PROCERES *vero* eorum quia ERANT MULTI NOMINE CARENT.

I am grateful to my former pupil, Dr. Wendy Davies, for drawing my attention to the significance of the *Flores* entry.

283.3 MEDRAUT: see p. 140 *Age*.
284.1 ALMONDBURY: EPNS WRY 2, 256.
286.3 GILDAS: 92, 3.
286.4 HERPES: it is possible that some of the Kentish objects catalogued in the British Museum as from Herpes did not come from there; but probable that most did; cf. Delamain *Herpes*.
287.1 PROCOPIUS: BG 4, 20.
287.3 BOULOGNE: Map 19A, and notes thereto; cf. *Cartularium Sithiense*, c. AD 850.
287.3 BROOCHES: said to have been in Boulogne Museum before 1940; none is known to have survived the war.
287.3 EGWIN: Fredegarius 4, 55; cf. 4, 78.
288.2 NORMANDY ... VILLAGE NAMES: Map 19B and notes thereto; see especially *Annales de Normandie* 10, 1960, 307 ff.; 13, 1963, 43 ff.
291.1 SAXONS ... OF BAYEUX: Greg. Tur. HF 5, 26; 10, 9.
291.2 SAXON PEOPLE: *Translatio Sancti Alexandri* 1; cf. Adam of Bremen 1, 4 *Saxones primo circa Rhenum sedes habebant [et vocati sunt Angli] quorum pars inde veniens in Brittaniam Romanos depulit; altera pars Thuringiam oppugnans tenuit illam regionem.*
291.2 DATE 531: Greg. Tur. HF 3, 7.

291.2 HADELN: *Annales Regni Francorum* AD 797. '*Haduloha ... ubi Oceanus Saxoniam alluit*' beyond the Weser, but not beyond the Elbe, therefore the region now called Hadeln.
291.3 SAXONS REBELLED: Greg. Tur. HF 4, 10 cf. 4, 14.
291.3 ROUGH POTTERY: Tischler *Sachsenforschung* 79.
291.3 BUTTL NAMES: see Map 17, p. 277 *Age*.
292.2 THURINGIA ... ANGLIAN POTTERY: Map 16 and notes thereto. The Anglian grave-goods of the Czech and East German museums have not yet been sufficiently studied to determine their date; it may prove possible to distinguish two movements, from the lower Elbe in the 5th century, and from Britain in the 6th century. Most of the stray English grave-goods in Hungary, Albania and elsewhere in the Balkans seem to be 6th-century, matched in cemeteries in Britain, but not on the Elbe.
292.2 -LEBEN NAMES: see Map 17. The names clearly remained in use for some time, into the earlier stages of German conquest of Slav territory.
292.2 SAXONS AND LANGOBARDS: Greg. Tur. HF 4, 42; 5, 15; cf. Paul the Deacon HL 2, 6; 3, 5–7. Since the Suevi were installed before the death of Clothair in 561, these Saxons left their homes earlier.

16 English Conquest (pp. 293–316)

293.1 CYNRIC, CEAWLIN, CUTHA: see p. 225 *Age*.
293.3 CUTHWULF: the story that he was Ceawlin's 'brother' is confined to guesses in late genealogies and insertions into the later texts of SC.
293.3 PLACE NAMES: see Map 20, p. 295 *Age*.
293.3 CUTTESLOWE: now commonly spelt Cutslow; cf. *Ant.* 9, 1935, 96 and EPNS Oxfordshire 267.
293.3 ESLINGAS: see p. 110 *Age*.
294.1 GEWISSAE: The word probably means 'confederates', either a federation of different English peoples, whose burial rite attests a mixed origin, or else translating *foederati*, the status accorded to them by the British. Their ornament demonstrates that they included many immigrants from the Saxon country on the left bank of the Elbe estuary, whose descendants in time predominated (cf. p. 324 *Age*), and, in contradistinction to the Mercian Angles, consented to be known by the collective national name of Saxons, which their British neighbours applied to them, as to other English immigrants.
296.1 ILCHESTER: see Map 21.
296.1 GLASTONBURY: William of Malmesbury *de Gestis Regum* 1, 27–28, in 601; Morfael, in or about 655; see p. 243 *Age*.
296.1 CANNINGTON: *ST 25 40*, MA 8, 1964, 237; *Christianity in Britain* 195.
296.2 INDEPENDENT MONARCHY: see p. 283 *Age*.
296.3 EAST ANGLIAN WARS: See p. 283 *Age*.
298.2 TRIBAL HIDAGE: see T and p. 492 *Age*.
299.2 WYE ... 584: see p. 227 *Age*.
299.3 KENTISH ... MIDLANDS: e.g. Leighton Buzzard, Chamberlain's Barns Pit II, which endured, and Totternhoe (Dunstable), Marina Drive, which did not long survive, *Arch. Jl.* 120, 1963, 161; below, vol. 6, p. 116; together with many of the sites listed *Arch. Jl.* 120, 190, beside others which contain Kentish material but are less specifically Kentish.

300.3 PIONEERS: see Map 22. The latest pagan burials, most of them of the early 7th century, extend into a few concentrated regions, between Bernicia and Deira; in the Peak District; in the border lands between the West Saxons and the Mercians, about the Cherwell and the Cotswolds; on the south-western borders of the West Saxons; and on the edges of the Weald. Pagan English burials have not been reported from the British lands of the north-west midlands, allied with the Mercians, though some Cheshire place-names ending in -*low* (burial mound), preceded by an English personal name, suggest some colonisation in the 7th century, perhaps beginning at the end of the 6th century; cf. p. 310.2 below.

301.2 BISHOP IN YORK: Bede HE 1, 29 cites a letter of Gregory the Great, dated 22 June 601, elevating Augustine to metropolitan status, and adding,
> we wish you to appoint and send a bishop to York, provided that if the city and its neighbourhood receive the Word of God, he also may consecrate 12 bishops, and exercise metropolitan authority.

301.3 HUMBER AND ... BEYOND: Bede HE 1, 25 says that in 597 the *imperium* of Aethelbert extended 'as far as the Humber, the great river that divides the southern and northern English'; on Aethelbert's death in 616 he describes the frontier as 'the river Humber and its adjacent borders' HE 2, 5. In both passages the language is careful; the reason for the variation may be that in the meantime Aethelbert lost all or part of Lincolnshire, to Aethelferth.

301.4 GOLDEN AGE: Bede HE 2, 16.

302.3 EDWIN AND THE WEST SAXONS: Bede HE 2, 9; SC 626.

302.4 EDWIN AND WALES: see p. 240 *Age*.

302.4 PENDA: see p. 240 *Age*.

302.4 OSWALD ... SEVERN: see A 635 and p. 240 *Age*.

302.4 ENGLISH REBELLION: A 636 *congregacio Saxonum contra Osualt*.

302.4 ATBRET IUDEU: Nennius 64–65, see P Giudi (probably Stirling). The word *atbret* is British, 'older than ... Primitive Welsh, and therefore not later than the seventh century', Jackson *Celt and Saxon* 38; cf. also P Winwaed.

303.2 PICTS AND SCOTS: Bede HE 2, 5.

303.2 PICTISH KING: Talorcan son of Enfrith; see p. 195 *Age*. Son of Oswy's elder brother, he had by Anglian law a better claim to the Northumbrian throne than Oswy himself.

303.2 ENGLISH UNDER-KING: see p. 195 *Age*.

303.2 EGFERTH: made Mercia tributary, before the death of Wulfhere (675), Eddius 20; constrained by archbishop Theodore to make peace after a disastrous battle on Trent in 679, where his young brother Aelfwini was killed, possibly at Elford *SK 18 10* near Lichfield, perhaps *Aelfwin's Ford*; Bede HE 4, 21; cf. Eddius 24.

303.2 EGFERTH ... IRELAND: Bede HE 4, 26; in Breg (eastern Meath north of Dublin).

303.2 EGFERTH ... PICTS: Bede HE 4, 26, SC 685. He was killed at Lin Garan, Nennius 57; at Dun Nechtain; Nechtansmere, Simeon of Durham HDE 9; Dunnichen *NO 51 48* near Forfar, north of Dundee; cf. P.

303.3 AETHELRED ... NO CIVIL WAR: he faced and survived one major rebellion, CS 692, 'battle against the son of Penda', which is probably not a doublet of the 679 entry; his enemy is more likely to have been Ine of Wessex than a relative or a Welsh invader.

303.3 EGBERT: he asserted Wessex independence in 803, and subdued Mercia twenty years later. 'The great battle between Egbert, king of the West Saxons and Ceolwulf, king of the Mercians, at *Cherrenhul* between Oxford and Abingdon, which Egbert won', Leland *Itinerary* (Toulmin Smith 2, 151), cf. *Ant.* 9, 1935, 99, probably preserves in Latin the full

NOTES TO *THE AGE OF ARTHUR* (pp. 300–310)

text of SC 823 (821) 'Ceolwulf was deprived of the kingdom.' The Saxon Chronicle dates the completion of the conquest of Mercia to 829, but Mercian independence was briefly re-asserted in the following year.

307.3 LATEST PAGAN BURIALS: there was no sharp and sudden end to the old funeral rites. Clothed burial lasted in some areas throughout the 7th century, and beyond. Some of the dead, especially wealthy women and young girls, were buried in their best clothes, with their finery. But in most large midland and southern cemeteries the pagan convention that deliberately buried objects intended for use in the after-life declined after the conquest and was almost entirely discontinued early in the 7th century. Strong evidence indicates the date at which weapons, emblems of office, pottery vessels and the traditional jewellery of ordinary women ceased to be normal in graves. The great royal barrows of the south, and some of the warrior graves of the Peak District, are securely dated to about the 630s by continental coins and ornament; the decorative styles of objects found in these tombs are slightly later than the latest normally observed on humbler brooches and ornaments in the large cemeteries, but not much later. Most pagan cemetery-burial ended a generation or more before the coming of Christianity. Pagan burial was not ended by conversion, but by the causes that made easy conversion possible; the grip of the old beliefs upon men's minds was already weakening before the Mercian and West Saxon kings were baptised.

307.4 BEANDUN: see P. Bindon, Devon, unlike Bindon, Dorset, and Bindon, Somerset, probably derives from *bean dun,* 'bean hill', EPNS Devon 636; cf. Hoskins WEW 8.

308.2 GLEVISSIG: see p. 228 *Age.*

308.2 MORFAEL: see p. 243 *Age.*

308.2 PENSELWOOD: see P. The suggestion that the battle was fought near Exeter and that the British withdrew northward towards Bridgwater (Hoskins WEW 15) is possible, but not probable.

308.3 POSBURY CAMP: *SX 80 97,* 'Possebury' in the 13th century, EPNS Devon 406.

309.1 CORNISH BISHOP: HS I, 674; cf. E Petroc.

309.1 BODMIN: HS I, 676 ff.; cf. T Gospel Books.

309.1 DUNGARTH: ACm 875.

309.2 MORCANT: cf. p. 230 *Age; moritur,* died, is commonly used of death in battle, e.g. ACm 558 (for 560) *Gabran ... moritur;* 580 *Gurci et Peretur moritur.*

309.2 INE ... MERCIAN SUPREMACY: In 701 Aldhelm secured the confirmation of the Pope's privileges for Malmesbury by both Aethelred and Ine; they came to an agreement, and so concluded, that whether it were peace or war between Saxons and Mercians ... the monastery should be ever in peace.

Aethelred signed first, as *Myrcena kyncg,* followed by Ine, *Wessexena cyng* BCS 106, end. In the 680s Wiltshire estates had been granted by Mercians alone (e.g. BCS 58, cf. 54); Ceadwalla and Ine had revived Wessex, but not thrown off Mercian supremacy. Coenred, who granted land near Shaftesbury in 704, could have been either king of the Mercians, or Ine's father, BCS 107.

310.1 ELISEG: ECMW 182 *necxit hereditatem Povo[i]s[et recepit?] per VIIII [annos?] e potestate Anglorum in gladio suo parta in igne.* The grammar is too eccentric for exact translation, but the meaning seems clear.

310.2 DERBYSHIRE: see Map 22, p. 305 *Age.*

310.2 NORTHUMBRIAN BORDER: the early place-names of Cheshire and south Lancashire are chiefly Mercian rather than Northumbrian. Peaceful settlement of some Mercian English in allied Welsh lands may have begun quite early, for early in the 7th century a Welsh churchman was said to have been disturbed by Englishmen shouting 'Ker gia, ker gia!' at their hunting dogs on the upper Severn, far beyond lands yet conquered, *vita Beuno* 8. But extensive settlement is unlikely before Wulfhere's accession; cf. p. 300.3 above.

310.3 BEDE ... ENGLAND: cf. e.g. for the territory *regio Anglorum* HE 3, 8; *Anglorum provinciae* 3, 3; cf. *Brettonum provinciae* 2, 2; for their dominion, *Anglorum regnum* 3, 24; 4, 26, etc.; for the population, *Anglorum populi* 1, 25; *natio Anglorum* 2, 2; 4, 26; *gens Anglorum* 2, 2; 3, 3; and *gentes Anglorum* 2, 3. These are samples of normal usage. 'Anglia' does not occur. 'Engelonde' in BCS 738, dated AD 939, may or may not belong to the original text.

311.1 CYMRY: cf. p. 41 *Age*.
311.2 SAXONIA: cf. p. 41 *Age*.
311.2 ANGLI SAXONES: first used in the later 8th century – by Paul the Deacon *Historia Langobardorum* 4, 22, about 790; cf. Willibald, *Anglorum Saxonumque vocabulo*, vita Bonifatii 4 (11), about 760. *Angul Saxones* is common in 9th-century charters, usually in Latin, but found no wider popularity; Latin variants were used by Florence of Worcester and a few other medieval writers, citing from West Saxon usage.
311.2 WEST ANGLI: and *Suth Angli*, used consistently by the chronicler Aethelweard, himself a prince of the West Saxon dynasty, as substitutes for West and South Saxons; but the substitution would not work for East and Middle Saxons, since East and Middle Angles already existed; it found few imitators.
312.4 ALDHELM: Bede HE 5, 18; cf. Aldhelm *Ep*.4 (also excerpted HS 1,202).
313.1 CONBRAN: Combran BCS 169 (745), Cumbran SC 755, possibly a nickname, 'the Welshman', more probably the name Conbran; cf. LL index, LL 122 etc.
313.1 CATWAL: BCS 186.
313.2 HENRY I: *Consuetudo West Sexe* (70) 5, Liebermann *Gesetze* 1,588.
313.3 LAET: the German word *litus*, or variants, including the *laeti* imported into Roman territory, denoted dependent cultivators, usually foreign, often conquered natives. The *laeti* of Kent were probably British; so Stenton ASE 300, cf. 311, and most who have studied the evidence in context.
313.3 DUNWALD, DUNWALLAUN: BCS 160, 175, 192 (about 747–772); cf. 332 (811) and 254 (788).
313.3 WELHISC: BCS 45, 72 (679, 688).
313.3 MABAN: Bede HE 5, 20; cf. Jackson LHEB 295[1].
313.3 MALUINUS: BCS 250.
314.1 NUNNA: very rare among the English, but a normal late Roman and British name; cf. Nonn(ita), mother of David, cf. E; Nunechia, wife of the early 5th-century British *magister militum* Gerontius; Nunechius, the name of two bishops of Nantes, Duchesne *Fastes* 2, 365; 367; and of a *comes* of Limoges, Greg. Tur. HF 6, 22; Ninian (E), p. 337 *Age*, called Nynia by Bede, Nyniga by Alcuin.
314.2 CHAD: etc., from British Catu-, Jackson LHEB 554.
314.2 CAEDMON: Bede HE 4, 24, Welsh Cadfan, Jackson LHEB 244, etc.; cf. p. 421 *Age*. Bede does not say that he was a 'cowherd', 'humble', or a 'lad'. He was 'elderly', *provectioris aetatis*, before he composed verses or entered a monastery. He had previously attended English-speaking dinner parties, where the *cithara*, 'guitar', or 'harp', was passed round in turn, but always left before his turn came, returning 'to his own house'. But on the

NOTES TO *THE AGE OF ARTHUR* (pp. 310–314) 73

particular night when his gift came to him, it fell to him to guard the stables (*stabula iumentorum*), for which he received payment from the steward, apparently of the monastery, next morning. The word *iumenta* means draught animals, oxen, horses or mules, who pull carriages or carts; not 'cows'. They were a valuable property, and the duty of night-guard clearly went by rota; adequate guard against thieves plainly required a number of people under a responsible person. The implication of Bede's words is that landowners undertook the duty in turn, supplying a guard from their dependants; Bede does not indicate whether the obligation fell upon all landowners, English and Welsh, or upon Welshmen only. It was an imposition likely to fall on men of Welsh status; Caedmon's name was Welsh, but his language was English, at least in his later years; there were doubtless many Welshmen born who normally spoke English, but were held to the legal status of their birth.

314.2 PENNINES ... STRATHCLYDE: *vita Cadroe* 17, Colgan ASH 497 and Skene CPS 116. In the early 950s Dyfnwal of the Clyde escorted Cadroe to meet the envoy of Eric Blood-Axe, king of York, *usque Loidam civitatem, quae est confinium Normannorum atque Cumbrorum*, 'as far as the city of Leeds, which is the border between the North Men and the Cymry'. The place could not be the Lothians, also called *Loidis*, Skene CS 1,241 note, which was not a *civitas* and was far from Eric's borders. The place-name and other evidence for the British reconquest of the Pennines in the earlier 10th century is discussed by Kenneth Jackson, in *Angles and Britons* 72 ff. Dyfnwal's short-lived reconquest, however, extended far to the south and west of the border there indicated; his suzerainty over remote and inaccessible Yorkshire dales implies the survival of a considerable Welsh-speaking population until the Norse settlement of the later 10th and earlier 11th centuries. That settlement was thorough enough to enable modern Norwegians to understand conversation in broad Yorkshire concerned with agricultural and topographical terms; what remained of Welsh speech and custom in Yorkshire was evidently extinguished after the devastation of the north by William I in 1069, except possibly in Dent.

314.2 WILFRED: lands, Eddius 17.
314.2 BRITISH ADMINISTRATION: see p. 221 *Age*.
314.2 BRITISH LAND TENURE: R.C.Shaw *Post-Roman Carlisle* 55 ff.
314.2 WILFRED ... VILLAGE: Eddius 18. Wilfred was in pursuit of a boy whom he claimed for his monastery, whose parents had fled to a British village to save the child. Wilfred was at *On Tiddanufri*, probably Tideover SE 32 49, in Kirkby Overblow, south of Harrogate; the British village was perhaps nearby Walton Head EPNS WRY 5, 43.
314.2 WALLERWENTE: the 'North People's Law' *North leodalage*, Liebermann *Gesetze* 1,460; cf. EHD 1,433; see T.
314.3 LONDON: VI Athelstan (*Iudicia Civitatis Lundoniae*) 6, 3; cf. IV Athelstan 6, 3.
314.3 CAMBRIDGE GUILD: Thorpe ALE 1,258, DAS 610; translated Kemble SE 1,514, and, less accurately, EHD 1,557, with the strange suggestion that *Wylisc* means 'servile'. It does not. For the meaning of *wealh*, see p. 315 *Age*.
314.3 BEANE: SC 913 *Beneficcan*, interpreted as *Bene fychan*, 'Little Beane' in Welsh, probably rightly; cf. Jackson LHEB 567. Many English rivers have Welsh names; but the retention of the Welsh adjective *fychan* argues that Welsh was commonly spoken when the English first settled by its banks, about the beginning of the 7th century, and perhaps for some time thereafter.
314.3 NORFOLK: Winnold House TF 68 03 at Wereham, cf. Tanner 355 and *Norfolk*

Archaeology 5, 1859, 297 ff., preserves the name of Winwaloe (see E) and incorporates much of the medieval monastic buildings. It was the site of a major fair on Winwaloe's day, March 3, until the late 18th century, superseded by Downham Market (*TF 61 03*) fair on the same day.

The cult of Winwaloe in Norfolk was not confined to Wereham. He is said to have had a church in Norwich (LBS 4, 361) and a widespread Norfolk weather rhyme on the windy first days of March runs

First come David, then come Chad,
Then come Winnell roaring mad.

The rhyme is cited LBS 4, 360; Arnold-Forster SCD 2,284. A radio broadcast request in the late 1950s elicited half a dozen versions, with slight variants, still known in different parts of Norfolk. David and Chad are extensively venerated in Britain on March 1 and 2; the observation of Winwaloe's day on March 3 is recorded only in Norfolk, and in Wales, Cornwall and Devon.

314.3 HERTFORDSHIRE: Wynnel's Grove *TL 41 35* in Cockenach, astride the boundary between Nuthampstead and Barley parishes, was *capella Sancti Winwaloei* in the 13th century, *Registrum de Walden* (BL MS Harley 3697) folio 189, printed Dugdale *Mon. Ang.* 1, 462–3; traces of what may be the chapel are visible in the wood, but have not yet been excavated. A stretch of the Icknield Way near Royston was called *Wynewalestrete* c. 1470, EPNS 175.

Both Wereham and Cockenach were granted to St. Winwaloe's Abbey at Montreuil-sur-mer in Picardy about the end of the 12th century. At first sight these grants might seem to be the reason why Winwaloe became patron of the places granted. But the late acquisition of a small dependent priory is insufficient to explain the wide and persistent honouring of Winwaloe's name in Norfolk; and in Hertfordshire the grants refer to the chapel, with its monks, as already in existence at the time when the grant was made, while the grantor's son undertook to maintain it in good repair. Moreover, a late name for a little chapel cannot by itself explain the local name for a major Roman and prehistoric highway five miles distant.

No medieval reason explains or links the grants of the two sites, remote from each other, to a foreign abbey without other English connections. The likely cause is that at the time of the grants both houses already bore the name of Winwaloe, but were doubtless in deep decay. The Life of Gwenael, Winwaloe's successor at Landevennec in Brittany, states that in or about the 590s he visited Britain and founded one or more houses; several are known in Wales and the west (see E), and they may have included Wereham and Cockenach, named, as often, in honour of the founder's teacher and master.

314.3 GUTHLAC: Felix *vita Guthlaci* 34. A band of Britons fired the monastery in a dawn attack, and wounded the saint who was wakened from a 'light sleep'. The incident was not an 'unquiet dream', nor were the British 'devils in disguise', as Colgrave, *Felix* 185 (for the translation, see *Ant.* 8, 1934, 193); Guthlac lived among British neighbours, for, at Crowland, he was a 'pattern to many a Briton', Cynewulf III c. 140 Kennedy p. 268.

314.3 11th CENTURY: BCS 991 and Ramsey Chronicle, cited H.C.Darby, *Ant.* 8, 1934, 194.

314.3 CAEDMON: see p. 314.2 above.

315.3 CAMBERWELL: the well from which the place is named has been excavated and found to be Roman British.

315.3 WEALH ... SERF: EPNS 1 i 18 (1924).

NOTES TO *THE AGE OF ARTHUR* (pp. 314–323) 75

315.3 SPECULATION: EPNE 2, 242–3 (1956).
315.4 WEST SAXON TEXTS: the texts are cited and discussed by H.P.R.Finberg *The Agrarian History of England,* vol. 1, 2 ch. 1; to whom I am indebted for permission to read the manuscript before publication.
315.4 INE: 23, 3.
315.4 WALL, WOOD: EPNE 2, 241; 244. These names are however far fewer than *wealh-tun*.

17 English Monarchy (pp. 317–334)

317.1 BEDE ... EMPIRE: HE 2, 5 (p. 329 *Age*); Aethelbert of Kent *imperavit* all the English *provinciae* south of the Humber; and was the third to hold such *imperium*. Bede adds details only of the Northumbrians, evidently commenting on a list already recognised. Its existence emphasises that the concept that the English should have one over-king who held 'empire' over all Britain was already established in the 7th century.
317.1 SAXON CHRONICLE: 827 (829), repeats the list, on Egbert's conquest of Mercia, adding Egbert, and gives these rulers the title *Bretwalda*, 'ruler of Britain', adapting the Welsh *Gwledic* (p. 206 *Age*).
318.1 ANGLES: see p. 265 *Age*.
318.1 SAXONS ... NO KING: Hucbald *vita Lebuini* 4.
318.1 FRANKS ... EXASPERATED: e.g. *Annales Laurissenses* AD 798 *perfidissimos primores Saxonum.*
318.2 OESC: see P Badon.
320.1 LEODE: Laws of Aethelbert 2.
320.1 REFERENDARIUS, GRAFIO: BCS 4; 5. The witness-lists are older than the body of the text; 'Hocca grafio' in 4 has been misunderstood by the copyist of 5, and turned into two persons, 'Hocca comes' and 'Grafio comes'.
320.2 FOUR LEADERS: cf. p. 233 *Age*.
320.3 YEAVERING: the excavator, Brian Hope-Taylor, has kindly allowed me to give this short description; cf. p. 214 *Age*.
321.3 GOODMANHAM: see p. 390 *Age*.
323.1 TAEPPA'S KINGDOM: the location of his tomb argues that his territory included south Buckinghamshire. Its splendour implies a wider kingdom. The then English settlements, whose ornament resembles that of the Taplow region, extended eastward along the Thames bank. Taeppa's 'Norrey' may therefore have been coterminous with Surrey, including the future Middlesex. In the poorly recorded conflicts that followed Aethelbert's death, Edwin of Northumbria overran Mercia and Wessex, and his ally Redwald was dominant in the south-east, probably through most of the 620s; it is possible that Taeppa then took London from the East Saxon allies of the enfeebled Kentish kingdom. It is also possible that the king buried at Broomfield was an East Anglian, temporarily installed as ruler of the East Saxons under Redwald's suzerainty; alternatively, it might be that Taeppa was himself an East Saxon, but since all known East Saxon kings, except Offa, bore names beginning with S for almost 200 years, the alternative is less likely.

The evidence does not suffice to determine the origin of Taeppa or the precise limits of his kingdom; but the magnificence of his tomb demonstrates that he was a great king who ruled north of the Thames in a generation when the history of the region is not known, between the collapse of the Kentish empire and the consolidation of Mercian control.

Whatever the vicissitudes of the London region (cf. p. 493.1 below) in these years, East Saxon control was probably reasserted by the middle of the 7th century; the weak record and uncertain dates of the East Saxon kings are discussed by Plummer *Bede* 2, 176.

323.3 FRONTIER PEOPLES: the term chiefly applies to the western districts of the Mercians and the West Saxons, and to the Bernicians in the north.

323.3 ANGLIAN CHRONICLE: p. 283 *Age*.

323.4 SAXON CHRONICLE: see pp. 103 and 317 *Age*; cf. A.

324.2 WEST SAXON RULERS: the older national name was *Gewissae* (p. 294 *Age*), probably meaning 'confederates'. It may have originated when Ceawlin and Cutha organised the separate southern English settlements into a single nation in the 570s and 580s, but was more probably the earlier name of the Berkshire English of the middle Thames about Abingdon, who began as an amalgam of immigrants from different parts of the continental homeland, who used differing burial rites, and ornament, and were also *foederati* of the British. They were known to the British as Saxons, as were all other English, and are first known to have used the collective term Saxons of themselves in the preamble to Ine's laws in the 690s, though the same laws describe the individual members of the population as English (p. 41 *Age*). Thereafter 'West Saxon' was the common and usual national name, though for centuries the old name Gewissae occurs as an occasionally literary variant in Bede, Asser and elsewhere.

324.3 WESSEX: the territorial name Westsexe is rarer than the ethnic term West Saxons. The adjective 'West' was required when other kingdoms also accepted the name Saxon. The English of the former *civitates* of the Trinovantes and Regnenses are also first recorded as East and South Saxons in the 690s (BCS 81, 87, 78 ff.), those of the London region as Middle Saxons in 704 (BCS 111). All four names were well established by Bede's time. The extant late copies of the 'Tribal Hidage' (p. 492 *Age*) use the terms Wessex, Essex and Sussex; since they are unacquainted with the term Middlesex, their usage may date back to the original of the document, probably drafted about 661. The name Saxon may have been first and most readily accepted by the Gewissae, since ornament that derives from continental Saxons of the lower Elbe is plentiful among the first immigrants, and continental Saxon political notions won acceptance in later generations (cf. note 324.4, Power of the Overking, below); but ancestry cannot explain the name of the East Saxons, whose archaeology and traditions have little to do with the continental Saxon area. A more compelling reason to accept a national name used by the British was doubtless dislike of the masterful assertion of sovereignty by the Northumbrian and Mercian Angles over all the English, that pressed acutely upon the West Saxons from the 620s, upon the East and South Saxons from the 640s and 660s.

324.3 WESSEX ... FIVE ... KINGDOMS: SC 626; Bede HE 2, 9; cf. p. 302 *Age*. The charters and some SC entries locate the kingdoms and name many of their rulers. The evidence has not yet been sifted, and has sometimes been swept aside by the easy pretence that the names are 'spurious'; it indicates however that the regions were in substance the future counties of Berkshire, Hampshire, Wiltshire, Somerset and Dorset. These kingdoms emerged from the former Roman *civitates*, Berkshire from the Atrebates, Hampshire and Wiltshire from the division of the Belgae (cf. p. 226.2 above), Dorset from the Durotriges, Somerset from the portion of

NOTES TO *THE AGE OF ARTHUR* (pp. 323–324) 77

          north-eastern Dumnonia subdued by the English in the late 6th century (see p. 294 *Age*), extended westward by later conquest. The subjugation of the rest of eastern Dumnonia in the mid and late 7th century added the new region of English Devon, which may thereafter have formed an additional kingdom. Some boundaries shifted; notably, some southern Atrebatic territory was incorporated in Hampshire.

324.3   THREE ... KINGS: in 661, while Cenwalh was High King, SC notes the deaths, presumably in the course of Wulfhere's invasion of Wessex, of king Coenberht, father of Ceadwalla, and of Cuthred, son of Cynegils' contemporary king Cwichelm (SC 614–636). The wording of many of the charters, and of the pedigrees inserted into SC, suggests that each kingdom had its own hereditary dynasty; Cuthred may or may not have been ancestor of Cuthred, king in Berkshire and northern Hampshire in Ine's time, c. 700 (BCS 101, 102, 155 etc.), and of Cuthred, High King of Wessex 741–756.

324.3   OVERKINGSHIP DISCONTINUED: Bede HE 4, 12 'the under-kings took over the government of the nation and held it divided between them for about ten years'. SC exploited a different tradition, that recognised a High Kingship continued, in name at least, by Cenwalh's widow for a year, by Aescwine from 674 to 676, and by Cenwalh's (grand)son Centwine from 676; Florence of Worcester (Appendix, *Genealogia regum West-Saxonum*, at 672, ed. Thorpe 1,272), on the authority of *Dicta Regis Alfredi*, adds Aescwine's father Cenfus, from a tradition that evidently intended the dates 672–674. The variant traditions are not in conflict; it is likely that these rulers claimed the high kingship at or about these dates; Bede's words show that the claims did not then succeed.

324.3   OVERKINGSHIP REVIVED: by Centwine, who is said to have claimed it from 676. He was acknowledged as 'King of the West Saxons' by his Northumbrian contemporary Eddius (ch. 40) in 680/681, at the end of Bede's ten-year period.

324.3   DIFFERENT DYNASTIES: the future form of the West Saxon monarchy was the result of a deliberate political decision taken at a particular time. The 60 years' unbroken rule of a father and his son from 611 to 672 had threatened to establish the High Kingship permanently in one dynasty. In 672 the West Saxon magnates refused to perpetuate its supremacy. Though Centwine briefly regained his ancestors' title, he failed to re-establish his dynasty. Ceadwalla, the young son of a former regional king, soon 'began to contend for the kingship' (SC 685), and succeeded. Three years later he abdicated; the political pressures and personal motives which induced him to do so are not fully recorded. He was succeeded by Ine, the son of a regional king who was still alive. Nothing is recorded of the ancestry of his successors, save that none of them is said to have been the son of his predecessor before 839; and that one of them retained Hampshire, presumably his own kingdom, when deprived of the High Kingship (SC 757). The principle of an elective monarchy, whose conventions limited the choice of the supreme ruler to the kings of regional dynasties, closely resembles the practice of the Irish, who for centuries chose their High King from among the heads of the several Uí Néill dynasties in turn.

324.4   POWER OF THE OVERKING: the decision to abolish a permanent dynasty in 672 automatically restricted the High King's power. It marked the dominance of those who clung to the continental Saxon tradition of effective government by local rulers, and rejected the continental Anglian tradition, powerfully asserted in Britain by the Mercians, of a strong central monarchy. It coincided in time with the consolidation of Mercian supremacy over the southern English, and with the replacement of the old national name of Gewissae (see p. 324.3, Wessex, above) by the collective ethnic term Saxon, and was reached when the influence of monks trained in Ireland, familiar with Irish hierarchical kingship, was at its strongest throughout Britain.

324.4 DIFFERENT TEXTS: closer study is likely to suggest when the differences are no more than varying formulae, and when they imply differing political conceptions. Occasionally an underking is termed *minister,* e.g. BCS 60, whereby Aethelred of Mercia granted Gloucester, c. 680, to Osric and Oswald *duobus ministris meis nobilis generis in provincia Huicciorum,* though they are elsewhere regularly termed *reges.*

324.4 REX: still used of regional West Saxon kings of the later 8th century; cf., e.g., SC 757.

325.1 KINGDOMS ... DETACHED FROM WESSEX: e.g. Wiltshire grants in 680–681 made to and by Cenfrith, *comes Mertiorum,* who is also called *patricius,* and *propinquus,* near relative, of Aethelred of Mercia, BCS 54, 58, 59.

326.3 COLLECTING TAXES: cf. p. 460 *Age.*

327.1 OSWY: William of Malmesbury *de Gestis Regum* 1, 50; he 'ruled (*praefuit*) the Mercians and the peoples of the other southern provinces', Bede HE 3, 24.

327.2 ALDHELM: e.g. BCS 108 *Ego Ine ... rex cum consilio et decreto praesulis nostri Aldhelm.*

329.1 EMPIRE: Bede regularly distinguishes the *imperium* of each over-king from his own *regnum,* e.g. HE 1, 25; 2, 5; cf. Plummer *Bede* 2, 43; 86. The Mercian charters and the 'Tribal Hidage' similarly distinguish between the *imperium* and the *regnum* of the Mercian kings; cf. Stenton ASE 234, and EHR 33, 1918, 433.

329.1 EMPEROR: BCS 289 *rector et imperator Merciorum regni.*

329.2 IRISH ... IMPERATOR: Muirchú 9; cf. Loegaire, p. 161 *Age.*

329.2 OSWALD: Adomnán *Columba* 1, 1 *totius Brittaniae imperator a Deo ordinatus*; earlier in the chapter *regnator Saxonum*; cf. p. 161 *Age.*

329.2 BRIAN BORU: Book of Armagh, folio 16 verso; cf. p. 167 *Age.*

329.2 ARMORICAN BRITISH: *vita Pauli Aureliani* 15; cf. p. 253 *Age.*

329.3 BONIFACE: *Ep.* 78 *imperator vel rex* referring to Aethelbald; cf. *Ep.* 75. Aethelbald calls himself *gentis Merciorum regens imperium* in an original charter, BCS 162, 'ruling the empire held by the Mercian nation'.

329.3 GWLEDIC: cf. p. 206 *Age.*

329.3 BRETWALDA: cf. p. 317 *Age,* and Athelstan's usage of *Brytaenwalda,* BCS 706, to translate *rector Britanniae* of BCS 705, dated AD 934.

330.2 10th CENTURY: occasionally used by Athelstan, e.g. *basileus Anglorum simul et imperator regum et nationum infra fines Britanniae commorantium,* BCS 700, dated AD 934, exactly defining notions of the respective meanings of king and emperor; cf. also BCS 746.

330.2 EDRED: king and emperor, e.g. BCS 874, 882, 884; Caesar BCS 909.

330.2 AETHELRED: e.g. KCD 1308 *rex Anglo-Saxoniae, atque Nordhymbrensis gubernator monarchiae*; *paganorumque propugnator, ac Bretonum ceterarumque provinciarum imperator.*

330.2 GREEK TITLES: e.g. *basileus orbis Britannie* KCD 1283; *basileus Albionis* KCD 1279 cf. note 330.2, 10th century, above.

331.2 ALCUIN: see E.

331.2 ALCUIN ... IMMENSE THREAT: *Ep.* 129, also printed HS 3, 509–511; cf. *Ep.* 17.

332.3 THREE PERSONS: Alcuin *Ep.* 174.

333.2 DAVID ... JOAB: Alcuin *Ep.* 178.

333.2 PRESSURES ... ADVICE: cf. Ganshof *Speculum* 24, 1949, 524. 'It was ... owing to Alcuin that he (Charles) went to Rome ... it was under the same influence that he accepted there the imperial dignity.' The story that Charles was taken by surprise when the Pope crowned him is unconvincing government propaganda, that could have deceived no one who knew what Alcuin had been advising, or had read his letters.

333.2 CHARLEMAGNE ... ROME: at the moment of his coronation Charles was not crowned 'western' emperor. He was crowned Roman emperor while the imperial throne in Constantinople was vacant. But the elevation of a new emperor in Constantinople made him and his successors western emperors.

333.2 ENGLISH PRECEDENT: English practice grew from past English, Welsh and Irish experience. Irish political practice was the main root of government by a High King over subordinate kings who acknowledged his precedence, but denied his authority. Continental circumstances prevented the emergence of a sovereign high-kingship on the English model and condemned the emperors to a high-kingship as weak as the Irish. For the next several centuries the main political relationships of European rulers, that are at present commonly classified as 'feudal', were of necessity obliged to reproduce many of the features of Irish government, which had underlain their formation at several removes. The study of 9th-, 10th- and 11th-century Europe is impoverished if Irish experience, secular as ecclesiastical, is disregarded.

18 Fifth-Century Church (pp. 335–355)

335.1 CHRISTIAN RELIGION: cf. pp. 12 and 23 *Age*.
335.1 ALBAN: and other personal names, see E. See also below, vol. 6, pp. 145–54.
335.1 AFRICA AND EGYPT: Tertullian *adversus Iudaeos* 7, written before 209; Origen *Homily 4 on Ezekiel*, *Homily 6 on Luke*.
335.1 ARLES: Mansi 2, 466 (HS 1, 7); cf. *Ant.* 35, 1961, 316.
335.1 ORTHODOXY: e.g. Hilary of Poitiers *de Synodis* Prolog. and 1, PL 10, 457, 459 (HS 1, 9); cf. passages cited HS 1, 7–13, from Athanasius and others.
335.1 CONTEMPT: e.g. the British bishops who rejected government subsidies at Rimini, p. 13 *Age*.
335.1 BISHOP OF LONDON: see E Augurius, and p. 14 *Age*.
335.2 CLERGY: e.g. the priest (Calpurnius) Odysseus, great-grandfather of Patrick (see E) about the beginning of the fourth century.
335.2 ARCHAEOLOGICAL EVIDENCE: summarised in JBAA 16, 1953, 1 ff.; 18, 1955, 1, ff. *Christianity in Britain* 37 ff., cf. 51 ff., 87 ff.
335.2 LONDON: see P.
336.1 VICTRICIUS' LETTER: *de Laude Sanctorum* PL 20, 443; a long extract is reprinted in HS 2, xxi.
336.1 MARTIN: cf. p. 26 *Age*.
336.1 POPE INNOCENT: *Ep.* 2 (PL 20, 471).
337.2 HALF A DOZEN ... MONKS: Pelagius, Coelestius, the Sicilian Briton and his fellow authors, Faustus, Constans Caesar (see E); Antiochus and Martyrius (Sicilian Briton *Ep.* 1) were monks in Britain, but might have been native or foreign by birth.
337.2 WANDERING MONKS: Fastidius, *de vita Christiana* 15 (PL 40, 1046), enjoins his widowed correspondent to delight in washing the feet of travelling saints.
337.2 SHRINE OF ALBAN: cf. p. 344 *Age*.
337.2 MARTYRS' SHRINES: Gildas 10; *sanctorum martyrum ... corporum sepulturae et passionum loca ... quam plurima*. He names St. Albans and Caerleon;

	St. Martha's, near Guildford, *TQ 02 48*, is probably another; cf. Arnold-Forster SCD 2, 559, cf. 509; and EPNS Surrey 244. The place-name Merthyr, usually joined with the name of a sixth-century saint, is common in south Wales, in and by the territories where Roman literate civilisation was deep rooted. Some of these shrines may have held imported relics maintained by monks.
337.2	BEDE: HE 1, 26.
337.2	SCHOOLS: see p. 409 *Age* and E Coelestius.
337.3	PATRICK: *Ep.*, 2 and 15; cf. E.
337.3	NYNIA: Bede HE 3, 4; cf. E Ninian and p. 191 *Age*.
337.3	CHURCH ... NAME: see p. 146 *Age*.
337.4	ROSNAT: see P.
338.1	EXCAVATION: see P Whithorn.
338.3	PELAGIUS: see E; cf. vol. 6 below, pp. 17–51; his *Commentary* on the Pauline Epistles, PL Sup. 1, 1110 ff.
338.3	JOHN CASSIAN: see E Cassianus.
338.3	JURA: cf. Greg. Tur. *Vitae Patrum* 1, and BHL Lupicinus, Romanus, 5073–4, 7309.
338.3	MONTALEMBERT: *Les Moines d'Occident* 1, 288 (English edition, 1,514).
338.4	HONORATUS: see DCB.
338.4	FAUSTUS: see E. The suggestion that he was 'Breton' rather than British is anachronistic. Faustus came to Lérins 40 years before the second migration to northern Gaul, a century before the third migration turned Armorica into 'Lesser Britain'.
339.1	AMATOR: see DCB, and p. 349 *Age*.
339.2	AUGUSTINE: and other European ecclesiastics; see DCB, cf. E.
339.2	AUGUSTINE: the texts of the Pelagian controversy are assembled in PL 45, 1679 ff.; 48, 319 ff.; 56, 490 ff.; cf. Mansi 4, 444 ff.; and are discussed in vol. 6 below, pp. 42–6.
340.1	ONE MAN: Sicilian Briton *de Divitiis* 8, 1–3.
340.2	LOOK YOU NOW: *de Divitiis* 6–7.
341.1	CAMEL: *de Divitiis* 18, 1–3.
341.2	LISTEN: *de Divitiis* 17, 3, concluding words.
341.2	MANKIND IS DIVIDED: *de Divitiis* 5 *tria enim ista sunt in quae humanum gens dividitur; divitiae, paupertas, sufficientia*.
341.2	ABOLISH THE RICH: *de Divitiis* 12 *tolle divitem et pauperum non invenies ... Pauci enim divites pauperum sunt causa multorum*.
341.2	THEOLOGIANS: cf. C.P. Caspari *Briefe*, page v.
341.2	UNIQUE: the nearest parallels to the Sicilian Briton's concepts are expressed by his contemporary John Chrysostom of Antioch, Patriarch of Constantinople 398–404; but Chrysostom's argument is less analytical, simple and direct, his practical conclusion less sharp and positive.
342.2	PROTESTANTISM: cf. e.g., G. de Plinval *Pélage* 405 *combien d'éléments inconsciemment pélagiens ont reparu dans le protestantisme anglo-saxon ou scandinave*.
342.2	WORKS COPIED: listed in Migne PL Supplement 1. Many MSS are known by the name of the monastery from whose library they come; the origin of those known only by the catalogue number of a major central library has not yet been systematically explored.
342.3	PELAGIAN WRITERS: Pelagius, the Sicilian Briton, Fastidius, and the author of *de Virginitate* were British, Coelestius probably Irish; Julianus of Aeclanum was Italian, the author of *de Divina Lege* of unknown origin. The writings of several other continental Pelagians have not been preserved; the writings of Faustus, also British, imply a Pelagian background in youth.

342.3 CITED IN BRITAIN: Gildas 38 cites *de Virginitate* 6 as the work of *quidam nostrum*, 'one of us', of our fellow countrymen; vol. 6 below, p. 27. The tract is one of half a dozen similar works similarly preserved, and it is therefore probable that the whole collection was known to Gildas, and approved by him; though the sentiment is repeated by the Sicilian Briton and others, the exact wording is used only in *de Virginitate*.

343.3 GERMANUS IN BRITAIN: Constantius *vita Germani* 12 ff., excerpted word for word by Bede HE 1, 17 ff.; cf. p. 62 *Age*. Prosper says that he was sent by Pope Celestine, Constantius that he was sent by a Gallic synod at the request of anti-Pelagians in Britain. Both are plainly right; a Gallic synod could not intervene without the Pope's approval, nor could the Pope wisely intervene without Gallic support.

345.2 PALLADIUS: see E.

345.2 PATRICK: see E and p. 64 *Age*.

345.3 POPE CELESTINE: Prosper *contra Collatorum* 21 (PL 51, 271).

346.4 PRELATES LEARNED: Patrick *Confessio* 13.

348.2 TWO PATRICKS: see E, and especially T.F.O'Rahilly *The Two Patricks*; J. Carney *The Problem of Patrick* and SILH 324 ff.; D.Binchy *Studia Hibernica* 2, 1962, 7–173; below, vol. 6, pp. 111–25; for older views cf. e.g. Todd *Patrick* and Bury *Patrick*.

348.3 INFORMATIVE TEXTS: the *Hymn of Secundinus* LH 1, 7 was probably composed in the 5th century, Kenney 260, CPL 16; but, though its author may have known Patrick, it gives little information about him.

348.3 MUIRCHU: see T and E.

348.3 ANONYMOUS LIFE: Colgan's *vita Secunda* TT 11 ff., cf. E Patrick; the texts and traditions that underlie this Life require study.

348.3 OTHER EARLY ACCOUNTS: Tírechán, 'Muirchú Book II', Probus, the Book of the Angel, etc. collected in Stokes VT and Colgan TT; several texts have been published independently; cf. Kenney 165 ff.; 319 ff.

348.4 VICTORICUS: see E; cf. also below, vol. 6, p. 112.

349.2 AMATOR: see E; Muirchú, and derivative texts, have Patrick ordained by Germanus and consecrated by Amator(ex), a neighbouring bishop; Muirchú's source did not make it plain to him that Amator was Germanus' predecessor, and died in 418; he understood *ordinatio* by two separate bishops to mean two contemporary bishops; since the bishops were successive, the original probably meant that he was ordained deacon by Amator, priest by Germanus.

349.4 FARTHER REGIONS: *Confessio* 51.

350.1 PATRICK ... FORGOTTEN: Kenney p. 324.

350.3 DOCCO: see E.

350.3 ST. KEW: founded long before Samson's visit, c. 530; cf. E Samson.

351.1 BISHOP CONSECRATED: the normal reluctance of popes and patriarchs to permit a multiplicity of bishops and a potentially independent metropolitan is emphasised by the exceptional nature of the privileges granted to Augustine among the English and to Boniface in Germany. Results were sometimes bizarre; until the 20th century, only one bishop was permitted in Abyssinia, and each new bishop was obliged to travel to Egypt for consecration. The mid seventh-century plague produced a comparable temporary difficulty in the English church; without sufficient bishops to consecrate new bishops, the episcopate could not have continued in Ireland in the fifth century after Patrick's death.

351.1 NORTHERN SEES: Few of the sees became permanent.

351.1 CHURCHMEN ... BRITISH: e.g. Mel (Mael), Mocteus; see E.

351.2 ARMAGH ... DEFERENCE: e.g. the bishop of Armagh is named first in the address of Pope John's letter to the Irish bishops in 640, Bede HE 2, 19.
351.2 ARCHBISHOP: Cogitosus, prologue (TT 518), writing not later than c. 650 (cf. E) calls Conlaed of Kildare (died 517, see E) *archiepiscopus Hiberniensium episcoporum* and describes Kildare as *caput pene omnium Hiberniensium eclesiarum ... cuius parrochia per totam Hiberniensem terram diffusam a mari usque ad mare extensa est* 'head of almost all the Irish churches ... whose diocese extends throughout Ireland from sea to sea'. The claims are no less extravagant than those put forward for Armagh half a century later; but are less remarked because they were not accepted, and not repeated. Some later Leinster clerics (e.g. Maedóc; see E) are entitled 'archbishop of Leinster', but not of Ireland.
351.2 DIOCESAN CLERGY: the sources are surveyed by Kathleen Hughes, CEIS especially pp. 79 ff.
351.3 BRIGIT: see E.
351.3 CONLAED ... CHAPLAIN: Cogitosus, prologue (TT 518) is explicit; Brigit was 'prudently concerned' that the Kildare houses should be governed 'properly in all respects', and because
> without a bishop who could consecrate churches and appoint clergy ... this was not possible, she summoned an illustrious hermit ... to govern the church with her, with the status of bishop, so that her churches should not lack clergy.

Nothing is said of how she got him consecrated, or by whom.
352.2 AILBE, CIARAN, DECLAN, IBAR, ENDA, KEBI: see E.
352.2 EUGENIUS, TIGERNACH: see E.
352.3 FAENCHA: she is likely to have been one of the numerous Irish girls to whom Patrick gave the veil; see E.
352.4 ROSNAT: Whithorn; see P and p. 337 *Age*.
353.1 ANGUS: see A 492.
353.2 POPE: the patriotic tale of the two-day British or Irish pope occurs in several Lives.
353.2 FINNIAN, MACCRICHE, ERLATHEUS: see E.
353.3 ETELIC: made uncle of Cadoc and of Paul Aurelian (E), both born about 500.
353.3 FINTAN: see E.
355.2 VOYAGES: cf. p. 384 *Age*.
355.2 CORNWALL: cf. p. 130 *Age*.

19 Sixth-Century Monks (pp. 356–388)

356.2 BRIOC: and other names; see E.
357.1 LIFE OF SAMSON: see E. The Life was written before the episcopate of Thuriau, bishop of Dol about 610.
363.2 LIFE OF PAUL AURELIAN: early spellings, e.g. Tigernomaglus (ch. 11); Quonomorius (ch. 8); villa Banhedos (ch. 8).
363.2 WILDERNESS: *ut heremi deserta penetraret, ibique a consortio mundalis vitae sequestratus ... vitam duceret* (ch. 6).
363.3 CHILDEBERT: often called 'Philibert' in the Lives.
364.2 PLOU- ... TRE-: Paul Aurelian (*vita* 12) found a still recognisable Roman estate (*fundus*) in the *Plebs Telmedovia*, now Plou-Dalmazeau (Map 14, D 2, number 22) which became 'one of his hundred *tribus*' wherein his followers built their *habitacula* (houses); Fracan (*vita Winwaloe* 1, 2)

found another estate, near St. Brieuc (Map 14 *N* 2) 'of the right size for a *plebs*', which 'is now named after its finder', today Plou-Fragan. Both Lives are 9th-century texts that used 6th-century written sources.

The organisational form of a *plebs* comprising a number of *tribus* containing houses has one precedent. Jerome's account of Pachomius' organisation of the Egyptian monks (PL 23, 69 ff.; 50, 275 ff.; preface 2, and *passim*) explains that 'three or four houses were federated into one *tribus*' with 'thirty or forty houses to one monastery', a *populus* or *plebs Dei*, a people of God; Bangor-on-Dee was also divided into seven *portiones*, equivalent to Jerome's *tribus*, 'none with less than 300 men', who necessarily lived in separate houses (Bede HE 2, 2).

The monastic terminology was riveted upon secular usage. *Plou-* and variants are the normal names of early district centres in Brittany and sometimes in Cornwall; *plwyf* is used for parish in Welsh, but does not occur in place-names. *Tre-* is the commonest form of village-name in all British lands where monasteries were numerous, Brittany, Cornwall, Wales and the Clyde kingdom (Watson CPNS 358 ff., with some possible extension as a suffix in Pictland), but not in Reged, between the Solway and the Mersey (EPNE 185; EPNS Cumberland 116), where monasteries were limited to a small region (Map 26). *Tref* (*trev* in Brittany) is the normal Welsh for village, equivalent to English *-tun*. *Ty*, house, and, in Brittany, *ker*, fortified enclosure, are also common in the names of farmsteads. Once established, the name forms remained in use, to give Treharris, Treherbert etc. in the 19th century; but very many of the personal names attached to *Tre-* are those of persons known to have lived in the 6th or 7th centuries.

The linguistic origin of *tribus* and *tref* is not known. It may derive from an Indo-European original, that might also underlie Germanic *terp*, *dorf*, *throp*, *thorp*, etc., but no such root is known; it does not occur among the very numerous Celtic place-names of the Roman world, and is unlikely to be connected with Gallic *Atrebates*, since, apart from linguistic difficulties, 'those who live at home (or in houses)' is an unlikely name for nation. Irish *treabh*, village, also exceedingly rare in place-names (Watson CPNS 357) is likely to derive from *tref*. The short vowel of *tribus* would by oral transmission be expected to give Welsh *trif*, or perhaps *trwyf*; but the term was no longer in normal spoken use in the late Empire; it was adopted by men who read what Jerome wrote; similarly the English read Jerome's *tribus* and pronounced it 'tribe', with a long vowel. The linguistic origin of *plebs, plou-, plwyf,* and of words for 'house', is clearer.

366.3 DEMETIA ... GLEVISSIG: Teilo is said to have instituted bishops in both kingdoms, in or about the 570s, LL 115; 131. The appointments corresponded with the creation of the separate Glevissig monarchy; cf. pp. 228 and 208 *Age*.

367.3 DAVID: see E. He was born *anno XXX post discessum Patricii <de Menevia>* ACm, at 458. The words *de Menevia*, 'from St. David's', are evidently a gloss added to the original by a copyist who mistook *discessus*, death, for 'departure', and allied it with a tradition that Patrick had sailed for Ireland in 432 from Porth Mawr, by St. David's. The round figure of 30 years after the death of Patrick, entered in most annals at various years in the 490s, gives a date in the 520s, consistent with baptism by Ailbe. He died in 589, A (AI; cf. AT, AC, CS). The corrupt entry or entries of ACm 601 *David Episcopus. Moni Iudaeorum* (perhaps for *Mons Giudiorum*, intending *Urbs Giudi,* Stirling), whatever their meaning or origin, do not evidence a belief in a variant death-date at odds with the annalistic tradition. *David Episcopus* might derive from an Irish annal, not otherwise preserved, concerning Mobhí of Inch (see E), who is sometimes called David in Irish texts.

368.1 PAULINUS: ECMW 139; cf. E.
368.2 RULE OF DAVID: Ricemarchus *vita David* 21–30. The words transcribed by Ricemarchus, *suffosoria vangasque invicto brachio terre defigunt* (22), are also cited by Gildas *Ep.* 4 *suffosoria figentes terrae,* and therefore derive from a sixth-century original. Ricemarchus cannot have copied Gildas, for even if he had known his Letters, he could not have identified the unnamed monk whom Gildas abused with his own hero.
368.3 ABSTINENCE ... : Gildas *Ep.* 2.
368.3 THEY CRITICISE BRETHREN ... : Gildas *Ep.* 3.
369.1 ABBOT: Gildas *Ep.* 4.
369.2 CASSIODORUS: see E.
369.3 ABBOTS: Gildas *Ep.* 5.
370.1 BREFI: see P.
370.1 DIFFERENT REGIONS: see especially Bowen SCSW, particularly the maps on pp. 38 and 52.
370.3 PLACES UP THE FOSSE WAY: see E David, Samson.
370.3 FOSSE WAY: beyond it, Elphin of Warrington, and of North Frodingham in the East Riding, was Welsh by name.
370.3 IRISH MONKS: see E Abbán, Columba of Terryglass; cf. pp. 386 ff. *Age.*
370.3 WINWALOE: cf. p. 314.3 (Norfolk).
372.1 WILFRED: Eddius 17.
374.3 SCATTERED HERMITS ... BRITISH: e.g. Daniel of Hare Island (*vita Ciarán Clonmacnoise* 25).
374.3 FIRST ORDER: *Catalogus.*
374.3 MONASTERIES: most were far removed from the seats of kings; the few that lie near to royal centres include Columba's Derry and Kells, and the Leinster houses of Kildare, Glendabough and Ferns.
375.1 TUATHAL: cf. p. 169.2 above.
375.3 SAINTS OF IRELAND CAME: Irish-language Life, Stokes *Lismore Lives* 2640.
376.1 FULL OF KNOWLEDGE: *vita Finniani* 34.
376.1 DAVID, CATHMAEL: Irish-language Life, Stokes *Lismore Lives* 2527 ff.
376.2 WINE: *vita Ciarán* 31.
376.2 AGRICULTURE: cf. p. 432 *Age.*
377.2 BLESSED IS GOD: *vita Ciarán* 33; cf. p. 169 *Age.*
377.3 CUIL DREMHNI: cf. p. 173 *Age.*
377.4 ADOMNAN: *Columba* 3, 3; 1, 1.
378.1 WHEN THE NEWS CAME ... : *vita Columbae* (O'Donnell) 2, 5 (TT 410); cf. ZCP 9, 1913, 268, paragraph 180.
379.3 TRADITION OF GILDAS: *vita Gildae* (Rhuys) 11–12 *Ainmericus rex ... misit ad beatum Gildam rogans ut ... veniens ecclesiasticum ordinem in suo regno restauraret* etc.; cf. *vita Gildae* (Caradoc) 5 *Gildas ... remanens in Hibernia studiam regens et praedicans in civitate Ardmaca.*
379.3 ELDERS OF IRELAND: Colgan TT 463 (50), also printed Reeves *Adamnan* 193, note a.
379.3 COLUMBAN ... GILTA: MGH *Epp.* 3, 158.
379.3 GILDAS' RULE: *Penitential* 17–18; 22; 27.
381.2 AGRICULTURE ... ECONOMY: cf. p. 432 *Age.*
381.2 SCIENTIFIC ENQUIRY: e.g. Virgilius, Dícuil, etc.; cf. p. 402 *Age.*

NOTES TO *THE AGE OF ARTHUR* (pp. 368-386)

381.3 LITERACY: some of Taliesin's poems in Welsh were probably composed as early, but were probably not written down until the 7th century.
381.3 DAGAEUS: *vita* (Sal.) 3; cf. 4-6.
381.4 KILDARE CHURCH: Cogitosus *vita Brigit* 35 (TT 523-4).
382.5 CHURCHMEN AND KINGS: e.g. Benedict Biscop; Ine and Ceadwalla, Coenred and Offa, Bede HA 2 ff.; HE 5, 7; 5, 19.
382.5 AETHERIA: CSEL 39, 35 ff.
383.1 XENODOCHIA: e.g. the 4th-century British frequented the *Xenodochium in Portu Romano* Jerome *Ep.* 77, last paragraph.
383.1 BONIFACE: *Ep.* 78.
383.1 BRITISH MONK: Greg. Tur. HF 5, 21; 8, 34, cf. E Winnoc, and p. 250 *Age*.
383.2 RADEGUND: see E John of Chinon, Radegund.
383.2 CARANTOCUS: *vita Columbani* 7; cf. E Carantoc of Saul.
383.2 NORTHERN GAUL: see Map 4, p. 89 *Age*; cf. p. 90 *Age*. Casual observation has remarked about a hundred place-names and church-dedications extending from western Normandy as far east as St.-Pol (de Léon), the proper name of the Dunkirk beaches, and Samson near Namur; systematic enquiry, so far confined to Canon Doble's study of the records of the diocese of Rouen, is likely to discover more. Many of these names are due to the Armorican British, some to migration direct from Britain. On the Belgian littoral, Winnoc's name is still prominent, though it is nowadays most obvious in the names of boarding-houses, restaurants and branded goods. The monks probably often preached where their countrymen had settled previously.
383.2 SPAIN: Excerpts from the texts are reprinted in HS 2, 99 ff. and discussed by E.A.Thompson in *Christianity in Britain* 201 ff., citing P.David *Galice et Portugal*.
384.1 VOYAGES: *Immrama* cf. Kenney 406 ff. CEIS 233 ff. Some of the Irish-language tales are translated in P.W.Joyce, *Old Celtic Romances*, the *Navigatio Brendani* in J.F. Webb, *Lives of the Saints*; cf. Selmer *Navigatio Sancti Brendani*.
384.1 BRENDAN AND MALO: see E. The two voyages, *vita I Brendani* 13; 64-66.
384.1 ITA: *vita I Brendani* 71.
384.1 SAILED WESTWARD ... : *vita I Brendani* 13.
384.2 THIS IS THE LAND ... : *vita I Brendani* 65.
385.1 BRITAIN ... HERESY: *vita I Brendani* 87.
385.1 MANUSCRIPTS: date, cf. Plummer VSH 1, xxi ff., commenting 'the compiler ... has earned our gratitude by preserving for us materials which exist nowhere else'; cf. xxxvii and Kenney 410 (ninth-century date).
385.1 ICELAND: see P.
385.2 YOUR KINGDOM ... : *vita I Brendani* 95.
385.2 FIFTY ROYAL TOWNS ... : *vita I Brendani* 80, where *oppida regum* probably means the raths of *tuath* kings.
386.1 ABINGDON: *civitatem que dicitur Abbaindun vel Dun Abbain vita Abbani* 14; cf. 13 *civitatem gentilem et deditam ydolis*. The early spellings *Aebbandun, Abbandun, Abbendun,* originally referred to another site, perhaps Boar's Hill, whence the name was removed to the later abbey and town DEPN 1; cf. MA 12, 1968, 26 ff.; see P. Medieval English tradition held that a Roman temple had formerly occupied the site; some 500 Roman coins are reported from Abingdon. The number is exceptionally large for a rural site away from a road; such concentrations are commoner in Roman temple-enclosures than on farms.
386.2 COLUMBA OF TERRYGLASS: *vita* (Sal.) 10; cf. E. The direct route from Tours to Ireland passed through no English area at this date. Columba's detour

suggests a visit to Abingdon, or possibly to Caistor-by-Norwich or Leicester, the nearest likely centres of royal cremation.

387.2 HOMELESS LAND: Reeves *Adamnan* 274; 266.

20 Seventh-Century Church (pp. 389–405)

389.1 BEDE: HE 3, 4.
389.3 AUGUSTINE: Bede HE 1, 26.
390.1 BRITISH ... MEETING ... AUGUSTINE: Bede HE 2, 2, at *Augustinaes Ac,* 'on the borders of the Hwicce and the West Saxons', perhaps Aust, *ST* 57 88, now the English end of the Severn Bridge.
390.2 THIS PRESENT LIFE ... : Bede HE 2, 13.
391.4 AEDAN: Bede HE 3, 5; cf. E.
392.2 WEST SAXON ... BAPTISM: Bede HE 3, 7; cf. 3, 22 (East Saxons), 3, 21 (Mercians, Peada).
392.2 BARKING AND CHERTSEY: Bede HE 4, 6.
392.2 BURGH CASTLE, BOSHAM: cf. E Fursey, Dicuil, Cedd etc.
392.2 BRIXWORTH: see P; cf. also Lyminge in Kent.
394.2 LINDISFARNE: Bede HE 3, 26.
394.3 WILFRED ... ENDOWMENTS: Eddius 17.
394.4 EASTER CONTROVERSY: see p. 399 *Age.*
394.5 WHITBY: Bede HE 3, 25, dated 664 HE 3, 26, after Easter, but early in the year, since Chad left for the south after the synod, but had not heard of the death of Deusdedit of Canterbury (14 July 664) until he reached Kent (HE 3, 28).
395.2 CHAD: Bede HE 3, 28.
395.3 CHAD AND THEODORE: Bede HE 4, 3.
396.2 PICTS, MERCIANS, IRISH: Eddius 19–20, Bede HE 4, 26.
396.3 HEXHAM: Eddius 22.
396.3 WORLDLY GLORY: Eddius 24.
397.1 FOUL WEEDS ... IRISH: Eddius 47.
397.1 RULE OF BENEDICT: the Rule is named, and chapter 64 cited by Bede *Historia Abbatum* 11; cf. 16. The Rule was probably set down before 550, and made extensive use of an earlier Rule, probably of about 500 or soon after, perhaps drawn up at Lérins or Marseille; the arguments are discussed by David Knowles, *Great Historical Enterprises,* 1963, 137 ff.
397.2 IONA CUSTOM: Bede HE 3, 4.
397.3 LLANDAFF: see T Gospel Books, *Liber Landavensis.*
399.2 CONFORMITY WITH ROME: summarised by Kenney 210 ff., Plummer *Bede* 2, 348 ff., etc.; see E Aed of Sletty etc.
399.2 KILDARE: cf. p. 351 *Age.*
399.2 MEMORY OF PATRICK: cf. p. 350 *Age.*
400.2 MONASTICISM IN EUROPE: the sources are summarised by Kenney 486 ff.
402.3 VIRGILIUS: see E.
403.2 ALCUIN: see E and pp. 331 ff. *Age.*
403.4 NATIONALITY ... MONASTICISM: much misunderstanding arises from the indiscriminate and undefined modern terminology of 'Irish' or 'English' missionary movements in Europe, particularly in accounts of the 8th century. Boniface and Virgilius of Salzburg disagreed deeply on matters of moment; but their disagreements had little to do with the accident that one was of English birth, the other Irish. Modern emphasis on their birth often leads to considerable confusion (cf. e.g. note to Map 29) and

sometimes tempts historians to exaggerate the importance of their fellow-countrymen and to belittle the impact of the foreigner upon their own history. The initial driving forces behind the monastic movement in Europe, north of the Alps and the Massif Central, were a blend of Irish zeal and English discipline. But after the first pioneering generations these influences, together with those of the environment of each monastery, worked with differing strength on different individuals, English, Irish, French or German, whatever their personal national origin.

21 Letters (pp. 406–428)

406.2 ROMAN EMPIRE: the evidence is surveyed in Jones LRE 991 ff.
406.2 ANKARA: Jerome *Commentary* on the Epistle to the Galatians 2(3) (PL 26, 357).
406.2 SEVERUS: Dialogues 1, 27.
406.2 SIDONIUS: *Ep.* 3, 3, 2, *sermonis Celtici squama.*
407.2 LONDON ARTISANS: Merrifield *Roman London* plate 101.
407.2 LATIN WORDS: Jackson LHEB 78–80 lists a selection.
407.3 BRITISH LATIN: Jackson LHEB 108 ff.
408.2 AETHERIA: the Rhone, ch. 18, 2. The date is probably early fifth-century, but might be later, as Meister in *Rheinisches Museum* 64, 1909, 337 ff. The Latinity is analysed and discussed by E.Löfstedt, *Peregrinatio Aetheriae*.
408.3 LATIN ... DIED: the late 6th-century Armorican British Latin of the first Life of Samson is as pedestrian as the language of Aetheria, but is still a living idiom; but in the 8th century Nennius is 'laboriously thinking first in Welsh and then translating', LHEB 121; cf. THS Cymm., 1946–7, 55–56.
408.3 MORI MARUSA: Pliny NH 4, 27, citing Philemon.
409.1 MAEGL: SC 577, which has 'the look of contemporary record' LHEB 677.
409.2 IRISH ... SCHOOLS ... PRESERVE LATIN: and Greek, see especially K.Meyer, *Learning in Ireland*, where, however, the statement of a 12th-century MS that 'all the learned of the whole empire fled abroad and increased the learning of Ireland' is unfounded; cf. LHEB 122 ff.
409.3 EDUCATION: the evidence for Roman education is collected and discussed by H.-I.Marrou, *Education in Antiquity,* and *Saint Augustin,* and is summarised by Jones, LRE 987 ff.
409.3 SICILIAN BRITON: away from school *Ep.* 1, 5; classes *de Divitiis* 12, 5; cf. E.
409.3 FLUENT GREEK: *eius responsionem Graeco eloquio prolatam* Augustine *de Gestis Pelagii* 4, cf. 2; and cf. 19 (Orosius).
410.2 WHITHORN: cf. P and E Maucennus.
410.2 COELESTIUS: cf. E; p. 339 *Age*; below, vol. 6, pp. 31–4.
410.2 ILLTUD: cf. E. His school is described in the Lives of Samson, written about 600, and of Paul Aurelian (9th-century), both of which used written texts of the 6th century.
410.2 SONS OF LAYMEN: e.g. Maelgwn, Gildas, Faelán, Colmán of Leinster (*vita Coemgen* 31), and others.
410.3 OUR THINKING: *vita Pauli Aureliani* 6.
411.1 GIMNASIA: e.g. *vita Kebi* 1.
411.1 COLLEGIUM: *vita Winwaloe* 1, 11.
411.1 CANE: *vita Niniani* 10; *Kentigerni* (Jocelyn) 5; cf. e.g. Ausonius *Protrepticon* 33; Augustine *Confessio* 1, 28; Sidonius *Ep.* 2, 10.
411.1 TEILO: LL 101, cf. 98, *stultorum philosophorum.* These attitudes are noticeably rare in the accounts of other saints.

411.2	TEACHERS ... GAUL AND BRITAIN:	for the modern myth of a migration of Gallic scholars see p. 409 *Age*.
411.2	MOCTEUS:	see E.
412.1	DRUSTICC:	see E Finnian of Moville.
412.2	CURRICULUM:	in Britain, Samson was at school from the age of 5 to 18 or 20; Leonorus from 5 to 15; Kebi from 7; Brioc from 10 or 12 to 24; Malo and Paul Aurelian from 'an early age', Paul to 16. The curriculum seems to have regarded Leonorus' 10 years as normal, Winninus stayed for 'the two *lustra*', the ten-year period, and Maudetus 'finished his curriculum in 7 years' and therefore 'did not complete his *decennium*'; cf. E. In Ireland, Brendan of Clonfert entered school at 5, Findchua (Bri Gobban: *Lismore Lives* 2834) at 7; in England Bede's education lasted from the age of 7 until his ordination as deacon 12 years later, Willibrord's from 'weaning' till the age of 20.
412.2	PAYMENT:	e.g. *vita Samsonis* (1) 7, cf. (2) 1, 5, *donaria secundum morem*; one cow, *vita Ciarán Clonmacnoise* 15.
412.2	FUNDS:	e.g. *vita Columba Terryglass* 5; in the early days of Finnian of Clonard's school his pupils took it in turns to provide the common meal, by labour, by purchase, or *per postulationem ab aliis*, by asking from others, lay neighbours.
412.2	STUDENT MEALS:	e.g. *Hisperica Famina* 303 ff.; cf. 222 ff.
412.3	AGILBERT:	Bede HE 3, 7.
412.3	IRISH EDUCATIONAL SYSTEM:	Bede HE 3, 27.
413.2	TECHNOLOGICAL SKILLS:	see pp. 433 ff. *Age*.
413.3	RUADAN:	vita 14; cf. *vita Finnian* of Clonard 24–26; cf. E.
414.1	ALDHELM:	*Ep.* 5.; cf. 3.
414.2	GREGORY:	HP, *Praefatio Prima*.
414.3	LITERATURE:	comment is here restricted to matter relevant to the history and impact of the Arthurian period. Space does not permit a balanced survey.
414.3	GILDAS:	see M. Winterbottom, *Gildas*, introduction.
415.1	MAELGWN'S BARDS:	Gildas 34, 6; cf. p. 219 *Age*.
415.3	VIRGILIUS MARO:	see E.
415.3	BONIFACE:	*Ep.* 9, written in youth to Nithard, is phrased in extravagant Hisperic. Boniface (Winfrith) was educated at Exeter and at Nursling, near Southampton, but in adult years abroad wrote normal European Latin; cf. E.
415.3	ALDHELM:	see E, and p. 498 *Age*.
415.3	WESTERN LATIN:	the main texts are summarised by Kenney, 250 ff.; cf. E Aldhelm, Boniface, Virgilius Maro. The word Hisperic is best confined to texts with fantasy vocabulary, as the *Hisperica Famina*, the word Western used for the wider literature, including Aldhelm.
415.3	HISPERIC:	named from the *Hisperica Famina*, ed. F.J.H. Jenkinson, Cambridge, 1908, including related texts; cf. M. Winterbottom *Celtica* 8, 1968, 126 ff., and Ker *Dark Ages* 31 note 4, etc.
416.3	CUNOBELINUS, BELIN:	The words of Suetonius, *Caligula* 44, *Adminio Cynobellini Britannorum regis filio* are transcribed by Orosius (7, 5, 5) as (*ad*) *Minocynobelinum Britannorum regis filium*; in Arthurian Britain the name was evidently read, with the corruption of a single letter, as *Minocyni Belinum*. The earliest person known to have been named Beli(n) was born about, or just before, the middle of the sixth century. The name was readily accepted because it occurred occasionally in Irish and Gallic mythology, though not as the name of a historical person (cf. CGH index p. 519); and 'Minocynus' resembled the Irish sea god Manannán, son of Lir, later adopted into Welsh literature as Manawydan.

416.4 COROTICUS: Muirchú 28, *musicam artem audivit a quodam cantare, quod de solio regali transiret* cf. p. 219 *Age*; the poet 'blasphemed' or 'satirised' the king, foretelling his end. To be effective, he is more likely to have sung in British than in Irish.

416.4 MAELGWN: Gildas 34, 6; cf. p. 415 *Age*.

416.4 NENNIUS: 62; cf. E.

417.1 OLDEST POEMS: see T. Most of the early poems survive in a few major medieval collections. Texts, not always accurately transcribed, were published by W.F.Skene FAB, with translations that outdo all other publications of bad verse in the English language. Most of the main MSS were published in transcript or facsimile by J.G.Evans 70 years ago, and several of the main poems have been edited by Sir Ifor Williams, with notes and introduction in modern Welsh, and by A.O.H.Jarman. Only the *Gododdin* has been accurately but literally translated in full, by Kenneth Jackson, but selections have appeared in most anthologies and histories of Welsh literature; cf. Works Cited, Sources, above, pp. 27–8.

417.3 DINOGAD: CA 88 (lines 1101 ff.), translated Parry HWL 22.

419.2 MAXIMUS' WIFE: Maximus first came to Britain in 367–368, his son was a child in 383, cf. PLRE I, Victor 14, and is shown on coin-portraits of 384 to 388 as a boy of 16 to 18. In 388 Maximus' daughters were apparently still unmarried, Ambrose *Ep.* 40, 32. He may have met and married his wife in Britain; her name is not known; several fourth-century empresses were named Helena.

420.2 ISIDORE: *Etymologiae* 9, 102, *Britones quidam Latine nominatos suspicantur eo quod bruti sunt*; cf. Heiric *vita Germani* 3, 246–247, *Britannia, brutis Barbara quo feritet gens ultro moribus omnis*.

420.2 CUANU: cf. E; ' "Britus son of Silvius son of Ascanius ... Aeneas the father of Ascanius, ancestor of Britan the odious". Thus our noble senior Guanach deduced the genealogy of the British from the Chronicles of the Romans', Irish Nennius (*Lebor Bretnach*) 6, translated into Latin, Zimmer, *Nennius Interpretatus*, MGH AA 13 p. 152. 'Guanach' is a misspelling of Cuana (cf. MGH p. 141), who probably died c. 640; cf. E.

420.3 LOEGRIUS: cf. e.g. the 14th-century pleas to the Pope, printed in Skene CPS, especially pp. 222, 243–247.

420.5 WELSH LITERATURE: surveyed by T.Parry and H.I.Bell: anthologies and translations, in OBWV, by Gwyn Williams, Conran, Bell, Graves, E.D.Jones and others include medieval and modern verse; cf. CSW 103 ff., and Works Cited, 1 (above, pp. 27–8).

421.3 ENGLISH LITERATURE: see especially Works Cited, 1: p. 16, above.

421.3 AETHELBERT: Attenborough LEEK; cf. Bede HE 2, 5.

421.4 CAEDMON: Bede HE 4, 24. The curious modern notion that he was a 'cowherd', of 'humble' origin, rests on inexact reading of Bede's words; cf. E and p. 314 *Age* (cf. note on 314.2).

421.4 CAEDMON'S VERSES: cf. Plummer *Bede* 2, 248–258 and subsequent literature; in the 19th century his name was read after verses inscribed on the Ruthwell Cross, in Dumfriesshire; cf. Sweet OET 125, etc.; the reading is doubted.

421.5 ENGLISH ... LATIN: see especially Manitius *Lateinische Literatur* and Laistner *Thought and Letters*.

421.5 SAXON CHRONICLE: see A.

421.5 MONASTIC ... RECORDS: Wilfred at Selsey, in the early 680s, was able to look up the day of Oswald's death in the 'books in which the burial of the dead was recorded' (Bede HE 4, 14). Selsey kept an up-to-date Martyrology, and is likely to have matched it with an annalistic record.

The probable form is an entry in an Easter-table *Occisio Osuualdi nonis Aug*, under the year 642, transcribed into a copy of a Martyrology under the 5th day of August.

422.2 IRISH LITERATURE: see especially Dillon and Chadwick *Celtic Realms* 239 ff.; Schoepperle, *Tristan*; and Works Cited, 1 (above, p. 18).

422.2 ROMAN WRITERS: especially Posidonius, most fully reported by Diodorus 5, 31; Caesar *de Bello Gallico*, especially 6, 13; Strabo 4, 4, 4; Ammian 15, 9, 8 citing Timagenes, where *euhages* misreads Greek *ouates*. The texts are summarised in N.K.Chadwick *The Druids* xiii ff.; cf. T.Kendrick *The Druids*; cf. A.Ll.Owen *The Famous Druids* 15 ff.; PRIA 60 C, 1959–60; cf. Jackson OIT, especially 39, ff.; etc.

422.3 FILID: the principal text is the Preface to the List of Tales in the Book of Leinster 189 b (24,915 ff.; 4,835), translated O'Curry 583 ff.

422.3 SECULAR SCHOOLS: cf. *Book of Aichill*, preface; cf. O'Curry 512, translated 50–51.

422.4 OGAM: O'Curry 464 ff.; Jackson LHEB 151 ff., where however the description of the staves as 'short', the 4th-century date, and the suggested origin among Irish colonists in Britain do not accommodate all the evidence. The script does not distinguish 'pagans' from 'Christians', Jackson LHEB 176, note 1. Varying sizes of sticks are envisaged in different tales. Some of them were long staffs cut from the trunks of small apple or yew trees (O'Curry 473, 475); others, as Patrick's 'wooden tablets', evidently Christian texts in Ogam characters, looked like swords (Book of Armagh 8 b 2, VT 300–301, with note), while others were much smaller. For the so-called 'Pictish Ogams', see p. 191.1 above.

423.2 REMOTE PAST: cf. p. 147 *Age*.

423.2 WINDOW ... IRON AGE: Kenneth Jackson OIT.

423.2 ANCIENT STORY: S.H.O'Grady, *Silva Gadelica*, vol. 1 (text), 2 (translation), contains a considerable collection, principally of tales set in the period of Finn or of the Historical Cycle; P.W.Joyce, *Old Celtic Romances*, translates a number of mythological tales, and some of the late extravagant and tedious *Imrama* (Voyages), that contrast with the more matter-of-fact Latin versions, as the Irish-language Saints' Lives compare with their Latin originals. The *Táin Bó Cualnge* (Cattle Raid of Cooley), of the Heroic Age, has been several times edited with translation. There are several translations of smaller sections of the literature; K.Meyer and others have translated a number of poems; cf. also M.Dillon and N.K.Chadwick, *The Celtic Realms*, 227 ff., 244 ff., and Kenneth Jackson, *The International Popular Tale*.

423.4 MACFIRBIS: O'Curry 122, reproduced CS, introduction p. xix.

423.4 LITERARY FORMS: cf. e.g. Carney *Medieval Irish Lyrics*.

424.2 MILKING A BULL: Adomnán, 2, 17, in a partially rationalised version.

424.2 FECHIN OF FORE: *vita* 9 (VSH 2, 79) *Res miranda atque novitate inusitata.* ... *Hoc enim possibile fuit illi solo qui produxit mel de petra, oleumque de saxo durissimo*. See E.

424.3 SENAN: *vita* 20 (Sal. 748–749), lines 673–711. Translation loses some of the wit of the original, which is reinforced by solemn rhyme and alliteration. The fourth verse here cited, lines 683–684 reads

  Nam, interruptis precibus, egre ferebat monachus
  ablucione parvuli sanctum liquorem pollui

The tenth verse, lines 697–700 reads

  Metitur quoque baculo que sit maris altitudo
  volens tantum procedere ut premineret pectore
  Huic inde, inquam, anxio ista erat intencio
  Ut non intraret alcius quam demonstraret baculus

426.2 ATTRACTA: *vita* 12, Colgan ASH 280, *taediosus factus est tibi Dominus Deus tuus.*
426.2 ADOMNAN: Irish Life, extract printed with translation, Skene CPS 408.
427.3 GEOFFREY'S ... FANCY: in the 12th century deliberate satire need not involve modern rational detachment. In all ages the human mind is capable of believing what it knows to be untrue; and to creative writers of fiction the characters they invent are easily invested with reality. The sharp classical and modern distinction between fiction and fact was alien to the complex psychology of Geoffrey and his age; neither he nor his readers found difficulty in accepting the reality of his inventions, when they had been written down, published to the world, and established in the consciousness of men. There was no contradiction between a conscious jest and a genuine belief in its truth. Geoffrey's academic contemporaries were open to the charge that they could not see the wood for the trees, but Geoffrey's artificial trees made a real wood, a concept of British history fully in accord with the beliefs and aspirations of his own day.

22 The Economy (pp. 429–444)

429.1 ANCIENT LAWS: see T, and pp. 445, 467 *Age*.
430.3 MORE PEOPLE LIVED ... OR ... DIED: neither the size of the population of Roman Britain nor fluctuations thereof have yet been closely studied. Modern estimates have risen from about half a million in 1937 (Colingwood) to about two million in 1968 (Frere), and there is no sign that the estimates have stopped rising. They have however been limited to generalisations about the whole province, and have been hampered by an assumption that it is commendable to strain the evidence to make the figure as small as possible. Avoidable error in either direction is equally undesirable.

Closer estimates will be possible when the archaeological records of a large number of localities have been examined, and interpreted in the light of what is known of Roman population-densities elsewhere, and of the earliest statistical record of Britain, the 11th-century Domesday Book.

At present it is only possible to note that in several parts of the country it is difficult to make the minimum Roman population implied by archaeological record as small as the population listed for the same areas in Domesday Book.

In the counties where the population is enumerated, Domesday Book lists a little under 300,000 adult males; the numbers of unlisted wives, children and other relatives are likely to multiply this figure about three to five times, giving a population in the neighbourhood of a million to a million and a half. To these must be added the population of Wales, of the northern counties excluded from the Survey, and various categories of unlisted persons, ploughmen in many regions, the occupants of houses and land entered as such, without numbers of people, and other categories. A substantial addition is needed to assess the mid-11th-century population. King William's devastation of the north is said to have cost 100,000 lives. The figure is patently a guess and doubtless exaggerated, but the casualties were plainly enormous; in Yorkshire the Survey listed 43 persons in one group of 411 manors, whose earlier population was necessarily much greater. Severe but less concentrated devastation is also reported in the Survey in many other parts of the country. It is therefore probable that the mid-11th-century population of the former Roman province was of the order of two to three million. If the thorough study of recorded Roman sites should suggest that the Roman population was normally somewhat greater, then it may argue an overall population of three to four millions.

The available evidence suggests that there were significant movements of population during the later Empire, but does not yet indicate whether the total population increased or decreased. The disasters of the Arthurian period however clearly reduced overall numbers. The urban and industrial population plainly declined; lands were wasted, and emigration and casualties removed people, though losses were doubtless partially offset by the weakening of imperial taxation, formerly a main factor in keeping down the birth-rate, and by the immigration of some tens of thousands of English.

These considerations rest on inference rather than information, but the document termed the 'Tribal Hidage' (see T and p. 492 *Age*), which lists a little over 200,000 hides in the midlands and the south, suggests the possibility that by the later 7th century population had fallen to a level not greatly in excess of the mid-11th century, when allowance is made for Wales, the north and the south-west. The Scandinavian invasions thereafter doubtless reduced native numbers, but added immigrants.

Until the evidence is more exactly studied, it is possible only to record that between the 4th century and the 11th the population is likely to have fluctuated between the outside limits of about 4,000,000 and about 2,000,000.

430.3 AUSONIUS' GRANDSON: 'Paulinus of Pella'; cf. Works Cited, 1 (above, p. 21).
431.1 GILDAS: ch. 26, 2; see p. 137 *Age*.
431.3 ANIMAL BONES: L.Alcock (*Dinas Powys* 36) tabulates an analysis of animal bones, together with comparable figures from three sites in the Wessex downland (Woodyates, Rotherley and Woodcuts), and from a number of Irish sites. The proportions are

	Dinas Powys	Wessex	Ireland
Cattle	20%	33–39%	70–97%
Sheep	13%	29–40%	1–15%
Pig	61%	2–13%	1–27%
Horse	under 1%	10–26%	1% or less

V.B.Proudfoot (MA 5, 1961, 106) catalogues the presence or absence of animal bones reported in the excavation of some 45 Irish raths, but not the quantities. Cattle were reported at 20 sites, sheep at 8, pigs at 15, horses at 11. The figures in general match Alcock's; horses seem more numerous, for a number of sites each produced horse-bones in small numbers. But among the animals named in the Book of Rights tribute-lists, sheep are relatively commoner; the figures total 25,220 cattle, 12,340 sheep, 6,410 pigs, in percentages 57%, 28%, and 15%.

432.1 LLANCARFAN AND LLANDAFF: see T Gospel Books.
432.1 THREE OR FOUR COWS: 25 times out of 30. The five more expensive values are 10, 14, 14, 25 and 70.
432.1 LLANDEILO: the Book of Chad, T Gospel Books.
432.1 WESSEX: Laws of Ine 70, 1.
432.1 BOOK OF RIGHTS: tributes summarised, ed. pp. 179 ff. The legend of the *Bóruma*, the cattle-tribute levied on Leinster (cf. A 125 x 138), gives a payment of equal numbers of cattle and pigs, some texts adding sheep. Cauldrons are required for the king's brewing, but not barley to supply them, nor brewed beer. The lists include cloaks, flitches and beeves, in much smaller quantities than the animals. The texts are late, long after

432.2 MONASTERIES ... MANY: their size varied. Initial numbers are often small; Winwaloe and Paul Aurelian (with sufficient slaves) began with 12 monks, Samson with 14 monks and 7 *famuli*, Lunaire and Tudwal with 72 monks. In developed houses, Brioc had 168, Gudwal 180, Petroc and Paternus 80. Lasrian of Leighlin with 1,500 and MoChuta with 867 claim unusually large communities. Brendan's numerous monasteries held 3,000 between them. Maedóc took 150 out to harvest. Cadoc, Illtud and Kentigern (at Llanelwy, St. Asaph) are credited with a division between *clerici* and *operarii illiterati,* analogous to that drawn by Cassiodorus in Italy; Illtud and Cadoc maintained the poor, and Cadoc also maintained widows; Cadoc, king as well as abbot, is also assigned a military force, giving totals of 300 to Illtud, 500 to Cadoc, 965 to Kentigern. The traditions that Mocteus of Louth and Ruadán of Lothra, until constrained, maintained clerics who did no agricultural work implies a similar division. These figures are not excessive, though in the nature of the transmission they are liable to inflation in honour of the founding saint. Bede's figure (HE, 2, 2) of over 2,000 in a single monastery of Bangor-on-Dee is exceptionally large. Their hierarchical organisation is matched by Kentigern's '*illos per turmas et conventus dividens*'. The implication of the evidence is that most houses could be numbered in scores or hundreds; their impact was due to their number rather than their individual size.

432.3 DAVID, CARTHACUS; and others. See E, under the saints named.

433.2 TOOLS: e.g. the schedule of goods to be divided on divorce, p. 445 *Age*; the price-list of 250 items (VC 3, 22, etc) is probably copied from a Wessex list, and concerns the English more than the Welsh.

433.2 WATERMILL: e.g. Carthacus, Ciarán of Clonmacnoise, Eugenius (in Gaul), Féchín and Mo Choemóg, Finnian of Moville, Fintan of Dunblesc, Gildas (in Brittany), Íta, Lugid, Gudwal (tidal), Flannan; canalisation, e.g. Féchín, Frigidian (in Italy), Moling. Usually, the nature of the mill is not specified; the donkey-mill does not appear; where the power is specified, it is water, occasionally tidal.

433.2 CORN DRYING: Cainnech (Sal.) 35; Ciarán 12, *rota de virgis contexta plena spicis igne supposito*; Finnian (*Lismore* 2629); poem, Mocteus *M.Don., M.Oeng.,* FM 535, also printed Todd *Patrick* 30. Three or four kilns have been excavated in raths (Proudfoot MA 5, 1961, 108; cf. 106), and the corn-kiln (*odyn*) is frequently mentioned in Welsh Law (ALW indices).

434.4 ULTAN: the Life is early, written when prayer with arms outstretched was still normal in Ireland.

434.4 NOBLEMAN OF MACHA: *vita Brigit* (Ultán) 61 (TT 534).

435.1 ANOTHER OCCASION: *vita Brigit* (Ultán) 80 (TT 537).

435.2 GERALD: ch. 12 (VSH). 'Gerald' is represented as an Englishman; a number of English followed Colmán of Lindisfarne, when he returned to Ireland, to found Mayo, in 664.

435.2 IUGERA: evidently translating Irish *immaire*; cf. a jumbled rehash of the story told in the *vita Geraldi,* in the Hymn of Colmán, preface, LH 1, 25; 2,12.

435.3 FLANNAN: (of Killaloe) ch. 31 (Sal.).

435.3 ANOTHER TRADITION: *Lebor na hUidre* 128, cited Plummer VSH xcvi 6.

436.3 LAW TRACT: the *Uraicecht Becc,* or 'Small Primer', ALI 5, 1; cf. MacNeill PRIA 36 c, 1923, 255 and *Celtic Ireland* 96 ff., dated by Binchy *Ériu* 18, 1958, 44 ff. to the '8th century or earlier' (p. 48), possibly contemporary with texts of c. 680 (pp. 51–52).

436.4 EXCAVATED RATHS: MA 5, 1961, 94 ff., especially pp. 94, 103 and selected plans p. 100.
436.5 LAW TRACT: ALI 5, 483, cited MacNeill *Celtic Ireland* 167–169.
437.3 STIRRUP: the metal innovation is well dated because it is preserved from numerous dated graves.
437.3 HORSE COLLAR: made of perishable material, and not buried in graves, and therefore less directly evidenced. Various early Slavonic forms are known, but cannot be closely dated; their ultimate origin seems however to be related to that of the stirrup. The evidence is discussed by Lefevre de Noëttes *Attelage,* and others.
437.4 NORICUM: the build of the animal, similar to the medieval Shire-horse, is most clearly demonstrated by Roman figurines in Austrian museums, notably at Wels, the Roman Ovilava.
437.4 MONKS ... SLAVS: cf. Map 29 and notes thereto.
437.4 SLAVS ... SUNDERED: cf. Map 17, p. 277 *Age.*
438.2 PICTS: cf. P.
440.2 CHURCHES OF WOOD: e.g. Cadoc and David in Wales, Goueznou in Brittany, Winniocus at Luxeuil in Burgundy (Jonas *Columban* 1, 15; 1, 17), Énda, Flannán of Killaloe, Mo-Choe and many others in Ireland, Fínán of Lindisfarne and Aedán at York in Northumbria. Cianán's stone church at Duleek and Ninian's at Whithorn were both regarded as exceptional, the work of foreign craftsmen.
441.2 WINE: in Britain; cf. e.g. Piro, p. 360 *Age*; in Ireland, Muirchú 18; cf. Stokes *Lismore Lives* 316; *vita Ciarani* Clonmacnoise 31; cf. *Lismore* 4402.
441.2 COLUMBA: Adomnán 1, 28. *Sulfurea de caelo flamma* that killed 3,000 sounds like a volcano; perhaps Etna, since Vesuvius is not known to have erupted during Columba's lifetime. Reeves' 'Istria' derives from a late martyrologist's guess; cf. P Caput Regionis (Kintyre).
441.2 COLUMBAN: Jonas 23 *navis quae Scottorum commercia vexerat*; cf. *vita Winwaloe* 1, 19 *mercatoribus transmarina negotia ausportantibus ... ad Scotos* (from Brittany).
441.2 PORTH MAWR, PADSTOW: cf. P.
441.2 FINNIAN: *vita Finnian Clonard* (Sal.) 4; cf. E.
441.3 JOHN THE ALMSGIVER: ch. 9; about AD 600. There is no reason to change the date given in the text.
441.3 VALUE: did not greatly change in many centuries. Over 700 years later, the Book of Ballymote was sold for 140 cows, Kenney 24.
442.1 BOOK OF TEILO: LL xliii; cf. T Gospel Books.
442.2 SILVER INGOTS: cf. e.g. H.Willers, *Die roemische Bronzeeimer von Hemmoor* 291, 'ex offi(cina) Isatis', found at London, Richborough, Coleraine in Ulster, Dierstorf (Minden) in Germany, and elsewhere.
442.4 WEST SAXON LAWS: Ine 25, ... *ceapie, do thaet beforan gewitnessum,* 'if a trader trade up-country, he shall do so before witnesses.'
442.4 KENTISH LAW: ...*gebycge,* 'if a Kentishman buy goods in London, he shall have reliable men, or the King's reeve to witness'. The law protects the Kentishman against suit for theft; he must prove by witnesses or oath that he had bought the *feoh* with his own *ceape,* or surrender it. Both words commonly mean property in general, and cattle in particular. Ch. 15, demanding surety for the foreign *ciepeman,* implies that traders felt the need of a local patron, for whose protection they presumably paid. The probable context of ch. 16 is that the Kentishman sold cattle in London and bought foreign imports; ch. 15 and the Wessex law appear

NOTES TO *THE AGE OF ARTHUR* (pp. 436–447)   95

              to envisage a travelling salesman of humble status and dubious honesty, nearer to the 18th-century 'chapman' than to the 'merchant'. These are the only references to traders in the 7th-century laws.

443.2   BOOK OF RIGHTS: p. 432 *Age*.
443.2   HOARDED WEALTH: p. 236 *Age*.
443.2   PENDA: Hostage, Bede HE 3, 24. Distribution, the *Atbret Iudeu* Nennius 65; cf. p. 302 *Age*.
443.3   ENGLISH MONEY: fines, etc., expressed in money values in the laws, may or may not have been paid in cash.

23 Welsh and Irish Society (pp. 445–465)

445.1   LAW: see T. The comprehensive collection of *Welsh Laws*, with translation and glossary, is the *Ancient Laws and Institutes of Wales* (AWL), ed. Aneurin Owen, 1841; vol. 1 contains the texts named Venedotian, Demetian and Gwentian Codes (VC, DC, GC); vol. 2 the 'Anomalous Laws' (AL), or 'Cyvreithiau Cymru', and various versions of the 'Laws of Hywel Da', the 'Leges Wallicae' (p. 749) (LW), 'Leges Howelli Boni' (p. 814) (HD), 'Powys Laws' (p. 881), a second 'Leges Howelli Boni', principally concerned with royal rights (p. 893), and the Statute of Rhuddlan (p. 909). A number of other MSS have been published since, usually without translation (cf. T), but the laws have not been collated; see CSW 73 ff.; WHR 1963 Special Number; T.P.Ellis *Welsh Tribal Law*.

              The comparable comprehensive collection of *Irish Laws* is the *Ancient Laws of Ireland* (ALI). The material is enormous. Among later works, R. Thurneysen and others, *Studies in Early Irish Law* (SEIL), is especially useful. The interaction of Irish and of Roman and Church law is clearest in the *Hibernensis*, cf. Kenney 247, of the early 8th century.

445.1   WELL INHABITED LAND: GC 2, 39, 28.
445.1   COHABITATION: VC 2, 1, 30–31; DC 2, 18, 10 etc.
445.1   BRAKE AND BUSH: VC 2, 1, 33 etc.
445.1   COMES OF AGE: e.g. VC 2, 28, 5 ff.; 2, 30, 3; 5.
445.1   GIRLS' PROPERTY: VC 2, 30, 3; the MS variant 'he wishes' contradicts the rest of the passage, and is clearly wrong.
445.2   VIRGIN BRIDE: e.g. VC 2, 1, 27.
445.2   CHILDREN'S UPBRINGING: e.g. VC 2, 28, 5–8.
445.2   IRISH LAW: cf. the texts cited in SEIL 187 ff.
445.3   DIVORCE: the principal sections of the laws are VC 2, 1; DC 2, 18; GC 2, 29; cf. LW 2, 19; HD 2, 23.
446.3   CHARGE OF IMPOTENCE: VC 2, 1, 66 (cf. 67, variant, 'rape'), discreetly translated into Latin rather than English.
446.4   IRISH ... DIVORCE: a number of the principal texts are surveyed in SEIL 241 ff.
446.4   HIBERNENSIS: 46, 8–10, Isidore *de Officiis* 2, 20, 12; the text describes and rejects grounds for divorce that were acceptable in Wales and Ireland.
446.4   CHURCH LAW: VC 2, 16, 2.
447.3   INHERITANCE: the principal Welsh texts are VC 2, 12; DC 2, 23; GC 2, 31; cf. AL 9, 26–27, LW 2, 11. Daughters' rights differed in north and south; cf. VC 2, 1, 64, DC 2, 23, 7 and scattered references; cf. AWL indices; the main Irish texts are summarised in SEIL 133 ff.
447.3   CENEDL: see p. 461 *Age*.
447.3   FINE: see especially *Senchus Mór* (ALI 1 p. 261 etc), and MacNeill *Celtic Ireland* 159 ff.

447.4 COMPENSATION: the assumptions of Roman and English law have prompted the notion that a 'blood-feud' must be invented to explain Welsh compensation laws. No evidence supports the assumption, and no word for such a 'feud' exists in Welsh. Germanic law permitted *faida*, legalised enmity (cf. note 485.2 below) in the exceptional cases when compensation was not paid; in the middle ages, in some Germanic and southern European lands, when customary sanctions broke down, *faida* developed into a chain of violence and counter-violence, that gave rise to the concept of 'blood-feud'. The notion is alien to early Welsh society, and belongs only to a political philosophy which maintains that 'human nature' is mutually destructive unless it is subjected to the authority of an élite.

448.4 RIGDOMNA: cf. MacNeill *Celtic Ireland* 114 ff; the evidence of the annals and genealogies argues that practice was more varied and less schematic than MacNeill suggests.

449.4 IRISH SOCIETY: cf. especially the 'Small Primer', p. 436.3 above, and the Book of Aichill.

450.4 DRESS: ALI 2, 146, 10 ff. I am indebted to Professor Binchy for drawing my attention to this passage, which prescribes colours for foster-sons, presumably those to which their fathers were entitled. The later texts e.g. LG 9, 8 (ITS 5,208); cf. Book of Leinster 2035 ff. (ITS 1, 64); FM 3664, cf. 3656; Keating 1, 25 (ITS 2, 123) ascribe their regulations to the mythical Bronze-Age kings of the second millennium BC, Eochu Etgudach ('Goodclothes') and Tigernmas; see also the poem LG 96, 2 (ITS, 435).

451.2 SENCHUS FIR NALBAN: CPS 308 ff., see p. 180 *Age*.
453.1 PICT INHERITANCE: cf. p. 192 *Age*.
453.2 TRAVELLERS: e.g., among many, Alexander Carmichael, reproduced in Skene CS 3, 378–393; cf. A.N.Palmer, YC 11, 1892, 176 ff., and other accounts.
453.3 CLAN: most of the evidence here discussed is assembled by W.F.Skene in *Celtic Scotland*, especially 3, 303 ff.
454.4 IN BUCHAN: grants inscribed in the Book of Deer.
455.1 CAMPBELLS: cf. the pedigree printed Skene CS 3, 458.
455.1 LENNOX: cf. the pedigree printed Skene CS 3, 475; P Dergind. The principal adaptations are to turn the Irish Loch Léin into Leamna (Lennox), Maine Munchain into Maine Leamna, and Dergind, p. 158 *Age*, into 'Gergind', equated with Circin or the Mearns.
455.2 SAVAGE AND RUDE: Fordun *Chron.* 2, p. 38, cited Skene CS 3, 307.
455.2 HIGHLAND CLANNA: Wyntoun *Chron.*, ed. 1879, 3, p. 63; *Scotichronicon* 2, p. 420, etc., cited Skene CS 3, 310 ff.
455.2 18th CENTURY OBSERVER: Gartmore MS (1747), cited Skene CS 3, 318.
455.3 DEGENERATE TO ... COMMON PEOPLE: cf. Sir John Davies' description, in 1607, of the means whereby *tanists* of 'septs' in Ireland 'did spoil and impoverish the people at their pleasure', cited Seebohm EVC 220. In Ireland, as in Scotland, English administrative notions turned local dynasts into 'chiefs' of 'tribes', or 'clans' or 'septs', and rewarded their loyalty to the conqueror by according them the legal right to exploit their own people. In Ireland succession to the 'chieftaincy' normally passed to any member of the *derbfine*, elected by show of hands and termed *tanist*, equivalent to the *rigdomna* of the greater dynasties; but in Scotland succession normally passed from father to son.
457.2 EOIN MACNEILL: 'more than any other' Kenney 81; on the clan, *Celtic Ireland*, 1921, 155–156; cf. p. 152, on Joyce's *Social History*, 'from book to book a thousand talkers and writers have said that the social organisation of

ancient Ireland in historical times was on a tribal basis, and they have called it the Clan System. Joyce ... is unable to find a single ancient authority to support it.' Nor has anyone else discovered such evidence. MacNeill protested that the 'cocksure people' who talked of tribes and clans in 1921 constituted a 'formidable body'; they still do. The recent mushrooming of 'clan-societies', the 'discovery' of 'clan-chiefs', the issue of 'certificates' and the proliferation of new 'tartans' serves modern commercial and political interests; it has no connection with the early history of Scotland, except that its confusion smears the dignity of genuine tradition and record, and tends to make them suspect associates of the current farce.

457.2 SKENE: cf. note 177.1 above.

457.2 TOO LITTLE HEEDED: e.g., among many instances, T.C.Smout *A History of the Scottish People*, 1560–1830, p. 24; 'Celtic society was clearly tribal, based on a real or fancied kinship between every freeman and the head of his tribe. The tribes apparently occupied fairly distinct areas of the country ... and possessed differing tribal laws'; cf. p. 334 'in the early 10th century ... the Highlands were tribal, in the exact sense that nineteenth-century Africa was tribal.'

Published in 1969, nearly 50 years after MacNeill wrote, and 100 years after Skene, this preamble to a history of a later period typifies the 'rubbish' that is still 'imposed' upon otherwise well informed authors, who have not themselves had occasion to study the evidence.

458.2 SLAVE: the modern word derives from Slavs, prisoners taken by Charlemagne and his successors, who were a mobile marketable commodity, as homeborn agricultural *servi*, serfs, were not, and lacked an appropriate descriptive term.

458.3 CAETH: the laws distinguish different kinds of *caeth*, domestic, agricultural, royal; and differentiate the voluntary *caeth*, a dependent stranger who prefers to give himself to the *uchelwr* rather than to settle as a king's *aillt*, from the purchased *caeth* (e.g. AL 6, 1, 72). The voluntary *caeth* appears to have enjoyed a status not greatly different from the English *hlafaeta*, 'loaf-eater', (p. 486 *Age*). Close research into the usage of the texts is likely to reveal more subtle shifts of meaning; but in general *servus* tends to mean *caeth* in legal language, whereas colloquial usage often wrote *servus* for *taeog*. The codes include both legal texts and some texts written in colloquial language, as the 'Privileges of Arvon' (VC 2, 2 etc.) and some of the 'Legal Triads'.

458.4 GILDAS: *Ep.* 3; cf. p. 368 *Age*.
458.4 SAMSON, HERVE, JUSTINIAN: see E.
458.4 WESSEX: Ine 74, 1; cf. p. 485.2 below (West Saxon).
458.5 TATHEUS, MALO, WINWALOE: see E.
459.3 PLEBES ... TRIBUS: cf. p. 364 *Age*.
459.3 SCHEMATISM: VC 2, 17, 6 ff.
459.3 MAINAUR: Book of Teilo (Chad) folio 216, memorandum 6, printed LL xlvii *mainaur Med Diminih*; cf. BBCS 7, 1935, 369, and, for the date, Jackson LHEB 47. The word, superficially similar to *manerium*, manor, was a gift to Norman lawyers, who so translated it.

459.4 VALENTINIAN III: Novella 31, CTh 2, pp. 129–132. It is theoretically possible that up to the late 450s the British government was able to accept and enforce imperial constitutions if it wished, or that Valentinian renewed older laws already in force before 410, and that the Welsh law re-enacts the Roman, but it is more probable that similar causes inspired similar legislation.

460.2   TIR CYVRIV: also called *tir kyllydus,* tax or rent-paying land; cf. especially VC 2, 12, 6 etc. Both king and lord might possess *tir cyvriv,* and on behalf of its *tref* allocate the *tref* land.

460.3   CYLLID: its main constituent was *dawnbwyd,* food-render.

460.3   GWESTVA: payable by free *uchelwyr,* VC 2, 17, 14–15, but not due from *tir cyvriv,* AL 5, 1, 28; 14, 32, 4 etc. It began as the entertainment of the king's household while on progress; it became a tribute of food, later a tax in money; when commuted to a money payment, *gwestva* was termed *tunc*; cf. 221.2 above.

460.3   CYLCH: cf. ALW indices, 'Progress'.

460.3   PROGRESS: cf. texts cited in *Angles and Britons* 156–157.

460.3   DISPENSING JUSTICE: *vita Gwynlliw* 16 gives a lively account of a dean riding hard through a night of wind and rain to be in time for the hearing of a case at a royal feast in Gwent.

460.3   PAYMENT: exacted by e.g. Maelgwn *vita Cadoci* 69; by 'Arthur', as a compensation fine, 22.

460.3   ANCIENT BREED: white cattle with red ears, in Britain, VC 1, 2, 2; cf. DC 1, 2, 6 and *vita Cadoci* 22 (red in front, white behind), exacted as the king's *saraad,* compensation-fine; white with red ears imported into Ireland from Britain, Cormac's *Glossary* 72, *Fir*; encountered in Brittany by Herbot (cf. E); cf. S. Baring-Gould, *A Book of Brittany* 277 (white cows). The breed perhaps survives in modern park-cattle, notably the Chillingham herd in Northumberland (*Ériu* 14, 1946, unnumbered page placed after the first of two pages numbered 169, citing several references in early Irish literature and one from 13th-century Flanders; cf. Whitehead *Cattle* and BBCS 23, 1969, 195). Excavated cattle-bones still receive rare and perfunctory examination, and it is therefore not yet possible to say whether or not archaeological evidence for these animals exists, or whether or where they were known in Britain in or before the Roman period.

460.3   FIRE PREVENTION: VC 3, 3, 13 ff. etc.

461.1   TRE'R CEIRI: RCHM Caernarvonshire.

461.1   DINAS POWYS: cf. p. 431 *Age.*

461.2   CANTREF: the principal texts are assembled and discussed in Lloyd HW 1,300 ff. The *cantrefi* were later subdivided into *cwmwdau* (commotes), to which the assembly was transferred.

461.3   CENEDL: cf. ALW indices, 'Kindred', 'Chief of Kindred', 'Caput Gentis', etc. The *cenedl is* frequently named in the codes, but most of the rulings about the *Pencenedl* are in AL.

461.4   LUIDT: Book of Teilo (Chad), folios 141 (memorandum 2) *luidt* and 18 (memorandum 3) *luith,* printed with facsimile LL xliii, xlv; for the date, cf. Jackson LHEB 43–46.

462.1   TEUYTH: *vita Wenefredi* 5 *Teuyth ... interpellans ut sibi fatteret quod de suo patrimonio deliberaret. Ille (Cadfan) refert 'O vir wenerande, nequaquam mihi vel tibi sortitur. Tamen sequestrare rus a provincie communione ne sibi sit inutile vel mee necessitati. Sed harum quamcumque villarum trium elegeris ad divinum officium tibi libere annuo, si placatus fueris, mihique reliquas relinque.'* The place was perhaps Whitford, near Holywell in Flint, *SD 14 78,* the only church in Tegeingl known to have been dedicated to Beuno; cf. Bowen SCSW 83, with figs. 22, 23; cf. Map 24, p. 359 *Age.*

462.4   SURVEYS: large extracts are printed in F. Seebohm, *Tribal System in Wales,* appendices, and discussed pp. 1 ff.

464.1   LLANCARFAN: the grants appended to the Life of Cadoc; cf. T Gospel Books.

The grants cited are 65; 62; 55; 60; 68. In another, 59, a nobleman 'commended' an estate to his son, with a rent-charge to the church.

464.1   LLANDAFF: T Gospel Books. Llandaff gives much detail of prices, rentals, extents, that concern its claims. In the one grant that the two have in common (LL 180 = *vita Cadoci* 67) Llandaff reproduces the reasons for the grant more fully, but leaves out many of the details of who made what gift to whom.

464.5   BOOK OF ARMAGH: folios 16 r to 18 v, also printed AB 2, 1883, 213 ff., and VT 334 ff., commonly known as the *Additamenta to Tírechán* 1–16. Sections 8 to 16 are in Irish. The scribe, Feradach, writing in 807, apologised for not translating into Latin passages that he found 'badly written in Irish; not because I am unable to write Latin, but because these accounts are barely intelligible in their original Irish', *finiunt haec pauca per scotticam imperfecte scripta; non quod ego non potuissem romana condere lingua, sed quod vix in sua scoti[c] a hae fabulae agnosci possunt*. Irish that was scarcely intelligible by c. 800 is unlikely to have been much less than a century old; the two datable grants (Cummén, II; Aed of Sletty, 16) are both late 7th-century, and the text transcribed by Feradach was therefore nearly contemporary with the original grants.

464.5   CUMMEN: *Add. Tírechán* II (VT 340). The genealogies place the chief, Eladach, about 680; Colmán (of Lindisfarne? E) was established at Inishboffin from 665 to 675.

465.2   FETH: *Add. Tírechán* (VT 338); Drumlease *G 83* in Callraige, Hogan 366, 152.

465.2   FOIRTCHERN: *Add. Tírechán* 4 (VT 336).

465.3   BINEAN: *Add. Tírechán,* 7 (VT 337); the scribe wrote *d[eu]s* for *dedit*; a later hand added *cui dedit* without erasing *d[eu]s*.

24 English Society (pp. 466–505)

467.2   LAWS: conveniently collected by Attenborough LEEK, based on ALE and the *Gesetze* of Schmid and Liebermann; extensively discussed by Seebohm TCASL–cf. EVC, TSW, and others: see T.

467.2   CHARTERS: the principal collections are BCS and KCD. The charters are comprehensively catalogued by Sawyer, and many are summarised by Finberg ECMW etc., and by Hart; see C, and p. 328 *Age*.

467.2   CHARTERS ... ALTERATIONS: among the commonest changes are the conflation of the witnesses to the original grant and to subsequent confirmations, that creates a superficial appearance of chronological contradiction and ensnares the incautious critic; and the alteration of rights and properties to suit the interest of the copier, with the insertion of words, and of the names of people and titles, places and regions, that belong to the copier's time, but were unknown at the time of the grant. The use of, for example, *Anglia* dates a copy to the 11th century or later, but frequently derives from an original that used a cumbrous old-fashioned term, as 'all the provinces of the English'.

467.2   FORGED ... GENUINE: the provisional system devised by Finberg, of marking texts by stars, whose number indicates the degree of alteration, is a considerable advance upon the crude categories employed in earlier inexact modern conventions of classification, but is no substitute for precise analysis of what is added to each text.

467.3   GRAVES ... SOCIAL DIFFERENCE: cf. p. 281 *Age*.

468.2 PLACE NAMES: EPNS, DEPN, EPNE; notes to maps 30 to 36; see P.
468.3 ELEMENTS: EPNE (cf. additions and corrections in JEPN 1), from which the meanings here given are cited.
468.3 STUDY OF ... -ING: J.M.Dodgson MA 10, 1966, 1 ff., and *Beiträge zur Namenforschung* (Heidelberg), NF, 2, 1967, 221 ff. and 325 ff.; 3, 1968, 141 ff., on whose work maps 30 and parts of maps 33 and 34 are based. Other maps are adapted from EPNS volumes, and from unpublished material kindly made available.
470.2 ARTOIS: see p. 287 *Age*.
470.4 TUN: EPNE 2, 188 ff. The word already meant a village in the 7th century, *Hlothere* 5. The suggestion in EPNE 2, 190 (5), that many or most began as 'single farms' and later grew into villages is unlikely and unwarranted, and contradicts the archaeological evidence. Later usage, translating *tun* as Latin *villa, ham* as *civitas*, contrasts an estate with a community, and does not concern size. Relatively few *-tun* names are likely to be earlier than the 7th century.
470.4 TUN ... SECONDARY COLONISATION: EPNE 2, 191 (9).
472.2 -BOTL: especially EPNE 1, 43–44. Its distribution in Europe is limited and localised; A.Bach, *Deutsche Namenkunde,* II 2 map 44, p. 333, para 610 ff., where the Carolingian date suggested is not probable; see Map 17.
472.2 -WORTH, -COTE: EPNE 2, 273 ff., especially 274 (3); 1, 108 ff.
472.2 -INGTUN: EPNE 1, 291 ff., especially 295 (5); *Teottingtun* (Teddington) distinguishes 'Teotta's village' from *Teottingatun*, the 'village of Teotta's people'. It is often impossible to tell the forms apart; but when they can be distinguished, *-ingatun* rarely forms as much as one fifth of the total, and it is therefore probable that *-ingtun* is normally the form of the great majority; but both forms imply lordship, and also secondary colonisation.
It is however not easy to discover names in any form of *-ingtun* attested before the middle of the 8th century. Their rarity is partly explained by the nature of the record; most such places were too small to figure in the works of Bede, Eddius, or other early writers; and charters commonly grant either royal land or small portions of estates, rather than centres of individual lordship. In some instances, however, the name of a settlement is recorded substantially earlier than its *-tun*. *Tun*, though it was the general word for a village in the 7th century, is itself rare in place-names of the late 7th and early 8th centuries. Closer study may therefore suggest that 7th-century settlements founded by an individual lord with his dependants were at first known by his name, followed by *-inga lond* or the like, but did not acquire their administrative centre and suffix *-tun* until some generations later. Records of *-cote* also begin late.
474.3 KENT: the custom of Kent is lucidly described by Jolliffe PFE, emphasising (p. 3) that 'the manors of Kent are more like those of Wales than of Oxford and Berkshire'. The suggestion that Frankish influence on Kentish ornament indicates that the Jutes of Kent and their customs came from the Rhineland (Leeds AASS 126 ff., developed by Jolliffe 102 ff.) was made when dates were less understood; Frankish ornament was favoured by the granddaughters of the first settlers, many of whom came from Jutland (Myres ASP 96, map 7; p. 289 *Age*). Third-generation ornament has nothing to do with the nationality of the first comers; the nationality of the first settlers is not determined by the fashions that their granddaughters favoured.
474.3 NINE LATHES: excluding Sutton, outside the early borders of Kent.
474.3 WELKECHILDELAND: BBA 1, 229, cited Jolliffe PFE 27, note 3.

474.3	NINE RAPES:	including Ytene, Meonwara and Wight, now in Hampshire.
476.1	WORTHS ... PENNINES:	Heworth, a suburb of York, stands alone in the North Riding; Ravensworth near Richmond is a variant of Ravensford.
476.1	BOTL STRONGHOLDS:	Newbottle, etc., by definition secondary, are omitted from Map 35.
476.1	WIDE RANGE OF NAMES:	the few that have been examined closely show their potential value; for example, -*wicham* and -*wictun*, derived from Latin *vicus*, are almost entirely confined to the areas of 6th-century burials, and are most plentiful where 5th- and early 6th- century cemeteries are commonest; cf. MA II, 1967, 87, map. p. 88.
480.1	INTENDS TO DEPART:	Ine 64–66.
480.1	CULTIVATED:	*gesette* means cultivated and tilled, usually by dependent cultivators, as Seebohm EVC 128, 136 ff., Vinogradoff GM 128, Aston TRHS series 5, 8, 1958, 65; rather than 'sown', as Maitland DBB 238 note 1, Liebermann *Gesetze* (on Ine 64) and others.
480.1	NOBLEMAN:	Ine 63.
480.1	UNAUTHORISED EMIGRATION:	Ine 39.
480.2	CEORL'S WORTH:	Ine 40, 42. Detached words from Ine 42 have been used to suggest the strip-cultivation of a later age; in context, they cannot relate thereto.
482.1	HEBERDEN:	BCS 144.
482.1	THURINGIA:	*Translatio S. Alexandri* 1.
483.3	SCOTS:	cf. p. 451 *Age*.
483.3	WELSH LAW:	cf. p. 448 *Age*.
483.3	HIDE:	cf. p. 487.2 below.
483.3	ONE TAXPAYER ... ONE HIDE:	cf. e.g. the equation in BCS 144; cf. note 487.2 (HIDE) and p. 499 *Age*.
484.1	ALFRED'S LAWS:	42, 7.
484.3	MANY LAWS:	e.g. Alfred 37; Edward II, 7; Aethelstan II 2; 8; 22, 1; III 4; IV 3; V Preface 1 and 2; 1.
485.2	WEST SAXON ... WELSHMEN:	Ine 74, 1. The law contrasts with *Lex Saxonum* 2, 5, which exposes the *litus* to *faida* without alternative.
485.2	RELATIVES ... RARELY:	e.g. if a killer escaped abroad, the relatives paid half the *leod* (*wergild*), Aethelbert 23; in Wessex, if no paternal kinsmen were discoverable, the maternal relatives paid one third, Alfred 30.
485.2	FAEHDE:	the word is the linguistic ancestor of modern 'feud', cf. note 447.4 above, but does not share its meaning of a chain of violence; see Du Cange, s.v. *Faida*. Among the Lombards, whose laws are nearest to the English, *faida* is glossed *vindicta mortis*, the simple avenging of death; Ine's *unfaedhe* (e.g. 28, 35, 74) concerns justifiable homicide, and Alfred's equivalent (e.g. 30, 42) is *orwige*.
485.2	RANSOM:	it extended beyond physical violence; relatives might ransom a penal slave, Ine 24, 1.
485.3	LORD:	see LEEK index.
485.3	NOBLEMAN'S LORD:	Ine 50.
485.3	GYLD:	see LEEK index, 'Associates', first named in Ine 74, 2. In Alfred 30–31 *gegildan* and relatives pay one third each; the *heafodgemacene* and perhaps the *gedes* of Wihtred 19; 21; 23 may be a Kentish equivalent. Under West Saxon supremacy, from the 9th century, West Saxon legal terminology tended to oust Kentish and other regional terms.
485.3	TOWNS:	the urban *frythegyld*, public-order guild, of noble and commoner (*eorlisce ge ceorlisce*), Aethelstan VI (*Iudicia Civitatis Lundoniae*, Preamble 1, 1; 6, 3), preceded separate trade-guilds.

486.2   SAXON LAW: *Lex Saxonum* 44 *qui defunctus non filios sed filias reliquerat, ad eas omnis hereditas pertineat.*

486.2   ANGLIAN LAW: *Lex Anglorum et Werinorum* 27 *ad filiam pecunia et mancipia, terra vero ad proximum paternae generationis*; cf. Bede HA II *quomodo terreni parentes, quem primum partu fuderint, eum principium liberorum suorum cognoscere, et caeteris in partienda sua hereditate praeferendum ducere solent*, with reference to Northumbrian Angles.

486.2   WEST SAXON ... MOTHER'S KIN: e.g. Alfred 8; 30.

486.3   FRIGMAN: Aethelbert 4, and regularly thereafter.

486.3   LAET: see p. 313 *Age*.

486.3   LOAF-EATER: *ceorlaes hlafaeta*, valued at only 6s, Aethelbert 25.

486.4   WERGILD: the essential information, contained in the laws of Ine of Wessex and Aethelbert of Kent, both 7th-century, is

WELSH OF WESSEX (Ine)   LAET OF KENT (Aethelbert)

theow	50s or 60s (23, 3)	
landless man	60s (32)	40s third class (26)
half-hide man	80s (32)	60s second class (26)
tax-payer's son	100s (23, 3)	—
tax-payer (*gafolgelda*)	120s (23, 3) ⎱	
one-hide man	120s (32) ⎰	80s first class (26)
horswealh	200s (14)	—
five-hide man	600s (24, 2)	—

ENGLISH OF WESSEX (Ine)

ordinary *wergild*		*fierdwite* fine (51)		compensation for *burgbryc* (45)
a man (normal)	200s (34, 1) ⎱			
aet twyhundum	200s (70) ⎰	*cierlisc*	30s	—
aet syxhundum	600s (70)	*gesithcundmon unlandagende*	60s	—
aet twelfhundum	1200s (70) ⎱	*gesithcundmon landagende*	120s	*gesithcundmon landhaebbende* 30s*
Cinges geneat (King's companion)	1200s (19) ⎰			
—		—		king's thane 60s
—		—		ealdormon 80s
—		—		King and Bishop 120s

*35s, MS.

ENGLISH OF KENT

Medume leodgeld (ordinary wergild)   100s (Aethelbert 21; Hlothere 3)
eorlcundman   300s (Hlothere 1)

Kentish law does not mention a distinct class of landed noble or royal companion. By the 9th century, the *ceorl*'s violated boundary fence (*edorbryce*) was compensated with 5s; the *syxhyndmon* had a *burg*, whose breach was met by 15s; the *twelfhyndmon*'s compensation was still 30s, but the bishop's and the *ealdormon*'s had fallen to 60s, the archbishop's to 90s; the king still received 120s (Alfred 40). The basic distinction of ceorl and *eorl* lasted well into the middle ages; cf. *Consuetudo West Sexe* 70, 1 *twyhindi, id est villani ... twelfhindi, id est taini* Liebermann *Gesetze* 1, 462 cf. 458.

Fragments of Mercian and Northumbrian law, preserved in the *Gesetze*, show similar classes and values.

This evidence is discussed at length by Liebermann *Gesetze, Seebohm* TCASL, Maitland DBB, Chadwick OEN and SASI, and others.

487.2   HIDE: Bede regularly wrote 'the land of so many families' (e.g. *terra LXXXVII familiarum*, HE 4, 13), or 'possessions of families', or 'of land', or 'of property' (e.g. *possesiones X familiarum, XII possessiones praediorum, XII possessiunculis terrarum*, all in HE 3, 24), described as 'by English measure' (e.g. *mensura iuxta aestimationem Anglorum* HE 2, 9; *quasi familiarum V, iuxta aestimationem Anglorum* HE 3, 4). Bede gives overall figures of 5 families for Iona HE 3, 4; 960 for Anglesey and 300 for Man HE 2, 9; 7,000 for Sussex HE 4, 13; 1,200 for Wight HE 4, 16; 600 for Thanet HE 1, 25; and 5,000 and 7,000 for South and North Mercia HE 3, 24; as well as for numerous individual estates. The figures for Sussex and Mercia agree with those of the 'Tribal Hidage' (p. 493 *Age*), and that for Thanet is proportionate to the total for Kent (15,000); but the assessment of Wight, 600 in the Tribal Hidage, was doubled, evidently after Ceadwalla's conquest, in or about 686. The hide and the individual family remained normally identical into the mid-8th century, since oaths in Ine's law were normally reckoned as of 30, 60 or 120 hides (e.g. 52–54; cf. 14; 19; 46), but in Northumbria as of 30, 60 or 120 cultivators (*tributarii* and *manentes*) Dialogue of Egbert (Archbishop of York, c. 750) 1. Oaths are discussed by Chadwick SASI 134 ff.

487.2   TRIBUTARII ... HIDES: in 725 the Heberden Charter of Nunna of Sussex granted twenty *tributarii* in the Latin text, but twenty hides in the English endorsement, which is probably contemporary. See note on 499.1.

487.3   UNCIA ... IUGUM: cf. pp. 459 and 5 *Age*.

487.3   RUSTIC DEIRANS: the nobleman Imma pretended to be a *rusticus* of the supply train, but his Mercian captors observed *ex vultu et habitu et sermonibus eius non erat de paupere vulgo sed de nobilibus* and sold him to a Frisian slaver of London, who allowed him parole to find his ransom, Bede HE 4, 22.

489.1   BENEDICT BISCOP: Bede HA 1.

489.2   BEDE ... EGBERT: *Epistula ad Egbertum* 10 ff.

491.2   ATTAIN ... RANK: the texts are discussed by Chadwick SASI 80 ff.

491.4   FOLC GEMOT: Alfred 22; 34; 38, 1. BCS 201.

491.4   REEVE: steward or bailiff, equivalent to the classical Latin *procurator*; the king's reeves, like the emperor's *procuratores*, were officers of importance; the later shire-reeve, or sheriff, was translated *vice-comes*, 'deputy earl', in medieval Latin, whence the modern title 'viscount'.

491.4   EALDORMAN: elder, or senior. The title was restricted to royal princes and great nobles; the *ealdorman* of a region was commonly its greatest magnate, sometimes equivalent to an underking.

492.1   HARROW: BCS 201.

492.1   INE ... HUNDRED: Ine 54, on *thaere Hyndenne*.

492.1   BARROWS: e.g. Loveden, Lincolnshire; Broadwater, Redbourn (Standard Hill), Hertfordshire; Effingham (Standard Hill), Surrey; Hassocks, Sussex, and many others; see S on Surrey.

492.1   THORSBERG: cf. e.g. the description in *Ant.* 26, 1952, 14.

492.2   LONDONERS: Aethelstan VI 3.

492.3   TRIBAL HIDAGE: BCS 297; Rolls 2 ii 296; see JBAA 40, 1884, 30 and n.s. 35, 1929, 273; EHR 4, 1889, 335; 27, 1912, 625; 40, 1925, 497; NQ 10th series 9, 1908, 384, and 192, 1947, 398 and 423; *Traditio* 5, 1947, 192; TRHS n.s. 14, 1900, 189, etc. See T.

493.1   SURREY: see p. 322 *Age*. Surrey and East Kent formed a distinct territory in the 5th and 6th centuries, until annexed by Aethelbert, in or soon after 584, when the East Saxons acquired London and its territory north of the Thames, the future Middlesex, under Aethelbert's suzerainty. On his death, during Redwald's brief supremacy in the 620s, king Taeppa (see p. 323 *Age*), known only from his tomb, appears to have ruled a substantial kingdom north of the Thames, which may have wrested London from the East Saxons for a few years. The name Surrey, southern region, doubtless balanced by a northern region across the Thames, may have been then brought into use. Thereafter the London region was for a while disputed between the West and East Saxons and Kent.

The enduring boundaries were drawn after Wulfhere's conquest, when Surrey was established as a distinct kingdom, whose ruler the copyist of a charter described as *Fritheuualdus provinciae Surrianorum subregulus Wulfarii Mercianorum regis* (BCS 34). Its northern boundary was sealed by the grant of almost all the Thames bank from Chertsey to Bermondsey to monasteries, and the London region on the opposite bank then or soon after became the *provincia* of Middlesex, though no *subregulus* is there attested. The Tribal Hidage lists the separate names of the small peoples who were organised into these two *provinciae*, in spellings that later copyists grossly corrupted, which have not yet been examined by philologists; but it did not know the names or existence of the future Surrey and Middlesex, and it is therefore probable that the original text was drawn up before Wulfhere's reorganisation created them.

493.2   DOMESDAY ... PERSONS: adult males are numbered. Since some men were unwed brothers, the number of families was necessarily a little smaller, perhaps nearer to 200,000.

493.3   HUNDREDS ... MET MONTHLY: cf. e.g. Edgar I 1; Edward II 8.

494.2   SHIRES: the word means a 'sheared' portion of a whole, and is rendered in Latin by *comitatus*, in English 'county', the territory of a *comes* used to translate English 'earl'. The shires and counties had differing origins. The earliest were the five, or six, constituent kingdoms of Wessex (pp. 324–325 *Age*), some of which were termed shires while still ruled by kings. Outside Wessex, the imperial arrogance of Offa abolished the monarchies of the old kingdoms of the south-east, to the distress of Alcuin (p. 331 *Age*), and restricted their rulers to the humbler style of *dux* or *comes*. In the 9th century, Egbert and his sons for a while themselves exercised the title of king of East Anglia or Kent, but the title 'king' lapsed in the course of the Scandinavian wars. East Anglia reverted to is two original 5th- and 6th-century constituents, the North and South Folk. The old south-eastern kingdoms retained their identity as counties, and as such were included under the generalised heading of 'shires', but, since they were not 'sheared' portions of a whole the suffix 'shire' was not and is not appended to the former kingdoms or *provinciae* of Sussex, Kent or Surrey, Middlesex or Essex, Norfolk or Suffolk.

In the east midlands, the tenth-century Danes organised the Hundreds, in their language *wapentakes*, military districts, into army-areas grouped round fortresses or boroughs. The West Saxon kings of the English applied their own word shire to these regions, and extended it to the west midlands, English Mercia. North of the Trent, the former

Mercian territory south of the Ribble remained part of Cheshire until the 12th century, while the Pennines, north of Danish Derbyshire, and all the English northwest, were grouped with the Danish kingdom of York in the huge county of Yorkshire. The old name of Northumbria or Northumberland was restricted to the former Bernicia, and the military border bishopric of Durham became a separate county. Cumberland retained its old name, 'the Welsh land', on its annexation by the English in 1092; Lancashire and Westmorland are creations of the 12th century.

The king's officer, or reeve, in each shire or county was termed shire-reeve, or sheriff, in principle not hereditary. The English term *eorl,* 'earl', originally the general word for nobleman, was influenced by its Scandinavian equivalent *jarl,* used for the head of an army or army-district, a midland shire, and was commonly used of hereditary rulers. In the 11th century it was chiefly used of the rulers of former kingdoms, Mercia or Wessex, but from the 12th century onward earls, in Latin *comites,* were increasingly appointed to individual counties, and in time *dux,* duke, came into use as the title of a superior earl, at first for royal princes.

496.3	OSRIC ... BAPTISED: Bede HE 4, 13.
497.1	BATH: BCS 43, dated 6 November 676.
497.1	GLOUCESTER: BCS 60; Finberg ECWM 158. *Oba* (huba), meaning *numerus mancipiorum, praedium*; and *sule* (sola), a measure; see Du Cange.
497.1	VICARIUM: Cartulary of Landévennec para. 45; cf. 46, 17 etc. The word renders the ecclesiastical and colloquial *plebs, plou-* etc.
498.3	ALDHELM: see pp. 415 and 496 *Age* and E.
498.3	PAGHAM: BCS 50, see John *Land Tenure* 8 and Finberg *Lucerna* 149.
499.1	NUNNA: BCS 144; see p. 482 *Age.* This is seo Landboc the Nunna cyng gebocade Eadberhte b' into Hugabeorgum xx hida.
499.1	AETHELRED'S GRANT REVOKED: Evesham Chronicle, cited Finberg ECWM 170.
499.1	TOKI: KCD 805.
499.2	CHURCH RIGHT: wording varies, e.g. *ecclesiastica ratio atque regula; monastica ratio* BCS 157; *ecclesiastica* (sic) *ius* BCS 182; *ius episcopalis sedis* BCS 76, etc.
499.2	GRAVER SCANDAL: Bede *Ep. ad Egbertum* 12.
499.2	WITHINGTON: BCS 156.
500.3	KIN RESTRICTION REMOVED: e.g. BCS 77.
500.3	BOOKED TO HIMSELF: BCS 451 *Aethelwulf ... ruris partem ... mihi in hereditatem propriam describere iusi; id est me ad habendum ... et iterum qualicumque prout me placabilis sit aeternaliter relinquendum* 26 December 847.
500.3	INE: BCS 142.
500.3	BEORTRIC: BCS 258.
500.3	KENTISH KING: BCS 496.
500.4	ALDHELM: e.g. BCS 108, cf. 109 etc., *Ego Ini ... rex, cum consilio et decreto ... Aldhelmi ... privilegii dignitatem monasteriis confero, ut ... absque tributum fiscalium negotiorum ... Deo soli serviant,* without reservation of the public services.
501.1	PUBLIC SERVICES: see p. 492 *Age.*
501.1	LOANLAND: e.g. Alfred *Soliloquies of Augustine,* preface; a man normally cultivates land loaned by his lord until he is granted 'bookland and perpetual possession'.
501.1	ENTAIL: Alfred 41.
501.2	EALDORMAN: Aelfred dux, BCS 558.
501.2	ILLEGITIMATE: so Maitland DBB 246, Stenton ASE 307. The objections of Chadwick SASI 171, note 1, are rightly rejected by John *Land Tenure* 16, note 2.

501.2   FOLK LAND: and Bookland. The problems are discussed, from the point of view of the later middle ages, by Maitland DBB 244 ff.; Pollock and Maitland, *History of English Law* 1, 37 ff.; Vinogradoff EHR 8, 1, ff.; GM 142 ff., 244 ff.; John *Land Tenure* 1 ff.; and others.
501.2   REEVE: Edward 1, Preface.
501.2   LONDON: *Libertas Londoniensis* 6.

NOTES TO THE MAPS
IN
THE AGE OF ARTHUR

1 **The Shape of Britain**: p. 7. Since drift-maps are not yet fully available, the surface boundaries are not always known. Attempts at over-precise indication are apt to mislead; boundaries are therefore approximate.

2 **Roman Britain**: p. 47. See the Ordnance Survey *Map of Roman Britain*; for Scotland, cf. maps 11 and 12, pp. 187, 189.

3 **Pagan English Settlement 1**: p. 59. Period A, AD 430/470. Only dateable sites are shown. Sites marked with a query as uncertain normally represent isolated objects of the period, or sites not yet adequately published, a few possibly not burials.

For details of the sites, see S; and, for most of them, Meaney *Gazetteer*. New discoveries and future study are bound to add new sites and to extend the date-limits of some of the sites here listed. The list endeavours to date known sites as closely and as fully as possible, and to enable the significance of new knowledge to be noted easily.

The sites are listed, as far as possible, from north to south and from west to east, by counties and within counties. For convenience, the sites shown on all the pagan English settlement maps (3, 6, 18, 21, 22; pp. 59, 107, 285, 297, 305) are here set down together.

New sites in areas previously settled are not listed or mapped in periods B-F. Only the earliest date of each site is given.

	Inhumation		Cremation		Mixed rite	Uncertain rite
	alone	with a little cremation	alone	with a little inhumation		
Large cemeteries	■	▮-	▬	▬▪	✚	
Cemeteries	☐	☐-	▭	▭▫	✢	
A few burials	‖		=			//
Single or family burials	ǀ		—			/
Barrow	⌒					
House or houses	△					
Excavated royal centre	▲					
Uncertain date	?					
Roman roads	---					

Map 3 p. 59 Period A 430/470

YORKSHIRE: ■York, Heworth SE 61 51; ☐York, The Mount SE 59 51; ■Sancton 1 SE 90 40.

LINCOLNSHIRE: ■Kirton-in-Lindsey SE 93 00; ■South Elkington TF 31 88; ☐Lincoln SK 97 71; ■Loveden Hill SK 90 45; ■Ancaster SK 94 43; ■West Keal TF 35 64.

NOTTINGHAMSHIRE: ■Newark SK 79 53.

LEICESTERSHIRE: ■Thurmaston SK 61 08; ☐Leicester SK 57 03.

WARWICKSHIRE: ■Cestersover SP 52 81.

RUTLAND: ◻Glaston SK 91 00; ■North Luffenham SK 93 04.

NORTHAMPTONSHIRE: ▮-Nassington TL 07 95; ■- Kettering SP 87 79.

HUNTINGDONSHIRE: ■Woodston, Peterborough TL 19 98.

NORFOLK: ■Castle Acre TF 79 15; ■Penstorpe TF 95 29; ■North Elmham TF 98 19; ▭Norwich, Catton TG 22 09; ▭Brundall TG 31 08; ■Caistor-by-Norwich TG 23 03; ■Markshall TG 22 03; ▭Shropham TL 98 93; ■Illington TL 94 89; △Thetford TL 86 82.

CAMBRIDGESHIRE: ✚Cambridge, St. Johns TL 44 58; ✚Cambridge, Girton TL 42 60; ‖Cambridge, Trumpington TL 45 55.

SUFFOLK: ■Lackford TL 77 71; ▯Ixworth TL 93 70; ‖Hoxne TM 18 77.

ESSEX: △Bulmer TL 83 38; △Little Oakley TM 22 28; ▯Feering, Kelvedon TL 86 19; ‖Bradwell, Othona TM 03 08; //Great Stambridge TQ 90 93; △■Mucking TQ 69 81.

BEDFORDSHIRE: /Harrold TL 95 57; ✚Kempston, Bedford TL 03 47; ✚Sandy TL 18 48; ?Egginton SP 96 25; ?Toddington, Warmark TL 00 28; ✚Luton TL 08 29.

OXFORDSHIRE: ▯Cassington SP 44 11; —Osney SP 50 06; ■Wheatley SP 60 04; △Dorchester SU 57 93.

BERKSHIRE: ▮-Frilford SU 43 96; ✚Abingdon SU 49 96; ✚Long Wittenham SU 54 93; ✣Reading SU 74 73; /Sonning SU 75 75.

HAMPSHIRE: ?Portchester SU 62 04; ?Droxford SU 61 18.

MIDDLESEX: ✣Shepperton TQ 06 67; ▯Hanwell TQ 15 79.

SURREY: △Ham TQ 16 71; ■Mitcham TQ 27 68; ✣Beddington TQ 30 65; ▮-Croydon TQ 32 65.

KENT: ■Orpington TQ 46 66; ▮-Riseley TQ 56 67; ■Milton, Sittingbourne TQ 90 64; ■Faversham TR 01 61; ▯Canterbury TR 14 57; ■Bekesbourne, Cowslip TR 20 55; ■Howletts TR 20 56; ■Sarre TR 26 66; ■Buttsole, Eastry TR 31 54; |Deal TR 37 52; ■Dover TR 30 43.

Map 6 p. 107 Period B 460/500

NORTHUMBERLAND: ?Howick NU 23 16; ‖Corbridge NY 98 64.

LANCASHIRE: ?Crossmoor SD 44 38; ▭Ribchester SD 65 35; —Manchester SJ 84 99.

YORKSHIRE: ‖Cowlam SE 96 66; |Rudstone TA 09 67; △Elmswell TA 00 57; ▯Driffield TA 04 57; ▯Sancton II SE 90 40.

LINCOLNSHIRE: ▯South Ferriby SE 99 22; ‖Flixborough TA 88 13; ▯Fonaby TA 11 03; //Cleethorpes TA 29 08; /Hatton TF 18 76; ▯Carlton Scroop SK 93 45; ▯-Caythorpe SK 96 49; ■Sleaford TF 06 45; ▭Baston TF 11 13.

NOTTINGHAMSHIRE: ■Kingston-on-Soar SK 50 27; ▭Sutton Bonnington SK 51 24; ▯Holme Pierrepoint SK 62 39; ‖Cotgrave SK 63 35; ▮Willoughby-on-the-Wolds SK 64 25.

LEICESTERSHIRE: ✚Saxby SK 81 19; ▯Glen Parva SP 56 98; ▯Wigston Magna SP 60 97.

RUTLAND: △■Empingham SK 94 07; ✣Great Casterton SK 99 08.

NORTHAMPTONSHIRE: /Helpstone TF 10 06; /Little Weldon SP 92 89; ✣Newton-le-Willows SP 83 88; ✣Rothwell SP 81 81; ▯Islip SP 98 79; /Cranford SP 94 77; —Addington SP 96 75; ✣Barton Seagrave SP 88 77; ✚Brixworth SP 74 72; ▭Pitsford SP 74 68; ▯Welton SP 57 66; ▯Holdenby SP 69 67; ▯Duston SP 72 60; /Milton SP 73 55; ▯-Marston St. Lawrence SP 54 43.

NOTES TO MAPS (6, 18)

HUNTINGDONSHIRE: ?Godmanchester TL 25 70; —Somersham TL 36 77; //Eynesbury TL 18 59.

NORFOLK: =Snettisham TF 58 34; =Walsingham Abbey TF 93 36; ▫Wolterton TG 14 32; ⇌North Runcton TF 64 15; /Thuxton TG 03 07; ▫Norwich, Drayton TG 18 13; ▪Rushford (Brettenham) TL 93 83.

CAMBRIDGESHIRE: ?Arrington (Wimpole) TL 33 50; ▫Barrington A TL 37 49; ▪Barrington B TL 38 39; ▮Haslingfield TL 41 52; ✚Little Wilbraham TL 56 57.

SUFFOLK: ▫Exning TL 62 65; ▫Undley TL 69 81; ▪Holywell Row TL 71 76; ▪Lakenheath TL 73 82; ▫Icklingham TL 77 72; △▪West Stow TL 79 71; =Ingham (Culford) TL 85 73; ▫Bury St. Edmunds TL 84 65; ▪Eye TM 15 74; |Coddenham TM 13 54; ▪Snape TM 40 59; |Ufford TM 29 52; //Waldringfield TM 28 44.

ESSEX: ✚Great Chesterford TL 50 43; —Ashdon TL 57 43; /Heybridge TL 85 08; =Colchester TL 99 25.

HERTFORDSHIRE: /Royston TL 35 40; △Stevenage TL 25 21; /Hertford TL 33 13; ?Ware TL 35 14.

BUCKINGHAMSHIRE: ?Bishopstone SP 79 11.

OXFORDSHIRE: ?Hornton SP 39 45; ▯Souldern SP 51 31; ▫Ewelme SU 64 92; /Oxford SP 50 06.

BERKSHIRE: △Sutton Courtenay SU 48 94; ▫Hanwell SU 48 88; ▫Blewburton SU 54 86; ▯Wallingford SU 60 89; ▪East Shefford SU 38 74.

HAMPSHIRE: ?Micheldever SU 50 39; ✚Worthy Park SU 50 32; ▪Droxford SU 61 18; △Portchester SU 62 04; ?Alton SU 71 38.

SUSSEX: ▪High Down, Ferring TQ 09 04; ▫Lewes, Saxonbury TQ 40 09; ▫Lewes, Malling TQ 42 11; ▫Selmeston TQ 51 07; ▮Bishopstone TQ 47 02; ▪Alfriston TQ 51 03.

SURREY: ▯Guildown SU 98 48.

KENT: ✣Northfleet TQ 62 73; ✣Hollingbourne TQ 82 54; ✚Westbere TR 19 61; ▪Bifrons TR 18 55; ▫Wingham TR 24 56; ▫Lyminge TR 16 40; ▫Lympne TR 10 35.

Map 18 p. 285 Periods C 490/530; D1 510/540; D2 530/560

One dot indicates period D1, two dots period D2.

NORTHUMBERLAND: D2 ‖..Benwell NZ 21 64.

DURHAM: C/D ?Castle Eden NZ 42 38.

CUMBERLAND: D 1/2 |..Birdoswald NY 61 66.

WESTMORLAND: D1 /.Brough NY 79 14.

YORKSHIRE: C ✣Saltburn (Marske) NZ 65 20; D1 |Kingthorpe SE 83 85; C △Wykeham SE 96 86; C |Ganton Wold TA 00 76; C ▫Hornsea TA 20 48.

DERBYSHIRE: C ▪King's Newton SK 34 26; D1 ⇌Swarkeston SK 36 29.

LEICESTERSHIRE: C/D /Loughborough SK 53 19; C ▫Rothley Temple SK 56 12.

WARWICKSHIRE: C ✚Baginton SP 34 74; C ?Long Itchington SP 41 65; C ▫Warwick, Longbridge SP 29 65; C ✚Stratford-on-Avon SP 21 54; C ✚Bidford-on-Avon SP 09 51; D1 ▫Stretton-on-the-Fosse SP 22 38.

WORCESTERSHIRE: D1 ▪.Beckford SP 98 36; D1 ▫.Broadway SP 11 37.

GLOUCESTERSHIRE: D1 ▫.Bishop's Cleeve SO 95 27; D1? ▯.Hampnett SO 10 15; D1 (?C) ▪.Fairford SP 14 01; D1? ‖.Chavenage ST 87 96; D1 ▫.Kemble 1 ST 99 98; D1? |.Minety SU 01 91.

OXFORDSHIRE: D1 ▢.Broughton Poggs SP 22 04; D1 ▢.Filkins SP 23 04; C ▰ Brighthampton SP 38 03.
WILTSHIRE: D1/2 ▰..Harnham Hill SU 13 28; D1/2 ▰..Petersfinger SU 16 29.
HAMPSHIRE: D1? /.Stockbridge SU 37 35; C/D1 ▰Chessell Down, IoW SZ 39 85.

Map 21 p. 297 Periods D3 550/590; E 570/610

NORTHUMBERLAND: ‖Galewood NT 95 32; /Lowick NU 01 39; ▢▲Old Yeavering NT 92 30; /Wooler NT 99 28; /Newham NU 16 29.
DURHAM: /Lanchester NZ 16 47; ▢Darlington NZ 28 15.
YORKS: ‖Catterick SE 22 98; /Fridaythorpe SE 87 59; ▢Sewerby TA 20 69; ▢▲Nafferton TA 06 58.
STAFFORDSHIRE: ▭Yoxall SK 14 19; ▢Wichnor SK 19 15.
DERBYSHIRE: |Duffield SK 36 44.
NOTTINGHAMSHIRE: /Tuxford SK 73 71.
LEICESTERSHIRE: /High Cross, Wibtoft SP 47 88; ▢Market Harborough SP 73 87; |Medbourne SP 80 93; ▢Caves Inn, Shawell (Tripontium) SP 53 79.
NORTHAMPTONSHIRE: /Naseby SP 68 78; |Clipston SP 71 81; ▢-Desborough I SP 80 83; ▢Desborough II SP 80 84; |Loddington SP 81 78; ‖Thorpe Malsor SP 83 78; ‖Cransley SP 83 77; ▢Badby SP 56 59; ▢Newnham, Daventry SP 59 59; ‖Norton (Bannaventa) SP 61 63; ‖Daventry SP 58 62; /Northampton II SP 77 61; ▰Northampton III SP 77 60; |Northampton IV SP 75 61; |—Irchester SP 92 66; /Aynho SP 52 32.
WARWICKSHIRE: —Brinklow SP 43 79; /Clifton-on-Dunsmore SP 54 76; | Napton-on-the-Hill SP 45 61; | Arrow, Ragley Park SP 07 55; | Aston Cantlow SP 13 59.
WORCESTERSHIRE: ▢Upton Snodsbury SO 94 54; ‖Evesham SP 04 43.
GLOUCESTERSHIRE: |Kempsford SU 15 97.
OXFORDSHIRE: ▢Lower Heyford SP 48 24; ‖Burford SP 24 12; ▢Minster Lovell SP 31 11; ▢Standlake SP 38 04.
BUCKINGHAMSHIRE: /Buckingham SP 68 36; ‖Tickford SP 88 43; ▢Newport Pagnell SP 88 44; /Oving SP 78 21; |Ashendon SP 70 14; /Winchendon SP 75 15; ▢Stone I SP 77 12; |Stone II SP 78 12; /Aylesbury SP 83 14; ▢Dinton SP 76 11; ▢Bishopstone SP 79 11; ▢-Kinsey SP 73 07; /Bledlow SP 77 01; ‖Ellesborough SP 84 07; |High Wycombe SU 89 91; |High Wycombe SU 90 91; ‖Hedsor SU 81 86.
BEDFORDSHIRE: |Farndish SP 92 63; ▲Felmersham SP 99 57; /Moggerhanger TL 14 48; /Shefford TL 13 38; /Langford TL 18 40; /Clifton TL 17 39; ‖Pegsden TL 12 31.
HUNTINGDONSHIRE: /Hemingford Grey TL 29 70.
HERTFORDSHIRE: |Ashwell TL 29 38; /Kings Walden TL 14 23.
MIDDLESEX: ‖Northolt TQ 14 84; //London TQ 33 81.
ESSEX: /Hockley TQ 84 93; /West Bergholt TL 96 28; /Dovercourt TL 24 31; /Dagenham TQ 49 84; ▰Rainham TQ 55 84; ◠Clacton TM 17 16.
SOMERSET: ‖Huish Episcopi ST 43 27; /Pitney ST 44 28; ‖Ilchester ST 52 23; ▢Queen Camel ST 59 25; /Ham Hill ST 48 17.
WILTSHIRE: ▢Purton SU 10 87; ▢Wanborough SU 22 82; ▢Bassett Down SU 11 80; /Barbury Castle SU 15 76; /Preshute, Temple Down SU 13 72; ▢Mildenhall SU 21

69; ‖East Grafton SU 29 60; /Wilton SU 09 31; ▫Winterbourne Gunner SU 18 35; /Winterslow SU 23 34.

BERKSHIRE: /Coleshill SU 23 94; /Ashdown SU 29 83; ⌒Lambourn SU 32 82; |East Garston SU 35 77; |Lockinge Park SU 42 87; ⌒Cuckhamsley SU 45 85; ⌒East Ilsley SU 50 81; ⌒Lowbury SU 54 83; ⌒Cookham, Cock Marsh SU 88 87; ‖Cookham SU 88 85.

HAMPSHIRE: /Silchester SU 64 62; ▫Shalcombe Down SZ 39 85; ▫-Bowcombe Down SZ 46 87; ‖Arreton Down SZ 53 87.

SUSSEX: /Chichester SZ 88 05; ▪Ocklynge TQ 59 00; ▫Eastbourne TV 60 99.

SURREY: ▲Farnham SU 84 46; |Banstead TQ 24 60; /Limpsfield TQ 42 53.

KENT: /West Wickham TQ 39 65; /Belmont Park, Throwley TQ 98 56.

Map 22 p. 305 Period F: 7th Century

NORTHUMBERLAND: ‖Hepple NY 98 00; ‖Great Tosson NU 02 00; /Sweethope NY 95 81; ⌒Capheaton NZ 01 79; |Barrasford NY 91 73; |Tynemouth NZ 37 69.

CUMBERLAND: ⌒near Carlisle NY 43 52; /Moresby NX 98 21.

DURHAM: /Hurbeck, Lanchester NZ 13 48; |East Boldon NZ 36 61; |Cornforth NZ 31 32.

YORKSHIRE: |Richmond NZ 17 02; |Ingleton SD 70 73; /Brough-by-Bainbridge SD 93 90; ‖Ripon SE 31 73; |Burton Leonard SE 34 66; |Occaney, Aldborough SE 35 62; ⌒Hawnby SE 52 89; |Lilla Howe SE 88 98; ‖Robin Hoods Bay NZ 94 05; |Hambleton Moor SE 55 80; ‖Yearsley SE 58 74; |Appleton SE 73 71; ▲York Castle SE 60 51; /York SE 60 52; ▫Aclam Wold SE 79 61; ▪Uncleby SE 82 59; ▫Painsthorpe Wold SE 82 58; ‖North Newbold SE 90 36; /Cave Castle SE 92 28; ‖Everthorpe SE 90 31; /Brough-on-Humber SE 93 26; /Beverley TA 03 39; /Leven TA 11 46; |Burton Pidsea TA 25 31; /Holderness TA 3 2; |Womersley, Pontefract SE 53 19; |North Elmsall SE 47 12.

LANCASHIRE: /Stalmine Moss SD 39 45; ⌒Wigan SD 56 05.

STAFFORDSHIRE: ▭Stretton SK 25 26; |Barlaston SJ 89 38; /Forsbrook SJ 95 41; ⌒Caulden SK 07 48; |Calton SK 10 50; |Musden (Ilam) SK 11 50; |Musden (Ilam) SK 11 50; |Castern (Ilam) SK 12 52; |Steep Lowe SK 12 56; ‖Tamworth SK 21 04; |Wetton SK 11 54; /Throwley SK 11 53.

DERBYSHIRE: ⌒Cow Law SK 10 72; ⌒Hurdlow SK 11 66; ⌒Grindlow SK 20 67; /Youlgreave SK 20 64; ⌒Brundcliff, Hartington SK 13 60; ⌒Cold Eaton SK 14 56; ⌒Benty Grange SK 14 64; |Alsop SK 16 55; ⌒Newhaven House SK 16 60; ⌒White Lowe SK 22 59; ⌒Standlow SK 15 53; /Galley Low SK 21 56; ⌒Tissington SK 15 52; ⌒Wigber Low SK 20 51; ⌒Wyaston SK 19 42; /Borrowash SK 41 34.

NOTTINGHAMSHIRE: /Nottingham I SK 56 39; /Nottingham II SK 56 39; ⌒Oxton SK 63 51; /Winkburn SK 71 60.

LEICESTERSHIRE: |Stoke Golding SP 39 97; /Hinckley SP 42 94.

WARWICKSHIRE: /Alcester SP 08 57; ‖Walton SP 28 52; ‖Compton Verney SP 31 52; ‖Lighthorne SP 33 55; /Burton Dassett SP 38 53; ▫-Long Compton (Rollright) SP 29 30.

NORTHAMPTONSHIRE: ‖Hardingstone SP 73 57.

WORCESTERSHIRE: ‖Wyre Piddle SO 96 47; /Bricklehampton SO 98 41; |Littlehampton SP 03 42.

GLOUCESTERSHIRE: ▯Ebrington SP 18 40; ‖Oddington SP 21 25; ▯-Blockley SP 18 36; ‖Leckhampton SO 94 18; ‖Withington SP 01 18; ▲Salmonsbury SP 17 20; |Stratton, Cirencester SP 01 04; ‖Cirencester SP 02 02; /Sea Mills, Bristol ST 55 78.

OXFORDSHIRE: ▯Lyneham SP 29 21; ▯▲Chadlington SP 33 21; /Spelsbury SP 35 21; |Great Tew SP 39 29; ◠Asthall SP 28 10; ▲▯Wilcote SP 37 13; ‖North Leigh SP 38 14; /Bampton SP 32 03; |Yelford SP 36 04.

BUCKINGHAMSHIRE: ◠Taplow SU 90 82.

HERTFORDSHIRE: /Hitchin TL 17 29; //Ippollits TL 19 27; ‖Redbourn TL 11 12; ▯Wheathampstead TL 17 14; /Hemel Hempstead, Boxmoor TL 03 05; ▯Verulamiufﬁ TL 13 07; ‖Furneaux Pelham TL 44 26; /Waltham Cross TQ 37 99.

ESSEX: ◠Broomfield TL 71 09; /Forest Gate TL 41 86; ▯Prittlewell TQ 87 87; ‖Great Wakering TQ 95 87; /Asheldam TL 97 01; ∎Saffron Walden TL 53 38; ‖Wendens Ambo TL 51 36; /Sturmer TL 69 43.

SOMERSET: ▲Worle Hall ST 36 64; ▯Saltford ST 68 68; ∎Camerton ST 68 57; ‖Buckland Denham ST 74 50; |Evercreech ST 64 38; /Shapwick ST 42 38; ‖Taunton ST 23 25.

DORSET: ◠Hardown Hill SY 40 94; |Maiden Castle SY 67 88; /Milton Abbas ST 80 01; ◠Woodyates SU 03 19; /Wor SU 01 17; |Oakley Down SU 02 17.

WILTS: |Roundaway Down SU 00 64; ▲Westbury ST 88 50; ‖Battlesbury ST 89 45; ‖Tilshead Lodge SU 02 47; |Shrewton SU 06 43; ◠Rodmead Down ST 81 36; ‖Sherrington ST 96 39; ◠Ford SU 17 33; ▯Winkelbury ST 95 21; |Ansty, Swallowcliffe ST 96 27; /Bishopstone SU 07 26.

HANTS: |Basingstoke SU 62 51; |Brown Candover SU 58 39; |Preston Candover SU 60 40; |Preshaw SU 58 24; ▯Southampton SU 43 13; /Boscombe Chine SZ 11 91; ‖Christchurch SZ 16 93.

SUSSEX: ▲Medmerry SZ 83 94; /Pagham SZ 88 97; |Arundel TQ 02 06; ‖Burpham TQ 05 09; ‖Blackpatch, Patching TQ 09 08; ‖Clapham TQ 08 09; /Thakeham TQ 12 18; ▭Hassocks TQ 29 15; |Kemp Town, Brighton TQ 32 04; —South Moulscombe TQ 32 06.

SURREY: ▯Hawkshill, Fetcham TQ 15 55; ▯Farthingdown TQ 29 58.

KENT: ‖Wrotham TQ 61 59; ▯Snodland TQ 69 62; ‖Aylesford TQ 72 58; ▯Maidstone TQ 73 56; ‖Harrietsham TQ 87 53; ‖Lenham TQ 90 52; |Westwell TQ 99 47; ‖Ashford TR 01 42; ‖Wye TR 07 46; ‖Crundale TR 06 49; ▯Smeath TR 07 39.

4 The British in Gaul: p. 89. Cf. notes 90.3, 90.5 above: and Doble *Saints in Normandy*. Only the registers of Rouen have been systematically examined; further research is likely to detect more dedications between the estuaries of the Seine and the Rhine. In the diocese of Amiens some well known foundations, as St. Winwaloe's Abbey at Montreuil-sur-mer, honoured British saints, but systematic evidence is not yet available. Clusters of such dedications suggest the likelihood of a 6th-century population of British ancestry; isolated sites do not.

Some sites may owe their names to the evacuation of relics by refugees from Scandinavian and other raiders; but present evidence does not clearly show whether houses without previous British connections took British names because they received such relics, or whether the refugees migrated to houses with which they already had links.

Places named Breteuil may have the same origin as those named Bretteville; cf. note 90.3 above.

NOTES TO MAPS (4-7)

5 The War Zone: p. 101.

AMBROS- PLACE-NAMES (see p. 100).

HEREFORDSHIRE Amberley *SO 54 47* DPNE 9
WORCESTERSHIRE Ombersley *SO 84 63*; Ambresdene and Ambresmedwe in Freckenham EPNS 268
GLOUCESTERSHIRE Amberley *SO 85 01* EPNS 95
OXFORDSHIRE Ambrosden *SP 60 19* EPNS 161
WILTSHIRE Amesbury *SU 16 41* EPNS 359
SUSSEX Ambersham *SU 91 20* EPNS 97; Amberley *TQ 02 13* EPNS 146 Amberstone *TQ 59 11* EPNS 435
ESSEX Ambersury Banks *TL 43 00* EPNS 22, in Epping Forest; Amberden *TL 56 30* EPNS 523, near Debden; Amberley *TL 67 24* EPNS 632, in Stebbing; Amberland *TQ 36 91* Folly Lane, Walthamstow; Amberland, Roydon *TL 41 09*; Emberdon, Matching *TL 53 13*; Ambyrmede, Wickham Bishops *TL 84 13* EPNS 106
KENT Amsbury, Hunton *TQ 73 51* PNK 161

The cluster of *Amber-* names in Derbyshire derives from the river Amber; Amersham, Bucks., and names in *Amble-, Ample-* etc. have a different origin. Further *Amber-* names may come to light when Hampshire, Berkshire and other southern and south-western counties are surveyed by EPNS.

MASSACRE AND BATTLE SITES (references in Meaney, *Gazetteer*)
The sites are marked on the map with the symbol X unless otherwise indicated.

WILTSHIRE Heytesbury *ST 92 42*; Knook *ST 95 44*; Roche Court Down *SU 25 35*; Old Sarum* *SU 14 32*; Alvediston [1] (Ebbesbourne Wake) *ST 96 25*
BERKSHIRE Uffington Castle (White Horse Hill) *SU 30 86*; Wallingford† *SO 61 89* (Hull and Reading Museums); Cookham† *SU 90 85* cf. *Ant. Jl.* 1, 1921, 316; *Arch.* 69, 1919, 13 [11-12]. etc.
SURREY Battersea† *TQ 26 76*, etc. (London Museum, BM)
BEDFORDSHIRE Dunstable, Five Knolls* *TL 05 10*; Puddlehill[1] *TL 00 23*
CAMBRIDGESHIRE Bran Ditch *TL 40 43*; Fleam Ditch *TL 57 54* (approximate); War Ditches, Cherry Hinton *TL 48 55*

many, but not all, of the burials at Dunstable, Five Knolls, and perhaps also at Old Sarum, may be gallows-burials of a later date.
[1] *single burial, fatal bone-wounds.*
† *concentrations of weapons in the Thames.*
Many single burials with shield and spear or sword without sign of 6th-century ornament may also be battle-casualties. They are most numerous in the same region.

6 Pagan English Settlement 2: p. 107. Period B 460/500. See Notes to map 3 above.

7 The Demetian Campaign: p. 128
1 *-cnwc* and *moydir* (Irish *bóthar*) names; after Melville Richards JRSAI 90, 1960, 133 ff.; Lochlann 2, 1962, 129.
2 The words *cil-, rath*, etc. do not imply that the places and sites were built or founded by Irishmen; they do imply that Irish words were in use locally when the names were given.
3 The military sites are

IN THE BRYCHAN DOCUMENTS
1 *Garth Matrun* ... Talgarth ...   *SO 15 33*
2 *Llan Maes* ... near Brecon ...   *SO 03 28*
3 *Lan Semin* ... Glasnevin ...   *SN 73 28*
4 *Methrum* ... Meidrim ...   *SN 28 21*
5 *Porth Mawr* ... Whitesands Bay ...   *SM 73 27*

NOT NAMED IN TEXTS
6   Caer Farchell ...   *SM 79 27*
7   Llan Marchell ...   *SO 14 42*

IN THE VITA CADOCI
Prologue
8 *Bochriu Carn* ... Fochriw ...   *SO 10 05*
9 *Altgundliu* ... ?Wentloog Castle?   *ST 25 03*
   (*palacium Gundlei*)

ch. 22

10 *Tref Redinauc* ... Tredunnock-on-Usk   *ST 37 94*

For the identification of the places, see L Theodoric.

8 Partition: p. 135. See Maps 6 and 13, pp. 107 and 209.

9 Fifth-Century Ireland: p. 153.

1 ROYAL CENTRES
(Those starred were probably not in use in the 5th century, but were venerated as ancient national centres.)
All Ireland ... Tara (Meath)
Northern Uí Néill ... Ailech
Dál Riada ... Muirbolc
Dál Araide ... Rath Mór
Dál Fiatach ... Dún Leithglaisse
Airgialla
         ... Airthir, Uí Bresail ... Emain*
         ... Uí Chrimthann ... Clogher
Meath
         ... Brega ... Duleek
         ... Tethba ... Uisnech* (anciently in Connacht)
Connacht ... Cruachu*
Leinster
         ... North (Uí Dunlange) ... Almu*
         ... South (Uí Chennselaig, Uí Bairrche) ... Dinn Ríg*
Munster ... Cashel

2 MONASTERIES
The name of the founder is given, with the date of his death, as entered in the Annals or indicated in the Lives, with the modern county and grid-reference.

Cianán of Duleek 491 Meath *O 06*
Mo-Choe of Nendrum 498 Down *J 56*
Énda of Aran early 6th? Galway *L 80*
Senán of Inis Cathaig (Scattery Island) early 6th? Clare *Q 95*

NOTES TO MAPS (8-14)

Darerca of Killevy 516 Armagh *J 02*
Boecius of Monasterboice 521 Louth *O 08*
Abbán of Moyarney early 6th Wexford *S 72*
Brigit of Kildare 525 *N 71*
Mocteus of Louth 533 *H 20*
Faencha and a few other names are recorded. It is likely that several other small houses were founded, especially for women, few of which retained later importance.

3 EPISCOPAL CENTRES (to 540, before the development of large-scale monasticism). The name of the bishop is given, with the date of death, as entered in the Annals, or indicated by the Lives, the modern county and grid-reference, and the ancient territory.
Patrick of Saul, Ulaid (Dál Fiatach), Downpatrick, Down *J 54* and Airgialla (Airthir, Uí Bressail) Armagh *H 84*, 459
Fiacc of Sletty, South Leinster (Uí Bairrche), Leix *S 77*, late 5th
Mael of Ardagh, Tethba, Longford *N 16*, 486
Mac Caille of Croghan, Uí Failge, Offaly *N 43*, 492
Mac Cuilín of Lusk, Brega, Dublin *O 25*, 496
Foirtchernn of Trim, Brega, Meath *N 75*, late 5th
Íbar of Wexford, South Leinster, *T 02*, Uí Chennselaig, 499
Declán of Ardmore, Munster (Dessi), Waterford *X 17*, early 6th?
Cerpán of Tara, Brega, Meath *N 95*, 505
Mac Cáirthinn of Clogher, Airgialla (Uí Chrimthann), Tyrone *H 55*, 505
Bronn of Cúil Irra (Killaspugbrone), Connacht (Uí Fiachrach Aidni), Sligo *G 63*, 508
Mac Nissi Aengus of Connor, Dál Araide, Antrim *J 19*, 509
Erc of Slane, Brega, Meath *N 97*, 512
Cairnech of Drumleen, Northern Uí Néill (Tír Eogain), Donegal *C 20*, and Duleek, Brega, *N 77*, early 6th
Conlaed of Kildare, North Leinster (Uí Dunlange), *N 71*, 516
Ciarán of Saigir, Ossory, Offaly *N 10*, c. 520
Beoaid of Ardcarn, Connacht (Brefni), Roscommon *G 80*, 522
Ailbe of Emly, Munster, Tipperary *R 73*, 528

Some of the five bishops in Brega were bishops of different Uí Néill High Kings; others may have succeeded each other. The Lives freely accord the title bishop to other saints, in some cases perhaps with justification. There is no sign that bishops' sees were yet fixed to a single centre in each kingdom.

11 **The Picts**: p. 187.
   Place-names: see especially K.H. Jackson in Wainwright PP, and Watson CPNS.
   Memorial Stones: cf. note 194.1 above. Half a dozen stones south of the Forth do not make the Lothians Pictish; nor do an equal number in the north-east make Caithness Pictish. Various archaeological objects are ascribed to the Picts because they are found in the same area; but are open to misinterpretation if the north-west is treated as Pictish.

12 **The Picts and their Neighbours**: p. 189. The most comprehensive mapping of the sites is in IANB. Most of the forts are pre-Roman. Whether those situated to the north and south of the Roman Antonine Wall differ significantly from each other can only be established by systematic enquiry.

14 **Brittany**: p. 255
   GRID Squares are designated between lines of longitude (letters) and latitude (figures),

as marked on the Michelin 1 km to 2 cm map. Letter squares run from A (= 8°40'
to 8°20') to Y (= 3°60' to 3°40') longitude; figure squares from 0 (= 54°20' to
54°00') to 9 (= 52°60' to 52°40') latitude. The letters and figures are marked in
the borders of the map. Each square is designated by a letter (reading downwards)
and figure (reading across) as Brest, E 3.

SITES shown on the map by a number are

1 Avranches V 1
2 Bangor-en-Belle-Ile L 9
3 Ile Brehat M 0
4 Ile de Batz G 1
5 Dinan R 2
6 Douarnenez E 4
7 Cap Frehel Q 1
8 Guingamp L 2
9 St.-Gildas-de-Rhuys N 8
10 Granville U 0
11 Huelgoat I 3
12 St.-Lunaire R 1
13 Laval Y 4
14 Landerneau F 2
15 Landévennec F 3
16 Landivisiau G 2
17 St.-Malo R 1
18 Mont St.-Michel U1
19 St.-Meen Q 4
20 St.-Nazaire Q 9
21 Ile d'Ouessant (Ushant) A 2
22 Ploudalmazeau D 2
23 Ploermel P 5
24 Pointe de Penmarc E 6
25 Pontivy M 4
26 Quiberon L 8
27 Quimperlé J 6
28 Redon R 7
29 Pointe du Raz C 5
30 Tréguier L 0
31 Trégastel-Plage J 0
32 Primel-Trégastel H 1
33 Ile Tristan E 4

15 The Homeland of the English: p. 263. See especially Genrich *Formenkreise* map
10, and Brøndsted *Danmarks Oldtid* figs. 176 and 246.

16 English Migration in Europe: p. 275. The material has not been surveyed, and
the sites shown here are therefore incomplete; see especially the collection in Weimar
Museum (examples in *Alt Thüringen* 1, 1953/4, 258, fig. 2), and Svoboda *Bohemia
in the Migration Period*, passim. The burials are recognised as Anglian or Saxon at
Weimar, but elsewhere are sometimes catalogued and labelled as 'Lower Elbe', or
'Iron Age' in general.

17 Pressures on the Continental English: p. 277.
Germanic place-names: see Bach *Deutsche Namenkunde* 2, maps 44–45, pp. 333–334;
cf. p. 588.
Slavonic place-names are taken from a modern map at 1: 400,000, ignoring those
that plainly have a modern origin, as Terezin.

1 Modern German names in *-au* may either transliterate Slavonic *-ow*, or else
preserve Frankish *-au*, 'island' or isolated settlement, equivalent to Old English *-eg*,
which is normally *-ey* in the endings of modern English place-names. Only
detailed research can distinguish Slavonic from Germanic *-au*. Slavonic *-ow*
names can therefore be recognised on a modern map only when they have not
been transliterated into German, and are therefore here omitted, since a
significant list should include many *-au* names.

2 Some places to the west of the Slavonic border bear German words for Slav, as
Windisch, and indicate that Slavonic settlement penetrated somewhat deeper
into western Germany at some time.

NOTES TO MAPS (15-20)

18 Pagan English Settlement 3: p. 285. Periods C 490/530; D 1 510/540; D 2 530/560. See Notes to map 3 above.

19 The English in Northern Gaul: A *Artois and Flanders* p. 288. The names are given as spelt on *Carte Michelin* 1 cm to 2 km., sheet 51; many of the differences reflect only modern dialect-variations. The origin of names in -*egem*, which extend farther eastward, and are there numerous, is not clear.
B *Normandy* p. 289. Two distinct settlements appear to meet and overlap to the west of Caen.

20 The English Conquest of the South: p. 295. Applied saucer brooches with a design of a Maltese Cross enclosing four outlined faces are most numerous among the Eslingas and at Kempston; a variant, similarly punched, with Six Faces, has a similar distribution. One group of Great-Squareheaded brooches, classified B 6 by Leeds, and described by him as a 'striking individual group ... the only group ... (with) ... a border of masks on the headplate as its distinctive feature' (Leeds *Corpus* 62) has a border of similar faces, freestanding, and is similarly distributed; three other Great-Squareheaded brooches, classified by Leeds in different groups, have the same distinctive headplate-border.

APPLIED SAUCER BROOCHES
   with *Maltese cross* design

CAMBRIDGESHIRE	Barrington A, *TL 37 49*, 5 burials, Ashmolean Museum.
	Barrington B, *TL 37 48*, with a girdle-hanger, Cambridge Museum (CASP 5, pl. iv).
	Haslingfield, *TL 41 52*, 2 burials, Ashmolean Museum (DSB 178 pl. xxvii 1).
	Linton, grave 72, *TL 56 47*, with wristclasp and squareheaded brooch, Cambridge Museum.
	Odsey (Ashwell Station), *TL 29 38*, ACR 254, Cambridge Museum.
SUFFOLK	Lakenheath, *TL 73 82*, with Great Squarehead A 3 (14), Cambridge Museum.
HERTFORDSHIRE	King's Walden, *TL 14 22*, St. Alban's Museum.
	Ashwell, 'near the station', see Odsey, Cambridgeshire.
BEDFORDSHIRE	Kempston, *TL 03 47*, 5 burials, British Museum; BB 275 pl. xlvii and 341 pl. lxviii a.
BERKSHIRE	Frilford, *SU 43 96*, 2 burials, Ashmolean Museum.
	East Shefford, *SU 38 74* (derivative), British Museum.
NORTHAMPTONSHIRE	Kettering, *SP 87 97* (fragment), Northampton Museum.

   with *Six Face* design

BEDFORDSHIRE	Kempston, *TL 03 47*, British Museum.
	Luton, *TL 08 22* (fragment), Luton Museum, and (derivative) *Ant. Jl.* 8, 1928, 180, pl. xxviii 1.
BERKSHIRE	Reading, *SU 74 73*, DSB 170 pl. xxvi 1; BB 315 pl. lviii 5.
GLOUCESTERSHIRE	Fairford, *SP 14 01*, 2 burials, DSB 164 fig. 5; 165 fig. 6.
NORTHAMPTONSHIRE	Nassington, grave 6, *TL 07 95*, with wrist-clasp, *Ant. Jl.* 24, 1944, 106, pl. xxiii a (o).

GREAT-SQUAREHEADED BROOCHES

Leeds *Corpus* type B 6, nos. 95–100, found at *Luton*, Beds., *TL 08 22*; *Market Overton*, Rutland, *SK 92 18*; *Fairford*, Gloucs., *SP 14 01*; *Mitcham*, Surrey, *TQ 27 68*; *Abingdon*, Berks., *SU 49 96*; *Haslingfield*, Cambs., *TL 41 52*; *Hornton*, Oxon., *SP 39 45*; *Marston*

St. Lawrence, Northants., *SP 54 43*; and *Coleshill*, Berks., *SU 23 94*. The other Squareheaded brooches with similar borders are A 2, 9 *Linton Heath*, Cambs., *TL 58 48*; A 2, 10 *Tuddenham*, Suffolk, *TL 74 70*; and A 3, 27 *Orwell (Barrington A)*, Cambs., *TL 37 49*. The concentration of finds in the Eslinga territory south-west of Cambridge suggests that this territory was Cutha's starting point and homeland.

PLACES named from Cutha (references in the appropriate EPNS county-volumes). 'Lost' place-names, no longer in use, are italicised.

BUCKINGHAMSHIRE	Cuddington *SP 74 12*.
OXFORDSHIRE	*Cudanhlaewe*, Cuxham, Watlington *SU 67 96*.
	Cudendone, Watlington *SU 68 95*.
	Cuddesdon *SP 59 04*.
	Cutslow, North Oxford *SP 51 11*.
GLOUCESTERSHIRE	Cudnall, Charlton Kings, Cheltenham *SO 97 21*.
WILTSHIRE	Cutteridge, North Bradley, Bradford *ST 87 56*.
SURREY	Cuddington *TQ 26 65*.
	Cudworth *TQ 28 42*.
KENT	Cudham *TQ 45 59*.
SUSSEX	*Cudnor*, Westham, Pevensey *TQ 64 04*.
	Cudlow, Climping, Bognor *SU 99 03*.

Cudanhlaewe and Cutslow in Oxfordshire suggest the burial mounds of two separate persons, both called Cutha, perhaps Cuthwulf and Cuthwine.

Further names may be recognised when the EPNS surveys of Hampshire, Berkshire and Kent are published.

A few *Cutha*-names are found outside the area of this map, in Devonshire and West Somerset, in Worcester, Shropshire and Cheshire, and in the Pennines.

The *Cutha*-names in Wessex are located on the left, Oxfordshire, bank of the Thames; as are the places that Cutha captured in 571. They suggest that Cutha's West Saxon kingdom lay east of the Thames, leaving the older Middle Thames territory west of the river, in Berkshire, to Ceawlin.

-*TUNS* taken in 571
   Limbury (Luton), Beds., *TL 07 24*.
   Aylesbury, Bucks., *SP 82 14*.
   Benson, Oxon., *SU 62 91*.
   Eynsham, Oxon., *SP 43 09*.

21 Pagan English Settlement 4: p. 297. Periods D 3 550/590 and E 570/610. See Notes to Map 3.

22 Pagan English Settlement 5: p. 305. Period F, 7th century. See Notes to Map 3. A number of sites here shown, that may only be described as 'late', might alternatively be shown on map 21.

23 The Seventh-Century Kingdoms: p. 319. Many boundaries were ill defined and short-lived. The immediate political allegiance of north-western England, and of Surrey and the London region, was variable and uncertain. The stronger kings of the West Saxons were sometimes able to assert authority over Kent and the South Saxons, and in Surrey. Their western border is shown as it was in the earlier 7th century; by the end of the century they had subdued all or most of Devon and of eastern Somerset. The Mercians at times exercised direct authority in north-western Wessex. The Northumbrians ruled

Carlisle and Galloway, but their authority did not endure; the extent of Northumbrian authority in northern Lancashire is also uncertain. London remained under the effective control of the Mercian kings; when and in what respect it was also subject to the East Saxon kingdom is uncertain.

24 Monks in Wales: p. 359. See especially Bowen SCSW.

25 Monks in Cornwall: p. 362. See especially Doble *Saints of Cornwall* and *LBS*, under the relevant names; cf. E.

26 Monks in the North: p. 371. Dedications to Columba, Kentigern, Ninian are listed in Reeves' *Adamnan* 289 ff., cf. 462; Forbes *Kalendars* 306; 372; 423 ff.; MacKinlay ACDS 2, 42 ff.; 180 ff.; 24 ff.; Arnold-Forster SCD 2, 144; 231; 223 ff. Many chantries, altars, and monastic and episcopal dependencies founded during the Middle Ages, listed by MacKinlay, are not here mapped; all however are located in the same districts as the ancient dedications, and most are immediately adjacent thereto.

27 Monks in Ireland: p. 373.
The modern county and grid-reference, the name of the founder and date of foundation, as entered in the Annals or indicated in the Lives, are given. Seventh-century foundations are placed in brackets. Fifth-century dates are in bold type. See E under the saints named.

Aghaboe Leix *S 38* Cainnech c. 550.
Aran Galway *L 80* Énda (c.470).
Ardstraw Tyrone *H 38* Eugenius c. 530.
Armagh *H 84* Patrick (c. **450**).

(Balla) Mayo *M 28* Mo-Chua 619.
Bangor Down *J 58* Comgall 558.
Begerin Wexford *T 02*, various saints, early 6th.
Birr Offaly *N 00* Brendan c. 550.

Clogher Tyrone *H 55* Mac Nissi Aengus (c. **490**).
Clonard Meath *N 64* Finnian c. 540.
Clonenagh Leix *S 39* Fintan c. 560.
Clones Monaghan *H 52* Tigernach c. 530.
Clonfert Galway *M 92* Brendan 561.
Clonmacnoise Offaly *N 02* Ciarán 547.
Coleraine Derry *C 38* bishop Cairpre c. 540.

Derry *C 41* Columba of Iona c. 545.
Devenish Fermanagh *H 24* Lasrian (Mo-Laisse) c. 540.
Dromore Down *J 25* Colmán c. 540.
Duleek Meath *N 77* Cianán (c. **470**).
Durrow Offaly *N 33* Columba of Iona c. 555.

Ferns Wexford *T 05* Aedán (Maedóc) c. 585.
(Fore) West Meath *N 57* Féchín c. 640.

Kells Meath *N 77* Columba of Iona c. 560?
Kildare *N 71* Brigit (c. **490**).
Killabban Leix *S 68* Abbán c. 500.
(Killala) Mayo *G 13* Cellach c. 630?

(Leighlin) Carlow *S 66* Lasrian (Mo-Laisse) c. 635.
(Lismore) Waterford *X 09* Carthacus 638.
Lothra (Lorra) Tipperary *M 90* Ruadán c. 555.
Lough Ree (Saints' Island) Galway *M 61*, various saints, mid-6th.
Louth *H 90* Mocteus (c. 495).

(Mayo) *M 27* Colmán of Lindisfarne 664.
Monasterboice Louth *O 08* Boecius (c. 480).
Moville Down *J 57* Finnian c. 560.

Nendrum Down *J 56* Mo-Choe (c. 470).

Rahan Offaly *N 22* Carthacus c. 580.
Raphoe Donegal *C 20* Columba of Iona c. 560.
(Roscrea) Tipperary *S 18* Crónán c. 610.

Saigir (Seirkieran) Offaly *N 10* Ciarán (c. 470).
Sletty Leix *S 77* (late 5th).
Swords Dublin *O 14* Columba of Iona c. 555.

(Taghmon) Wexford *S 91* Fintan (Munnu) c. 615.
Terryglass Tipperary *R 89* Columba of Terryglass c. 545.
Tory Island Donegal *B 84* Columba of Iona c. 560?

28 Monks in the English Kingdoms: p. 393.
Houses founded by IRISHMEN (those starred were, as far as is known, short-lived, and of limited influence): Lindisfarne, Hanbury, Burgh Castle*, Malmesbury, Abingdon, Bosham*. ANGLO-IRISH houses, founded by the immediate pupils of Aedán of Lindisfarne and others: Tyninghame, Coldingham, Melrose, Coquet Island, Gateshead, Ebchester, Hartlepool, Gilling, Whitby, Lastingham, Barrow, Bradwell, Tilbury. ENGLISH foundations: Jarrow, Wearmouth, Beverley, Bardney, Partney, Wenlock, Pershore, Fladbury, Evesham, Bredon, Crowland, Peterborough, Oundle, Ely, Gloucester, Bath, Bradford-on-Avon, Chertsey, Bermondsey, Barking. BRITISH AND ROMAN origin: St. Albans, Glastonbury. POSSIBLY OF BRITISH origin: Carlisle, Dacre, Burton, Repton, Dunwich. NORTH ITALIAN CHURCHES: Brixworth, Wing. (Wenden's Ambo, Saffron Walden, Essex, may be as early.)

DEDICATIONS
  to *David*: Holme Bridge, Airmyn, Yorkshire; Farnsfield and Holme, Nottinghamshire; Wettenhall, Cheshire; Caldecote, Warwickshire; Newbold-on-Stour, Worcestershire; Moreton-in-the-Marsh, Gloucestershire; Barton, Somerset; Exeter. Dewsbury *SE 25 22* (the *burh* of Dewi, or David, EPNS WRY 2, 184), whose church, dedicated to All Saints, was evidently rededicated by the English, may also have originated as a foundation in honour of David.
  to *Gulval*: (Finstall) Worcestershire.
  to *Melor*: Amesbury, Wiltshire.
  to *Samson*: York; Cressage, Shropshire; Colesbourne, Gloucestershire; Cricklade, Wiltshire; Milton Abbas, Dorset; Norwich?
  to *Cyngar*: (Docco): Congresbury and Banwell, Somerset.
  to *Winwaloe*: Norwich; Wereham (and Downham Market) Norfolk; Cockenach, Nuthamstead, Hertfordshire, cf. 314.3 note above.
See Arnold-Forster SCD and Baring-Gould LBS under these saints, and E.

29 Monks Abroad: p. 401. See Kenney 486 ff.; Jedin *Atlas*, especially map 25. The question-marks draw attention to the 8th and early 9th century Christianity of the Greater Moravian empire, where the impact of Virgilius of Salzburg and of other offshoots of the work of Boniface, Permin and their successors, is difficult to assess. The architecture of many churches suggests an Anglo-Irish origin. The material is comprehensively surveyed by V.Richter in *Magna Moravia* 121–360, with plans of nearly 500 churches, and an immense bibliography; the argument is however obscured by rigid word-play and an unreal antithesis between the terms 'iroschottisch', 'angelsaechsisch', 'Carolingian', 'Bavarian', 'Benedictine' etc.; cf. the short discussion and views summarised by Hruby *Staré Město* 177–178. Influence from the second generation of the Anglo-Irish foundations in German lands was considerable, whatever the labels applied to them. The artificial term 'iroschottisch' mistakes both the national and religious realities of the monks in central Europe; cf. note 403.4 above.

30-36 English Colonisation 1-7: pp. 469 ff. Maps 30, 33 and 34 are based, with permission, on those of J.M.Dodgson MA 10, 1966, 7 ff., and on map 21 above. Maps 31–36 make use of additional material, published and unpublished, collected by EPNS.

31 Central Bedfordshire: p. 471. For the cemeteries see below, vol. 4, pp. 109-27. The *-inga(s)* names are Wooton Pillinge *TL 009 405*; Worthy End *TL 038 339*; Lidlington *SP 991 388*; Kitchen End *TL 074 332*; EPNS Beds. 87; 150; 77; 161.

32 Settlement by ... Individuals: p. 473. The *-ingtun* symbol is an approximate indicator. It is at present possible to distinguish between *-ingtun*, *-ingatun*, and *-ingastun* only in a few counties; and early evidence is wanting for many names. It has not yet been possible to distinguish systematically the places with these terminations that begin with a personal name from those prefixed by a geographical, folk or other name.

Where information is available, a considerable majority of the places with these endings appear to derive from *-ingtun* prefixed by a personal name, implying a colony planted by a great man, accompanied by followers and dependants. The proportion of personal *-ingtun*s among the various forms of the ending seems to increase towards the west country. The symbols on the map are not therefore strictly comparable with those for *-worth* and *-cote*; they do not indicate a recorded number of individual settlements, but a category of names within which such settlements are likely to be numerous. Closer local study is likely to give a more accurate view of the proportions in different districts of settlements by substantial independent freemen, by dependent cottagers, and by lords.

33, 34 Kent etc.: Essex etc.: pp. 476, 477. Places called Sheepcote and Saltcote are omitted.

35 The North and West: p. 478. Based on EPNE maps 3, 4 and 8, corrected by separate county-volumes, and by other information when available. The names Newbottle, etc., are omitted, since by definition they do not belong to the earliest phase of settlement in their region.

36 -Botl ... in the South: p. 479. Based on EPNE map 8 and other information, when available; the names Newbottle etc. are included to show their relationship to other *-botl* names.

INDEX TO
THE AGE OF ARTHUR

Italic figures refer to the notes.
An asterisk (*) indicates a note on the name or word concerned.
The letters f (*filius*) and m (*mac* or *map*) mean 'son of'; f. means 'following'.
Bold letters, as A, refer to the sections of *Arthurian Sources* (p. 1, above).
Modern conventions on the spelling of names vary, and are often arbitrary; thus, Aethelbert or Ethelbert are nowadays equally familiar, Athelbert unfamiliar, but Athelstan prevails over Ethelstan or Aethelstan. The most recognisable form is normally used. Irish names are normally given in plain English spelling.

Aarhus Map 15
Aballo 138
Abbán 375, 386, 513, *232.2, 370.3*, Maps 9, 27 **E**
Abbandun; see Abingdon
Abbots 397 f.
— 'of Heaven' 398
— 'of Rome' 398
Aben; see Abbán
Abercorn 195. Maps 26, 28
Aberdeen 178. Maps 10, 20
Aberfoyle Map 26
Abergavenny 229. *124.3*. Map 7
Aber Lleu 236
Abernethy 191. Map 26
Aberystwyth 120, 370
Abingdon 60, 82, 99, 132, 211, 226, 268, 281 f., 370, 386, 513. *303.3, 324.2*. Maps 13, 3 **P, S**
Abulci 49.4
Abyssinia 345. *351.1*
Achm 254 f. Map 14
Aclam Wold Map 22
Adda 233 f., 515
Great Addington Map 6
Adeon 418 f.
Adminius *416.3*
Adomnán 161, 165, 170, 175, 182, 193, 377 f., 384, 400, 424 f., 438, 516 **E**
Adrianople 20, 512
advenae 458
Aeclanum *342.3*
Aed m Ainmere 173, 515
— m Bricc 432 **E**
— of Sletty 175, 399. *464.5* **E**
— Guaire 170
— Slane 435
Aedán m Gabrán 181 f., 194 f., 235, 515
— of Ferns; see Maedóc
— of Lindisfarne 391 f., 514. *440.2* **E**
Aegidius 53 f., 88 f., 114, 251, 291, 513
Aelfwini *303.2*

Aelle of Deira 233 f., 515
— of Sussex 94, 103, 113, 271, 513 **L**
Aeneas 420
Aengus; see Angus
Aesc; see Oesc
Aescwine *324.3*
Aeternus 68
Aethelbald 303, 310, 327, 329, 421, 517
Aethelbert 226, 239, 293 f., 300 f., 309 f., 307, 317 f., 322, 329, 421. *301.3, 486.4, 493.1*
Aethelbert (Hengest?) *266.3*
Aethelferth 195, 235 f., 300 f., 326, 391, 515, 518. *301.3*
Aethelred 303, 327, 497 f., 517 **E**
Aethelred II 330
Aethelric 234 f., 320, 515
Aethelward *311.2*
Aethelwulf *500.3*
Aetheria 382, 408
Aëtius 39, 40*, 77 f., 513. *28.1*
Agilbert 411 f. **E**
Agned *111.5*
Agricola, Julius 151
— Bishop 72, 243 **E**
— Longhand 125 f., 158, 168, 203, 207 f., 256, 357, 366
agweddi 445
Aigynd *287.3*; see Egwin
Ailbe 352 f., 367, 383 **E**
Ailech 167. Map 9
Aileran 423
Ailill Molt 167, 513
aillt 459
Ainmere 169 f., 182, 379, 515
Aircol; see Agricola
Airgialla 157, 167
Airmyn Map 28
Airthir Map 9
Aithech Tuatha 151, 450
Aki 499
alae 50

122

INDEX (CORRECTED) TO *THE AGE OF ARTHUR*

Alamanni 10, 14, 18, 41, 91, 93, 114, 256, 265, 276, 284. *52.1*
Alan of Brittany 259
— of Dol *198.3*
Alans 22, 266
Alaric 21, 22, 73*
Alba 42, 155 f., 186, 197*. *159.2* P
St Alban 335 E
'Albania'; see Albany
'Albanus' 420, 427
Albany 42, 187, 219, 420, 455
Albinus 257 E
Albion 42
Alcester Map 22
Alclud 239; see Clyde, Dumbarton P
Alcuin 331 f., 403, 503, 516. *494.2* E
Aldborough Maps 2. 22
Aldfrith 196, 303, 321, 397, 416, 423, 517. *176.2*; see Fland Fína
Aldhelm 208, 312, 327, 414 f., 421, 496, 498 f., 517. *309.2* E
Alexander 87
Alexandria 13, 345, 441
Alfred 484, 501, 503, 517
Alfriston Map 6
Alleluia Victory 62. *228.1*
Aller, Map 16
alltud 459
Almondbury 281
Almu Map 9
Alnwick *110.1*
Alps 27, 65, 159, 274 f., 394, 495, 518. *403.4*
Alsop Map 22
Alton Map 6
Alton Priors 299
altrix 357
Alvediston Map 5
Amargein 157
Amator 26, 339, 343, 349*, 512 E
Amberden Map 5
Amberland Map 5
Amberley 100. Map 5
Ambros- names 100. Map 5
Ambrosden 100. Map 5
St Ambrose 23 f., 71, 83, 182, 512 E
Ambrosius the Elder 48, 71, 73, 518 L
Ambrosius Aurelianus 37, 43, 48, 71, 72, 95 f., 116, 132, 272, 405, 430, 506 f., 513, 515, 518 L
America 42, 355, 385, 400
Amesbury 100, 256. Maps 5, 28
Amesbury Banks Map 5
amici 286
Amiens *90.3*. Maps 4, 19
Amlaut *210.3*
Amlethus 265
Ammian 12, 15 f., 23 f., 157. *50.4*
Ammon 356
Amon *90.5*
Amsbury Map 5
Anastasius 513
Ancaster Map 3
Andalusia 22

Anderida 99. *49.4*; see Pevensey
Anderetiani 49.4
Anderlecht 287
Andover 313
Andredsleag 94
Aneirin 122, 231, 237, 416 f.
Angel 42, 74, 106, 261, 270, 292, 492, 513. Map 15
Angelcyn 42, 311
Angers 91, 257
Angles 41 f., 110 f., 261 f., 271 f., 318, 270, 486. *310.3*. Map 15; see Anglo-Saxon, Engle, Saxon P
— East 41, 82, 94, 99 f., 106 f., 110 f., 218, 229, 270 f., 281 f., 287, 296 f., 301, 311, 313, 322 f., 326 f., 386, 402, 466 f., 470, 490, 493. *272.3, 283.2, 494.2*. Maps 13, 23
— Middle 41, 112, 136, 218, 270 f., 281 f., 291, 293, 298 f., 311, 313, 325 f., 398, 470. *331.2*. Maps 13, 23
— West 42, 311*
Anglesey 125, 239 f., 353, 370. *487.2* L
Anglesqueville Map 19 B
Angli; see Angles
Anglia; see Angles
— East 85, 138, 239; see East Angles
Anglian Chronicle 283*, 296
Angligena 42, 311
'Anglo-Saxons' 42*, 311*f., 420; see Archaeology, Angle, Saxon P
Angus of Munster 353, 433, 513
Angus of Alba 158
Ankara 406
Anna 356
Annals 144*, 200, 218, 222, 240, 335, 348, 406, 423, 443 A
annona 220 f.
Anstey Map 22
Anthemius 91, 513
'Anticipators' 16, 213; see *Supervenientes*
Antioch *341.2*
Antiochus *337.2*
Antonine Wall 123, 186, 215. Map *12*
Antonius; see Donatus
Antrim 154, 441
Applecross Map 26
'Appleton' 138
Appleton Map 22
Aquitaine 22, 58, 114, 266, 274, 286, 406; see Prosper
Arabia 128
Arabs 20, 514, 516
Aran 353 f. Maps 9, 27; see Enda
aratra 487, 502
Arcadius 21, 74, 512
arcani; see *areani*
Archaeology, especially 30, 32*f., 200*, 267 f., 293, 300, 335, 373, 467
'Archbishop of Ireland' 351*
Archenfeld 229, 365 f.; see Ariconium, Ercig
Ardagh Map 9
Ardcarn Map 9
Arderydd; see Arthuret P

Ardgal 168 f.
Ardmore Map 9
Ardstraw Map 27
areani 16
Arecluta *122.3*; see Alclud, Clyde, Dumbarton P
arglwyd 461, 488
Argoed Llwyfain 234 P
Argyll 157, 180, 190, 451, 545, 518
Arians 13, 25
Ariconium 365. Maps 7, 24; see Archenfeld, Ercig
Arius 13, 14
Arles 335. *12.3*; see Hilary
Armagh 151, 347 f., 399 f., 434. *147.3*, *379.3*. Maps 9, 27
Armes Prydein 417
Armorica 8, 20, 46, 80, 96, 121, 198, 228, 249 f., 274, 402, 419, 429. *146.2*, *383.2*; see Brittany, Tractus Armoricanus
Arnhem 287
Arno 360
Arreton Down Map *21*
Arrington Map 6
Arrow Map *21*
Art 155; see Cormac
Arthmael 146. *251.4* E
Arthur, especially 43, 70, 87 f., 103, 116*f., 143, 165, 168, 176, 202, 210, 272 f., 281, 292 f., 299 f., 329, 347, 367, 405, 419, 430, 455, 506f., 513, 518. *124.2*, *139.2* L
— of Demetia 170.3
Arthur's Leap, Seat 137
Arthuret 218, 232, 515 P
artifex 440
Artois Map *19* A
Artorius 95, 116
Arun 94
Arundel 98, 482. Map *22*
Arvon 216, 418. *458.3*
Ascanius *420.2*
Asclepiodotus 427
Ascelin *116.2*
Ashdon Map *6*
Ashdown Map *21*
Asheldam Map *22*
Ashendon Map *21*
Ashford Map *22*
Ashwell Maps *20*, *21*
Asser *125.1*
Asthall Map *22*
Aston Cantlow Map *21*
Atbret Iudeu *443.2*; see Giudi
Atecotti 15, 177*, 190. Map 2 P
Athanasius 13. *335.1*
Athelstan 503
Atlantic 355, 384, 388, 433; see Exploration
Atrebates 210, 218. *324.3*, *364.2*. Map 2
Attacotti; see Atecotti
Attila 74, 91
-au Map *17*
Augurius 14. *335.1* E
Augusta 15; see London
Augustine of Canterbury 389 f., 421, 496, 514. *351.1* E
— of Hippo 18, 39, 71 f., 339 f., 408 f., 512. *45.2* E
Aulne Map *14*
Aurelian(us); see Ambrosius, Paul L
Aurelius; see Caninus L
Ausonius 3 f., 9, 19, 20, 27, 430
Autun 10
Auvergne 93, 222, 407, 513
Auxerre 25, 339; see Amator, Germanus
Auxilia Palatina 60.3
Avallon 138; see Aballo
Avars 413, 437
Avitus 88, 513
Avon (Bristol) 210, 307
Avon (Warwick) 5, 284, 298, 325
Avranches Map *14*, 1
Axe 307
Axminster 307
Aylesbury 226. Maps *20*, *21* S
Aylesford 81, 513. Map *22*
Aynho Map *21*

Bacauda 8, 22, 90, 253
Badby Map *21*
Badon 37, 39, 43, 105, 111 f., 123, 126, 133 f., 140 f., 168, 210, 212, 227, 271 f., 280, 293, 299, 318, 356, 375, 513, 517, 518. *111.5* P
— second battle 230, 309
Baetán (m Ninnid) 515
Baginton Map *18*
baile 449 f.
Bainbridge; see Brough
-bald; see -botl
Baldock 442
Balkans 10, 19, 20, 278 f., 430. *190.4*
Balla Map 27
Bally- 451
Baltic 113, 265, 269, 278 f., 408
Bamburgh 183 f., 214, 231 f., 515; see Din Guayrdi
Bampton Map *22*
Banbury 227, 271, 298
Bangor-en-Belle-Isle Map *14*, 2
— -on-Dee (Iscoed) 238 f., 370. *364.2*, *432.2*. Map 24
— -on-Menai 370, 397, 514. Map 24
—, Ireland 376, 379, 381, 392, 414, 514. Map 27
— Orchard *241.3*
Banhed(os) 257, 363; see Castle Dore
Bannauc 121
Bannaventa Map *21*
Banstead Map *21* S
Banwell Map *28*
Barber's Hill *64.3*
Barbury Castle 225. Map *21*
Bardney Map *28*
Bards 226, 411 f., 422 f.
Bardsey Island Map 24
Barking 392, 517. Map *28*
Barlaston Map *22*
Barley *314.3*

INDEX (CORRECTED) TO *THE AGE OF ARTHUR*

Barnstaple 51
Barrasford Map 22
Barrectus *124.2*
Barrington Maps *6, 20* S
Barrowash Map 22
barrow burials 467
Barrow-on-Humber Map 28
'Barruc' *125.1* E
Barton, Somerset Map 28
Barton Seagrave Map *6*
basileus 330.2
Basingstoke Map 22
Bassas *111.5*
Bassett Down Map *21*
Baston Map *6*
Batavis 54
Bath 79, 112, 211, 227 f., 308, 310, 496. Maps 13, 20, *28*
Batheaston 113
Bath (House) 458
Battersea Map *5*
Battlesbury Map 22
Batz 253. Map 14.4
Bavaria 21. Map 29
Bayeux 291. Map 4
Beachey Head 94
'Beandun' (Bindon) 307. *211.2* P
Beane *314.3*; see Beneficcan
Beauly Firth 178
Beauvais *90.3*
Béc m Dé 162 E
Beckford Map *18*
'Bedcanford' 515; see Bedford
Beddington Map *3* S
Bede xiv f., 39, 40*, 176, 229, 233 f., 270 f., 296, 301 f., 310 f., 317, 321 f., 329, 337, 389 f., 397, 411, 416, 421, 427, 468, 483, 489, 499, 505. *144.2, 412.2, 432.2, 487.2* E
Bedford 60, 136, 211, 269, 293. Map *3*; see Bedcanford S
Bedfordshire 51, 470
Bedwyr 120
Beetgum *34.1*
Begerin Map 27
Bekesbourne Map *3* S
Belgae 6, 9, 73, 80. *226.2, 324.3*. Map 2
Belin f Manocan 416*, 419
Belmont Park Map *21*
Benedict Biscop 397, 413, 416, 489, 496. *382.5* E
— of Nursia 360, 365, 404 f., 513 E
Benedictine Order 405. Map 29
— Rule 397*
'Beneficcan' *314.3*; see Beane
Benli 63
Bénne Brit 155*
Benignus 155 E
Bennius 155
Benson 226. Map *20*
Benty Grange Map 22
Benwell *51.1*. Map *18*
Beoaid Map *9*
'Beorgford' (Burford) 310

Beornhaeth *195.3*
Beortric 500
Beowulf 266 f., 272, 421, 513. *261.2*
Berachus 432, 434 E
West Bergholt Map *21*
Berkshire 221, 225, 312. *125.1, 324.2, 324.3, 474.3*. Map *20*
Berlin 279. Maps 16, 17
Bermondsey *497.1* Map *28*
Bernicia 68, 77, 106, 195, 214, 217, 231 f., 300 f., 326 f., 489, 515. *300.3, 324.3, 494.2*. Map 13 P
Berroc *125.1*
Bethlehem 23
Bethune Map 19 A
Beuno 432, 434, 462*. *310.2*. Map 24 E
Beverley Maps 22, *28*
Bewcastle 234
Bicoir *116.2*
Bidford-on-Avon 284. Map *18*
Bieda 104
L. Bieler xv
Bifrons Map *6*
Bignor 482
Billingas 482
Billinghurst 482
Bindon ('Beandun') 307. *211.2, 308.3* P
Binean 465 E (Benignus)
Birdoswald 140. *51.1*. Map *18*
Birr *375.3* Map 27; see Brendan
Biscay 93, 127
Biscop; see Benedict
Bishops, especially 351, 398, 496
Bishops Cleeve Map *18*
Bishopstone, Bucks. Maps *6, 21* S
— Sussex Map *6*
— Wilts Map 22
Blaan 434 E
Blackpatch Map 22
Black Sea 113, 265
Blathmacc 435
Blavet Map 14
Bledlow Map *21*
Blenheim Palace 3
Bletchley 137
Blewburton Map *6*
Blockley Map 22
'Blood feud' *447.4*
Bluchbard 416
Bobbio 376, 402
Bochriu *120.2*. Map 7, 8
Bodmin 309, 366. Map 25
Bodmin Moor 5
Boecius 191, 411. Maps *9, 27* E
Bognor Map *20*
Bohemia 32, 108, 114, 156, 264, 274 f., 286, 292, 438 P
Boia 129 L
-bold; see -botl
East Boldon Map 22
boneddig 458
Boniface 308, 383, 402, 415*, 516. *351.1, 403.4*. Map 29; see Winfrith E

Book of Aichill *422.3, 449.4*
— Armagh 464*
— Ballymote *441.3*
— Chad see Teilo
— Durrow 384, 440
— Kells 440
— Leinster *422.3*
— Lindisfarne 440
— Llancarfan 200, 432, 439, 464*
— Llandaff 200, 208, 210, 432, 439, 464*
— Rights 432, 443
— Teilo (Chad) 432, 439, 442. *459.3*
—; see Lebor
Bookland 459
Bordeaux 3,4,9, 19,223. *12.3*; see Ausonius
Sir Bors 119
Boructuarii 270
bóruma 151. *432.1*
Boscombe Map 22
Bosham 386. Map 28
bothach 450
-botl 291, 472 f. Maps 35, 36
Boudicca 36, 99
Boulogne 287. Maps 19 A, 19 B
Bourges 91. *12.3*
Bowcombe Down Map 21
Bowes 234, 237
Bowness-on-Solway *156.3*
Boxmoor Map 22
Bradford-on-Avon 230, 308. Maps 20, 28
North Bradley Map 20
Bradwell-on-Sea 398. Maps 28, 3; see Othona
Bran 236
Brandenburg 402
Bran Ditch Map 5
Bratislava 266
Breaca 130 E
Brechin 180
Brecon 126 f., 168, 228, 366. *127.1*. Maps 7, 13
Bredon Map 28
Brefi 370. Maps 7, 24 P
Brefni Map 9
Breg(a) 355. *303.2*. Map 9
Bregion *111.5*
Brehat Map 14, 3
Bremen Map 15
Brendan of Birr 170, 174, 377 f. Map 27 E
— of Brandenburg 402
— of Clonfert 173 f., 384 f., 440, 513. *412.2, 432.2*. Map 27 E
Brest 254. Map 14
Breteuil *90.3*
Brethan 464
Brettenham Map 6
Bretteville 90*, 251. Map 4
Bretwalda 329* f. *317.1*
Brian Boru 161, 170, 329
Briccius *146.1*
Bricklehampton Map 22
Bridei m Bili 195 f.
— m Meilochon 174, 181, 183, 192 f., 206, 515 L

Bridgwater *308.2*
Bridlington 16
Brigantes 149. *192.2*. Map 2
Brighthampton Map 18
Brighton Map 22
Brigit 146, 162, 165, 169, 191, 351 f., 375, 389, 400, 411 f., 434, 513. *146.2, 158.2*. Maps 9, 27 E
Brigomaglus *51.1*
Brinklow Map 21
Brioc 356, 363. *412.2, 432.2*; see St. Brieuc E
Bristol 210, 350; see Sea Mills
Lesser Britain 251, 254, 259; see Brittany
Britan *420.2*
British 41* and passim; see Welsh
Brittany 8, 20, 117 f., 126, 130, 222, 249 f., 290, 356 f., 406, 432, 458, 497, 512, 513, 518. *146.2, 159.2, 314.3, 364.2, 433.2, 440.2*. Map 14; see Armorica, Llydaw P
Brittu 63
Britus *420.2*
Brixworth 392. Maps 6, 28 P
Broadwater *429.1*
Broadway Map 18
Brocagnus 130
Brochs 188*f., 453
Brockweir 229 P
Bro Guerech 259
Broichan *193.1*
Bronn Map 9
Brooches 32, 188 f., Map 20
Broomfield 322, 467. *323.1*. Map 22
Brough-by-Bainbridge Map 22
— -on-Humber 16. Map 2, 22
— -under-Stainmore *51.1*. Map 18
Broughton Poggs Map 18
Brown Candover Map 22
Brundall Map 3
Brundcliff Map 22
Brunhilde 402, 514
Brunswick Maps 16, 17
Brussels 287
Bruttius 63
Brutus the Trojan 420
Brychan 126 f. Map 25
Bryneich 214; see Bernicia
Brynn 244
Brytwalda 329
Buchan *61.2*
Buckingham Map 21
Buckinghamshire 136, 322, 394
Buckland Denham Map 22
— buddle Map 35
Budic f Daniel 130 f., 228, 254 f. *93.2, 96.3*
— of Cornubia 259
— *comes* 497
Builc; see Morcant
Builth Maps 13, 23
Bulgarians *190.4*
Bulmer Map 3
Burford 3, 10. Map 21
burg 488. *486.4*
Burgh Castle 392. Map 28

INDEX (CORRECTED) TO *THE AGE OF ARTHUR*

Burgh-by-Sands *156.3*
Burgus Cavi *124.2*
Burgundians 22, 38, 56, 90, 114, 265 f., 323. *90.5, 264.3*
Burpham Map 22
Burton Bassett Map 22
— Leonard Map 22
— -on-Trent Map 28
— Pidsea Map 22
Bury St. Edmunds Map 6
Bute 434
-büttl 291, 472. Map 17; see -botl
Buttsole Map 3

South Cadbury 99, 137* **P**
Cadda 313
St Cadfan 239, 370. *240.2* **E**
King Cadfan 462
Cadfan *314.2*
Cadman; see Cadfan
Cadoc 120, 122, 174, 227 f., 367, 369 f., 376, 411, 439, 464, 513. *353.2, 432.2, 440.2, 464.1.* Map 24 **E**
Cad-; see Cat-
Caedbad *211.4*
Caedmon *314**, 421, 516 **E**
Caen *116.2*. Maps 4, 19 B
caer 459; see ker-
Caer Banhed; see Banhed
— Bullauc 497
— Farchell 129. Map 7, 6
— Gai *124.2*
— Greu 233, 515
— Gybi Map 24; see Llangybi
— leon 6, 111, 125 f., 138, 156. *337.2.* Maps 2, 7
— Luitcoet 242; see Lichfield, Wall
— narfon 51, 216. *158.2.* Map 24; see Segontium
— narfonshire 125, 168, 461
— Rhun 67, 217
— sws *124.2*
— Weir (Durham) *68.1*
— went 207, 350, 366, 369, 410. Maps 2, 7, 24; see Gwent
Caesar Brittaniae 330
Caesarea 144
caeth 458*
Cai 120
Cáin Adomnán 175
Cainnech 440. *433.2.* Map 27 **E**
Cairenn 157
Cairnech Map 9 **E**
Cairpre of Coleraine Map 27 **E** (Coirpre)
— of Kerry 158
cais 221
Caistor-by-Norwich 60, 76*, 77, 298. *386.2.* Maps 2, 3 **S**
Caithness 180, 196 f. *188.2, 191.1, 195.1.* Map *11*
Calais Map 19 A
Calchvynydd 211, 232. Map 13 **P**
Caldecote Map 28
Caldey Island 357, 370, 410. Map 24

Caledo(nes) 188. *186.3* **P (Caledonii)**
Caledonia 188. *190.4*
calligraphy 440
Callraige *465.2*
Calpurnius 95. *335.2*; see Patrick
Calton Map 22
'Calvus Perennis' (Mael Suthain) *161.2*
Camberwell 315
Camber 420, 427
Cambria 215
Cambrian Annals 229 f., 233, 309 **A, G**
Cambridge(shire) 60, 82, 85, 102, 109 f., 226, 268 f., 271, 282 f., 293, 314. Maps 13, 20 **S**
Camelot 138. *137.3* **P**
Camerton Map 22
Camlann 140, 283, 513
Campbells 455
Camulodunum 138
Canao (Conan) 256 f.
Candida Casa 337; see Rosnat, Whithorn **L**
Candidus 333; see Witto
Brown Candover 313. Map 22
Preston Candover 313. Map 22
Caninus (Cynan) 203 **L**
Canmore (Bighead); see Malcolm
Canterbury 74 f., 309, 357, 383, 392 f., 414, 439. *394.5.* Maps 2, 20, 3 **P**
'Cant Guic' 250; see Quentovic, Etaples, Le Touquet
Canturguoralen 74
Cantium (Kent) 218
cantref 474
Canu Aneirin 231, 243; see *Gododdin*
— Llywarch Hen 231, 241
— Taliesin 231
Capel Marchell *127.1*
Cap Frehel Map 14, 7
Capheaton Map 22
Cappadocia 25
caput 5
Caradawc 418
Caradoc Vreichvras 210 f., 251. *226.2*
Caradog 42
Caranteus *124.2*
Carantoc 121, 123 **E**
Carantoc of Saulcy 383 **E**
Cardiff 51, 126, 168, 208, 220, 397, 431, 442, 461. Map 7
Cardigan 66, 68, 126, 204, 356, 366, 397. Map 13
Carhaix 254 f. Map 14
Carlisle 17, 68, 138, 177, 198, 214 f., 234. *68.1.* Maps 2, 10, 13, *18*, 22, 23
Carlton Scropp Map 6
Carmarthen 49, 52, 66, 126, 316, 432. Maps 2, 7, 24
Carmarthenshire 125, 207 f.
Carolingians xiv, 507. Map 29
Carpathians 264
Carthacus 432. Map 27 **E**
Carthage 409
Cashel 160. Map 9

cassatus 502
Cassington Map *3*
Cassian; see John Cassian E
Cassiodorus 3, 67, 369, 404, 410 f., 459. *432.2* E
Castern Map *22*
Great Casterton Map *6*
Castle Acre Map *3*
— Collen Map *7*
— Dore 118, 257, 361, 363. *256.3*; see Banhed
— Eden Map *18*
Caswallon 42; see Catwallaun
Cat 186
Categirn 81
Catel(l) 63, 95
'Catellius Brutus' *63.2*
Catellius; see Decianus
Cathair Mór *161.4*
Cat(h)en 215 f.
Cathmael (Cadoc) 376 E
Catlow 214
Cato of Dumnonia 121 f., 210, 251
Catraeth 237 f., 515. *234.2*; see Catterick P
Catraut 211; see Calchvynydd P
Catterick 234 f. Maps 13, *21*; see Catraeth P
cattle (white) *460.3*
Catton Map *3*
Catuvellauni 61, 211, 218. Map *2*
Catwal 313
Catwallaun Lauhir 125, 168, 204
Catwallaun m Cadfan 240 f., 302 f., 391, 427, 515
Cauci 149
Caulden Map *22*
Cauuus (Caw) 124*. *122.3* L
Cave Castle Map *22*
Cave's Inn Map *21*
Cavos; see Cauuus
Caw 121, 124; see Cauuus
Caythorpe Map *6*
Ceadwalla 309 f., 313, 324, 517. *321.3, 382.5, 487.2*
Ceawlin 226 f., 293 f., 299, 324, 515. Map *20*
Cedd 398. *399.2* E
Celestine 345. *334.3* E
céli 449
Celidon 111, 219. *110.1* P
Cellach Map *27* E
Cellan 402 E
Celtic 149, 406 f.
Cenél Crimthann 158
— Conaill etc. 160
—; see Cinél
cenedl 447, 461, 485
Cenfrith *325.1*
Cennaleth 194
Cennfaelad 422. *168.5*
Cennselach; see Uí
Centwine *324.3* G
Cenwalh 308 f., 324, 326, 515

Ceolfred 397
Ceolred 517
Ceolric 324
Ceolwulf 302
ceorl 472, 486 f.; see *cierlisc*
Cerdic of Elmet 239
— of Winchester 103 f., 113, 272, 293, 323 f., 513
Ceredig 42; see Ceretic
Ceredigiaun; see Cardigan
Ceretic of the Clyde; see Coroticus
— f Cunedda 204, 210
— Interpreter 74
Ceridwen 426
Cerpán of Tara Map *9* E
Cestersover 442. Map *3*
Cetgueli; see Kidwelly, Ystrad Tywi
Chad 314, 395 f., *394.5* E (Ceadda)
Chadlington Map *22*
Chadwick xvii
Chamavi 262
English Channel 17, 29, 35, 44 f.; see Icht
Channel Islands 257
Charlemagne xiv, 327, 329 f., 403, 516
Charles Martel 516
Charlton Kings Map *20*
Charters 328, 467*, 495 C
Chavenage Map *18*
Chelles 402
Chelmsford 322
Cheltenham Map *20*
Chemnitz 279
Chepstow 208, 458
Cherbourg 291. *80.3.* Map *4*
Cherenhul *303.3*
Cherry Hinton Map *5*
Chertsey 392, 517. *493.1.* Map *28*
Cherwell *300.3*
Cheshire 5, 221, 310, 474. *300.3, 494.2.* Map *20*
Chessell Down Map *18*
Chester 5 f., 22, 51, 67, 111, 125 f., 138, 238 f., 515. Maps 2, 13, 24
Great Chesterford 272. Map *6*
Chesterholm *51.1*
Cheviots 17, 123, 177, 198 f., 228
Chichester 94 f. Maps 2, 13, *21*
childe 474
Childebert 253, 361 f.
Childeric I 91 f., 253, 513
Chilterns 307
Chinese 437
Chinon 383
Chramn 257 f., 514
Christchurch Map *22*
Christianity, especially 12 f., 23 f., 191 f., 335 f.
Churchover; see Cestersover
Chysauster 449
Cian 154
Cian Gueinth Guaut 416
Cianachta 154 f., 160
Cianán of Duleek *440.2*. Maps 9, *27* E
Ciarraige Luachra Map *9*

INDEX (CORRECTED) TO *THE AGE OF ARTHUR*   129

Ciarán of Clonmacnoise 169, 375 f., 411, 432, 440. *433.2*. Map 27 E
— of Saigir 130, 166, 352 f. Maps *9*, 27 E
cierlisc 487; see *ceorl*
Cil- Map *7*
Cimbaed *147.3*
Cinél Gabráin 180
— Loarn 184*
— 160, 447 f., 485; see Cenél
cingulum 51
Circin 186, 188. *455.1* P
Cirencester 5, 9, 79, 211, 227, 284 f., 296, 299 f., 307. Maps 2, 13, 20, 23, *28, 22*
Cissa 94
cives; see Cymry
civitas 2, 17, 29, 69, 134, 207, 210 f., 214, 351, 366, 430, 450. *470.4*
Clackmannan 215
Clacton Map *21*
Clan MacDuff 158
Clan Morgan 158
clanna 160, 453 f., 461
Clapham, Sussex Map *22*
Clare 353
Cleethorpes Map *6*
Clemens 403
—; see Quintilius
Clermont Ferrand 90, 96, 251; see Sidonius
Clifton, Beds. Map *21* S
— -on-Dunsmore Map *21* S
Climping Map *20*
Clipston Map *21*
Clogher Maps *9*, 27
Clonard 325. Map 27; see Finnian
Clonenagh 376. Map 27; see Fintan
Clones Map 27
Clonfert 375. Map 27; see Brendan
Clonmacnoise 375, 441. Map 27; see Ciarán
Clothair I 257 f., 261, 514
Clothair II 290, 402
Clovis I 114, 127, 138, 284, 287, 365, 513. *251.3*
Clovis II 402
Clyde 1, 17 f., 36, 41, 44, 121 f., 168, 177 f., 186 f., 215 f., 220 f., 231 f., 303, 370, 387, 398, 415 f., 420, 452, 513, 515. *364.2*. Map 23; see Arecluta, Alclud, Dumbarton, Strathclyde P
Clyro *124.3*
Clytno Eidin 216
Cockenach *314.3*. Map *28*
Cockmarsh, Cookham Map *21*
Coddenham Map *6*
Coed Clwydgwyn *220.1*
Coel Hen 54, 68, 213 f. P (N. Britons)
Coelestius 339 f., 410. *65.2, 337.2, 342.3* E
'Coelestius' (Coel Hen) 213
'Coelius' (Coel Hen) 213
Coenberth *324.3* G
Coenred 517. *309.2, 382.5* E
Coenwulf 329, 492
Cogitosus 381. *351.2* E

Cogwy; see Maes Cogwy
Cohors IX Batavorum 53
— I Cornoviorum 69
cohortes 50
coiced 154
Coifi 390
coins 30 f.; see currency, money
Colchester 52, 54, 60, 76*, 100, 137 f., 211, 283. *200.2*. Maps 13, 23, *6*
Cold Eaton Map *22*
Coldingham Map *28*
Coleraine 168. *442.2*. Map 27
Colesbourne Map *28*
Coleshill Maps *20, 21* S
Collas 157
collegium 411
Collen 370 E
Colmán of the Britons 465; see Colmán of Lindisfarne E
— of Cule 375 E
— of Dromore Map 27 E
— of Hungary 402 E
— of Leinster *410.2*
— of Lindisfarne 395. *435.2*. Map 27 E
Colmán's Hymn *435.2*
Cologne 10, 20. *12.3*
coloni 430
coloniae 75.4
Colonisation 472 f.
Columba of Iona 165, 169 f., 181 f., 190 f., 199, 218, 375 f., 387, 389 f., 422, 424, 440, 465, 514, 518. *146.2*. Maps 26, 27 E
— of Terryglass 375 f., 386. *223.2, 370.3*. Map 27 E
Columban 165, 376, 379, 383, 400 f., 414, 441, 514 E
Columbus 385
comarb 465
Comberton 98, 314 f.
Combrogi; see Cymry P
Comes Brittaniarum 49*
comes 251.3, 494.2; see count
Comgall of Bangor 376, 400, 414, 514. Map 27 E
— of Dál Riada 180
commanipulares 201
compensation 447; see *faehde*
Long Compton Map *22*
Compton Verney Map *22*
Compton Wynyates 3
Conall m Néill 160, 162
— of Dál Riada 181, 515
— Cernach *161.4*
Conan; see Canao, Caninus, Cynan
Conang *116.2*
Conbran 313, 314*
Congar 350; see Docco E
Congresbury 350. *137.3*. Map *28*
Conlaed 351*f., 359, 381. Map 27 E
Conn 154 f. *149.3*
Connacht 151 f., 160 f., 168, 375, 384, 440. Maps *9*, 27
Connor Map *9*

Conomorus 55, 251, 256 f., 361 f., 514. *96.3*; see Mark
Conotigirnus *90.5*; see Kentigern E
Constans Augustus 2, 10 f., 512
Constans Caesar 22, 350. *337.2* E
Constantine I 2, 10, 12 f., 144, 335
Constantine III 21 f., 29 f., 37, 46, 48 f., 52, 63 f., 202, 350, 512, 518. *52.2*
Constantine of Dumnonia 203
Constantine Gorneu 241
Constantinople 2, 13, 21 f., 27, 91, 93, 222, 329 f., 345, 507, 516. *341.2*
Constantius I 427
Constantius II 2, 10, 13, 512
Constantius presbiter 63 f., 343 E
Conway 67, 210, 217
Cookham 102. Maps *5*, *21*
Coquet Island Map *28*
Coracles *56.2*
Corbie 402
Corbridge 304. *51.1*. Maps *2, 10, 6*
Corcc 160
Corcodemus *65.2* E
Coritani 111, 218, 284, 298. Map *2*
Cork 412, 441
Cormac m Airt 141, 155 f., 160, 166, 423
— m Cuilennáin 158. *147.3*
— Ua Liatháin 384 E
cornage 222
Cornforth Map *22*
Cornish 309, 315
Cornouailles 254. Map *14*
Cornovia *68.3* P
Cornovii 55, 63 f., 68 f., 111, 123, 125, 168, 210, 230, 238, 254, 286, 298, 308, 350, 361, 513. Maps *2, 13*
Cornwall 49, 68 f., 108, 118, 126, 130, 222 f., 254, 309, 350, 361, 408, 432, 441, 449, 506. *314.3*, *364.2*
Coroticus of the Clyde 18, 416, 513
'Corsoldus' 92, 274
Coscrach *116.2*
— *257.1*
-cote 472 f. Maps *32* f.
Cotentin 291
Cotgrave Map *6*
Cothriche 149; see Patrick
Cotswolds 3, 5, 49, 56 f., 60, 97, 139, 202, 208, 227, 284, 299 f. *300.3*
cottar 502
de Coulanges 164
Council of the Province 57, 84
count; see *comes*
Count of the Coast 5, 15 f.
— Saxon Shore 5
county; see shire
Coventry 284
Cowall 180
cowgeld 221
Cowlam Map *6*
Cow Law Map *22*
Cowslip Map *3*
cowyll 445
craftsmen 440

Cranford Map *6*
Cransley Map *21*
Cray 81
Crayford 81 f., 513
Crediton 308
Creoda 298 f., 324
Cressage Map *28*
Cretta; see Creoda
Cricklade Map *28*
Crida; see Creoda
Crimthann 17, 157 f., 160, 168, 512. *160.1*
—; see Uí Chrimthainn
Crínán *198.1*
Croghan Map *9*
Cromarty Firth 178
Crónán Map *27* E
Crossgates *51.2*; see Scarborough
Crossmoor Map *6*
Crowland 272. *314.3*. Map *28*
Croydon 109, 226. Map *3* S
Cruachu Map *9*
Cruidne 196
Cruithne 42, 149*, 154 f., 171, 186; see Picts P
Crundale Map *22*
Cuanu 420 E
Cuckhamsley Map *21*
Cuckmere 103
Cud- place names Map *20* S
Cúil Dremhne 173*f., 377, 387
Cúil Irra Map *9*
Cuillus 121*, 123
Culford Map *6*
Culhwch and Olwen 120
cumal 162, 436 f., 450, 465
Cumber 21, 98, 316. *314.2*; see Cymry
Cumberland 156, 198, 214, 219, 239, 449, 457, 474 f. *51.1*, *146.2*, *494.2*
Cumberlow 315
Cumberton 98
Cumbran; see Conbran
Cumbria 198
Cumbrogi; see Cymry
Cummén 464*
Cumméne 182 f. E (Cuimíne)
Cunedag *66.2*; see Cunedda
Cunedda 66 f., 124 f., 202, 204, 210, 218, 513. *124.2*, *158.2*
Cuneglassus 203, 416
Cunobelinus 215, 409, 416; see Kynvelyn
Cunomaglos 252
Cunorix 125; see Cynric L
Cupetianus *124.2*
Curnan 170
Currency 430, 436
Cutha 226 f., 293, 324, 515. *272.3*. Map *20*; see Cuthwine, Cuthwulf
Cuthbert of Canterbury 383 E
— of Lindisfarne 396 E
Cuthred 310. *324.3*
Cuthwine 226 f., 323. Map *20*
Cuthwulf 226 f., 293 f., 323. Map *20*
Cutteridge Map *20*

INDEX (CORRECTED) TO *THE AGE OF ARTHUR*

Cutteslowe 293. Map *20*
Cuxham Map *20*
Cwichelm 299, 307. *324.3*
Cybi; see Kebi E
cylch 221, 460
cyllid 460, 462
Cymen 94
'Cymenes-Ora' 94 P
Cymri 98, 142, 239, 419, 431, 442, 458; see *Combrogi*, Welsh P
Cynan of Edinburgh 237
— Meriadauc 250, 256 f., 411
Cynddelw 217
Cynddylan 241 f., 247 f., 417, 490
Cyndrwyn 241
Cynegils 302, 307 f., 324, 515
Cynewulf 421
Cyngar; see Congar E
Cynric 125, 225 f., 293 f., 324, 515
Cyn-; see Kyn-
cyulae; see keels

Dacia 156
Dacre Map *28*
dadenhudd 463, 499
Dadera 154
Dado; see Ouen E
dael 481
Dagaeus 376, 381, 392, 411, 440 E
Dagda 146
Dagenham Map *21*
Dagobert I 259, 402, 514 E
Daire 441
Dal Araide 171. Map *9*
Dal Cais Map *9*
Dal Fiatach 172. Map *9*
Dalmatia 53
Dal Riada 124, 168, 180 f., 192 f., 235, 451 f., 487, 513, 515, 517. *116.2*, *191.1*. Maps 9, 27; see Aedán P
Damascus 515 E
Damasus 23 f., 27, 512
Damnonii 18. Map *2*
Danes 57, 108, 258, 261, 268, 278 f., 309, 318. *276.1*, *494.2*. Map 17
Daniel Dremrud 256. *93.2*
— of Bangor 370, 514 E
— of Hare Island *374.3* E
Danube 10, 19, 49, 53 f., 148, 264 f., 276 f., 286, 405, 438, 518. *148.2*, *278.3*. Maps 16, 29
Darenth 8, 81, 109, 158
Darerca 41. Map *9* E
Darius 148
Darlington Map *21*
Darlugdach 412 E
Dart 158
Dartford 82
Dartmoor 5
Daventry Map *21*
St David 130, 146, 165, 227, 355, 367*f., 370, 376, 379, 392, 400, 432, 439, 458, 514. *208.1*, *314.1*, *3*, *440.2*. Maps 24, 25, 28 E

King David I 146
'David' (Charlemagne) 332
Deal Map *3*
Debden Map *5*
Decangi 210. Map 2 P
Deceangli 210
Decebalus 156
Decianus 17. *68.2*
Declan 352. Map *9* E
Dedications 146 f.
Dee 6, 64, 268, 370, 372
Deer Map *26*; see Book
Deganwy *210.1*
Degsastan 183, 238, 515
Deira 77, 195, 217, 233 f., 283, 298 f., 320 f., 326 f., 395, 489. *300.3*, *487.3*. Map 13; see Deur, Yorkshire, East Riding P
Déisi; see Déssi
Isle of Delight 384; see Iceland
Demetae 207. Map 2
Demetia(ns) 18, 68, 125 f., 158, 168, 203, 208, 220, 227, 340, 355, 357, 366, 397, 410 f., 513. *116.2*, *124.2*, *170.3*. Map 13
Demett 497
Denbigh *127.1*
Denmark 2, 61 f., 272, 287. *148.2*. Map 15
denn 470
Dent 214*, 314. Map 13 P
Déols 91
derbfine; see *fine*
Derbyshire 218, 288, 310. *494.2*
Dergind; see Mag Dergind P
Derguenid 158
Derry 167, 169*, 182, 377 f., 513. *374.3*. Map 27
Derventio Statio 158
Derwent 158
Desborough Map *21*
Déssi 155 f., 352. *125.3*. Map *9*
Deur 77; see Deira
Devenish 381. Map 27; see Lasrian
Devil's Dyke, Norfolk *57.2*
Devizes 299
Devon 49, 68, 105, 229, 307 f., 402, 472, 475, 480, 490. *314.3*. Maps *20*, *23*
Dewsbury Map *28*
Diarmait m Aed Slane 435
— m Cerbaill 157, 169 f., 217, 300, 377 f., 383, 513
— m Murchada 149
Dícuil, geographer 483. *392.2* E
— of Bosham 386 E
Didier 402*
Dieppe Maps 4, 19 B
Dierstorf *442.2*
Dinan Map 14, *5*
Dinas Emrys 99
Dinas Powys 220, 431, 442, 461
Din Draithou 121, 158; see Din Tradui
— Guayrdi 231; see Bamburgh
DinlleWrecon 241. *245.2*; see Wrekin

Dinn Rigg Map 9
Dinogad 417
Dinton Map 21
Din Tradui; see Din Draithou
Diocese 5
Diocletian 25
Diodorus 422.2
Dobunni 73, 218, 227, 284. Map 2
Docco 69, 350, 356, 361, 379, 405, 408, 410, 513. Maps 24, 28 E
doer 449
dofraeth 221
Dol 259, 361. *198.3*. Map 14
Dol 91; see Déols
Dolau Cothi Map 7
Domesday Book 493, 502. *430.3*
dominus 4
Domitian 151
Domnann; see Fir Domnann
Domnall Brec 183 f., 195 f.
— m Robartaig 402
Domnoc *140.3*; see Dyfnauc E
Domnonée 257 f., 361. Map 14; see Dumnonia
Donald; see Domnall, Dyfnwal
Donatives 89
Donatus; see Antonius Donatus, Dunawt
Doncaster *240.3*
Donegal 375
Dorchester, Dorset 296. Map 2
— on Thames 60, 307, 309, 439. *34.1*. Maps 28, *3* S
Dornoch 178
Dorset 97, 210, 229, 302, 307, 347. *308.2, 324.3*
Douarnenez 258. Map 14, 6
Douglas 112. *111.5*
Dover Map *3*
Dovercourt Map 21
Down 154
Downham Market *314.1*. Map 28
Downpatrick 166, 349. Map 9
Downs 225 f.
North Downs 303
South Downs 94
Drayton, Norfolk Map *3*
Dremrud; see Daniel
Dresden 265, 279. Maps 16, 17
Drest; see Drust
Driffield 77, 217, 282. Map 6
Dromore Map 27
Drostanus 257.1; see Drustanus
Droxford 271. Maps *3, 6*
Druids 176, 377, 422, 449, 456
Drum Ceat 182, 412, 452 P
Drum Lease 465
Drumleen Map 9
Drust 56, 186 f., *257.1*
Drustanus 257*; see Tristan
Drusticc 412
dryhten 485
Drysgl; see Kynvelin
Dubglas 112

Dublin 197. *303.2*
Dubricius 357 f., 365 f., 513 E
duces 220, 331, 365; see duke, *dux*
Duffield Map 21
duke *494.2*
Duleek *440.2*. Maps 9, 27
Dumbarton 180, 182, 239. Map 13; see Alclud, Clyde, Strathclyde
Dumfries 62*, 68, 215, 219
Dumnonia(n) 49, 51, 68 f., 105 f., 121 f., 138, 158, 203 f., 210, 220, 225, 229, 239, 243, 251 f., 302, 307 f., 312, 355, 364, 370, 429. *324.3*. Maps 2, 13, 23; see Damnonii, Fir Domnann
Dunadd 183
Dunawt (Dunaut) 214 f., 234 f.; see Donatus E
Dunblane Map 26
Dunblesc *433.2*
Duncan m Crínán 198*
Dúngal of Pavia 403 E
Dungarth 309
Dunkeld Map 26
Dunkirk *383.2*. Map 19 A
Dúnlang; see Uí Dúnlange
Dún Leithglaisse Map 9
Dún Nechtáin *303.2*; see Dunnichen, Nechtansmere P
Dunnichen *194.1, 303.2* P
Dunoding *214.4*; see Dent
Dunotinga regio *214.4*
duns 188 f., 453
Dunstable 8, 60 f., 79, 82, 99, 102, 112, 136, 211, 280, 442. *299.3*. Maps 13, 5 S
Dunwald 313
Dunwalinglond 313
Dunwallaun 313
Dunwich *140.3*. Map 28
Durham 69, 198, 221, 475. *68.1, 494.2*
Durotriges 73, 210. Map 2
Durrow 375. Map 27; see Book
Duston Map 6
Dux Britanniarum 5, 33, 54, 201, 213 f. *49.4*
Dwyryw 244
Dyfed 207; see Demetia
Dyfnauc; see Domnoc E
Dyfneint 69, 105; see Devon
Dyfnwal 123 f., 215 f., 220, 513. *314.2*
Dykes 434
Dyrham 6, 227 f., 515

Eadberth; see Edbert
ealdorman 486.4
Eanfrith 195
earl *494.2*; see *eorl*
East; see Angles, Anglia, Boldon, Garston, Grafton, Hendred, Ilsley, Riding, Saxons, Shefford
Eastbourne Map 21
Easter 347 f., 394 f.
East Goths; see Ostrogoths
Eastry Map *3*
Ebbesbourne Wake Map *5*

INDEX (CORRECTED) TO *THE AGE OF ARTHUR*

Ebchester Map *28*
Ebicatos 125*
Ebissa 61, 75, 213
Ebrington Map *22*
Ebroin 516
Ecclefechan 219
Ecdicius 96*f., 407
Echwyd 232 f. P
Eda Glinmaur; see Adda
Edbert 42, 498. *499.1*
Eddius 396. *324.3*
Edgar 330
Edinburgh 123, 155, 183, 197 f., 234 f., 304. *124.2, 234.3*. Maps *10, 13, 23*; see Eitin P
Ediovinchus 22
education 409 f.
Edred 330
Edward 42
Edward the Elder 501
Edwin 141, 195, 206, 238 f., 301 f., 320 f., 325, 390, 489, 514, 515. *195.2, 323.1* L
Effingham *492.1* S
-eg Map *17*
Egbert of Iona 175, 270, 400 E
— of Wessex 303*, 309, 317, 324, 331, 396, 517
— of York 489 E
-egem Map *19*
Egferth 195, 303, 517
Egginton Map *22* S
Egwin 287
Egypt 25, 50, 53, 222 f., 335, 338, 357 f., 364, 404, 410, 441. *351.1, 364.2*
Eider 265. Map *15*
Eidin; see Edinburgh, Eitin P
Eigg *192.2*
Einiaun 210
E(i)niaun *137.1*
Eitin 183 P
Eladach *464.5*
Elafius 80*
Elbe 33, 52, 62, 65, 257, 261 f., 269, 278 f., 291, 513. *32.2, 146.2*. Maps *15, 16, 29*
Eleuther(ius) (Eliffer) 54, 214, 513
Elford *303.2*
Elidyr 216
Eliffer; see Eleuther
Eligius (Eloi) 259, 402, 514 E
Elim *149.3*
Eliman 120
Elise(g) 63, 310
South Elkington Map *3*
Ellesborough Map *21*
Elmet 238 f., 493. Maps *13, 35* P
North Elmham Maps *28, 3* S
North Elmsall Map *22*
Elmswell 77. Map *6*
Eloi; see Eligius E
Elphin m Urien 236
Elphin of Warrington *370.3*
Elvan 244
Elvodug 39
Ely 157*. Map *28*

Emain 349. *147.3*. Map *9*; see Armagh, Navan
Emberden Map *5*
Emchath *193.2*
Emden Map *15*
emeriti 490
Emesa 202
Emly 352. Map *9*
Emperor 317 f.
Empingham Map *6*
Emrys 99 f.
Ems Map *15*
enclosures 438
Énda 166, 352 f., 374 f., 411, 513. *440.2*. Maps *9, 27* E
England, especially 310 f.
Engle, Englisc 41
English Channel; see Channel
Enhinti 227
Enniaun; see Einiaun
Enoch 356 f
Eochaid 157, 512. *160.1*
Eochu Etgudach *450.4*
Eogan Albanach 157
— m Gabráin 182
— m Mog 154 f.
— m Néill 160
Eoganacht(a) 144, 155, 158, 160
eorl 486 f.; see earl
eorlcund 487
Eormenric the Goth 265 f.
— of Kent 281
Eowa 302 f., 325
Episford 81; see Aylesford, Horseford
Érainn 151
Erc of Slane Map *9* E
Ercig 229, 365; see Archenfeld, Ariconium
erenach 465, 498
Erfurt 278, 403
Eric Blood-Axe *314.2*
Erlatheus 353 E
erogator 220*f.
Erp; see Drust
erw 459
Esbjerg Map *15*
Esla 294
Eslingas 110*, 226, 273, 280, 293 f. *272.3*. Map *20*
Eslington *110.1*
esne 486
Essendon *110.1*
Essex 84, 94, 110, 136, 269, 271 f., 283, 306. *94.3, 324.3, 494.2*; see East Saxons
estron 459
Ests 265
Etaples 250. Map *19* A
Etelic(iaun) 208, 355 P
Ethel-; see Aethel-
Etna 119, 137. *441.2*
Eudav Hen 418
Eugenius 352, 411. *433.2*. Map *27* E
Eusebius of Caesarea 144*
— of Vercelli 25

Evercreech Map 22
Everthorpe Map 22
Evesham Maps 21, 28
Evreux 90.3
Ewe Close 449
Ewein 206
Ewelme Map 6
exactores 460
Exeter 296, 308, 350, 366, 370, 458. *308.2, 415.3*. Maps *2, 28*
Exmoor 5
Exning Map 6
exploration; see voyages
exploratores 49.4
-ey Map *17*
Eye Map 6
Eynesbury Map 6
Eynsham 226. Map *20*

face-payment 446
faehde; see *faida*
Faelán *410.2* E
Faencha 166, 352 f., 411. Map *9* E
faida (faehde) 485. *447.4*
Fairford 284. Maps *18, 20*
fairs 430, 443
fáith 422; see *vates*
Falmouth 130 f. Map 25
family 445, 483
famine 435
Farmoutiers 402
Farndish Map *21* S
Farnham Map *21* S
Farnsfield Map *28*
Farthingdown Map 22 S
Fastidius 45, 46, 56, 84, 342 f., 356, 408, 512. *35.2* E
Faustus 84, 338*, 408, 513. *35.2, 337.2, 342.3* E
Faversham Map *3*
feast; see Tara
Féchín 424, 435. *433.2*. Map *27* E
federates 88; see *foederati*
Feering Map *3*
rí Féinnidh 156
Felmersham Map *21* S
Fens 314
Feradach *464.5*
Ferchar Foda 184, 517
Fergus of Dál Riada 124, 168, 180
'Fergus of Spain' *155.2*
Fermanagh 149
Ferns 227. *374.3*. Map 27; see Maedóc
Fernvael 42
South Ferriby Map 6
Ferring Map 6
Fetcham Map 22 S
Feth 445
Fethanlea 227 P
feud *447.4*; see compensation, *faida*
Fflamddwyn 234 f., 242
Fiacc Map *9* E
Fiachna Lurgan 235
fianna 156

Fib 186
Fife 183, 186 f., 411
filid 156, 422, 449
Filkins Map *18*
Fínán of Inis Cathaig 425
— of Lindisfarne *440.2* E
Findbarr 130 E
Findchua of Bri Goban *412.2*
fine 447, 485. *167.4, 455.3*
Fingar 130 E
Finn m Cumail 156 f., 423
Finn Folcwalding 266
Finn's Burg 266 P
Finnian 353 E
— of Clonard 169, 375, 380, 392, 411, 442, 513. *166.2, 412.2*. Map *27* E
— of Llancarfan 227, 370 E
— of Moville 172 f., 377, 412. *433.2*. Map *27* E
Finnian's Penitential 379 f.
Finstall Map *28*
Fintan Crubthir 353 E
— of Clonenagh 376. Map *27* E
— of Dunblesc *433.2* E
— of Mumu 432
Fir Domnann 151. *149.3*
Firth; see Beauly, Cromarty, Dornoch, Forth
Fitzalan 198, 259
Flaald *198.3*
Fladbury Map *28*
Fland Fína 423; see Aldfrith
Flanders 149, 286. *146.2*. Map *19*
Flannán 435. *433.2, 440.2* E
Fleam Ditch Map *5*
Fleury *249.2*; see Vitalis
Flint 442. *63.1, 462.1*
Flixborough Map 6
flooding 78
Fochriw Maps *7, 8*
foederati 286. *60.3*; see federates
Foirtchern 375, 465, 498. *65.2, 166.2*. Map *9* E
folcgemot 491, 501
folcriht 486 f., 493
-fold 470
folkland 501*
Fonaby Map 6
Ford Map 22
Fore 435. Map 27; see Féchín
Forest Gate Map 22
Forfar *303.2*
Forsbrook Map 22
Fort Augustus 180. Map *10*
Fort William 180. Map *10*
Forth 1, 17, 41 f., 62, 65, 121 f., 177 f., 183, 186 f., 192, 195, 215 f., 238, 240 f., 302, 306, 387, 452, 518. *61.2, 124.2, 188.2, 197.3*
Fortrenn 184, 186 f., 196; see Uerturiones P
Fortuatha 450
Fosse Way 60, 296, 372
fosterage 445

INDEX (CORRECTED) TO *THE AGE OF ARTHUR* 135

Fowey 118, 361, 363, 441. Map 25; see Castle Dore
Fracan 251 f., 432. *364.2*
Franks 1, 10, 14 f., 21 f., 32, 53, 90, 95 f., 114, 127, 137, 202 f., 211, 220 f., 234, 251 f., 261 f., 273, 276 f., 282 f., 306, 318 f., 329, 376, 400 f., 414, 440, 485, 496. *52.2, 276.1, 278.1, 474.3.* Map 17
Fraomar 18*. *52.1*
Freckenham Map 5
Cap Frehel Map 14, 7
'Frenessicum Mare' 61; see Forth
Freothulf 234
Freuer *245.2*
Fridaythorpe Map 21
Frigidian *433.2* E
frigman 486
Frilford Maps *3, 20*
Frisia(ns) 41, 58, 62, 92, 108, 214, 258, 261 f., 270 f., 278 f., 486, 516. *52.1, 276.1, 487.3.* Maps 15, 17 P
Frithewald *493.1*
North Frodingham *370.3,*
frythegyld 485.3
fuidir 450
Fulda Map 16
Fullofaudes 15
Fünen Map 15
Furneaux Pelham Map 22
Furnes Map 19 A
Furness 234; see Jocelyn
Fursey 400, 402, 516. *392.2* E
Fustel de Coulanges 164

Gabrán 180 f., 191 f., 513
Gadeon; see Adeon
Gael 148.,
gaerstun 470, 480
gafolgelda 315, 502, *486.4*
Gaius Campus 241; see Winwaed
Galatians 406
Galenga 149
Galewood Map 21
Galgenberg 291
Galioin 149
St Gall 402 E
Galla Placidia 22
Galley Low Map 22 S
Gallic 407 f.
'Gallic Migration' 411
Galloway 190 f., 232, 337, 345. Maps 13, *23*
Gangani 149
Ganton Wold Map *18*
East Garston Map *21*
Garth Matrun Map 7, 1
Gartnaid *180.3*
Garton Map *18*
Gateshead Map 28
gavell 463
Gavidius 13 E
gedalland 480 f.
gedes 485.3
Gelligaer 126. Map 7
Gemmán 375 E

genealogies 143 f., 201 G
geneat 486.4
Gentiles 10, 52, 273. *60.3*
Geoffrey of Monmouth 118, 259, 427
geology 5 f. Map 1
Geraint 308. *64.1*; see Gerontius
Gerald of Mayo 435 E
Geren; see Geraint, Gerontius
'Gergind' *455.1*; see Dergind P
Germanianus 68, 214 f.
'German(us) m Guill' *64.3* E
Germanus of Auxerre 44, 62 f., 72 f., 80, 339 f., 343 f., 346, 361, 512, 513. *18.2, 64.1, 228.1* E
Gerontius comes 11
— Magister Militum 22, 63
— of Dumnonia 69, 104 f., 123, 210, 251; see Geraint
gesith 480 f., 488. *476.1, 486.4*
Gewissae 226, 282, 294*, 298 f. *41.3, 324.2 f*; see West Saxons
ghestum 221.2; see *gwestva*
Gildas 35 f., 43 f., 54 f., 61 f., 68, 87 f., 116, 122 f., 132 f., 137 f., 174, 188, 200 f., 210, 217, 219, 226, 240, 247, 250, 259, 268, 286, 331, 347, 356 f., 365 f., 375 f., 385, 400, 408, 410, 414 f., 431, 458, 514. *124.2, 342.3, 368.2, 433.2* E
St.-Gildas-de-Rhuys Map 14, 9
Gildo 21
Gilling Map *28*
Gilta (Gildas) 379
Gippingas 282 f.; see Ipswich
Girton Map *3*
Giudi Urbs *302.4, 367.3*; see Iudeu, Stirling P
Glamorgan 121, 207 f., 227 f., 350, 357 f., 366, 369 f., 431; see Glevissig, Gwlad Morcant
Glasgow 123, 155, 198, 215, 239, 370. Maps 10, 26
Glasnevin Map 7, 3
Glaston Map *3*
Glastonbury 138, 158, 243, 296, 370. Map *28*
Glen *111.5*
Great Glen 178 f., 197, 452 f.
Glendalough *374.3.* Map 27
Glen Mór; see Great Glen
Glen Moreston 183
Glen Parva Map *6*
Glen Saxon *62.1*
Glevissig 208, 210, 219, 228 f., 232, 254, 259, 308, 353, 363, 366, 397, 515. Map 13; see Glamorgan
'Glivis' 208; see Glevissig
Gloucester 5 f., 97, 126, 138, 202 f., 211, 227, 230, 239, 284 f., 308, 310, 366, 497. Maps 2, 27, *13, 20, 24, 28*
Gloucestershire 6, 102, 307, 475, 496
Godmanchester Map *6*
Gododdin 105. Map 13; see Votadini, Manau Gododdin P
Gododdin 122, 231, 417; see Canu Aneirin
Goodmanham 77, 321, 390

Gospel-Books 440, 464*; see Book T
Goths 3, 19 f., 30, 56, 58, 84, 90 f., 96, 114, 127, 131, 138, 220, 234, 264 f., 286, 323, 345, 365, 369, 430, 512, 518
   Ostrogoths 19, 113 f., 262 f.
   Visigoths 19 f., 38, 58, 114, 127, 512
Gouet 252. Map 14
Goueznou *440.2* E
Gower 208, 229
Gowrie 180
Gradlon 92, 251
graf(io) 320, 490
East Grafton Map *21*
Granville Map 14, 10
Gratian 19 f., 23, 31, 512
Great; see Addington, Casterton, Chesterford, Glen, Stambridge, Tew, Tosson, Wakering
Gregorian chant 391
Gregory the Great 165, 234, 301, 389, 398, 402, 514 E
— of Tours 131, 202, 222, 228, 250 f., 291, 357, 383, 414. 514 E
Grind Low Map *22*
Groningen Map 15
Guallauc 215, 234; see Wallace
Guanach *420.2*; see Cuanu
Gudwal *432.2, 433.2*
Gueint Guaut; see Cian
Guengarth 464
Guildford *337.2* S
Guildown Map *6* S
Guiner 130* E
Guingamp Map 14, 8
Guinnion *111.5*
Gulval Map *28* E
Gundlei Map *7, 9*; see Gwynlliw
Guoloppum; see Wallop
Gurci 233. *309.2*
Guthlac 272, 314* E
'Gwawl' 212
Gwedian 361
gwely 448 f., 462, 485
Gwenael *223.2, 314.3* E
Gwendoleu 214 f.
Gwent 202, 207 f., 228 f., 254, 308, 366. Maps 13, 23
gwestva 460*. *221.2*
Gwgawn 233
Gwiawn *241.3*
Gwion Bach 426
Gwlad Morcant; see Glamorgan
Gwledic 220, 329 f. *317.1*
Gwynedd 145, 210, 216, 219 f., 238 f., 366, 397, 399, 514. Maps 13, 23; see Uenedotia P
Gwynlliauc 208, 369
Gwynlliw 120, 208; see Gundlei
gwyr nod (viri noti) 460
Gwyrangon 74 f.
gyld 485*
gymnasia 411

Hadeln 291
Hadrian 151 f.
Hadrian's Wall 17, 50*f., 54, 61, 68, 111, 123, 137, 140, 152, 213 f.
Hadugat 291 f.
Hael 246, 443
Haeloc 259
J.B.S.Haldane *253.2*
Halifax 310
-ham *470.4*
Ham Map *3*
Hambleden 8
Hambleton Moor Map *22*
Hamburg 278*, 291. Maps 15, 16
Ham Hill Map *21*
Hamlet 265; see Amlethus
Hampnett Map *18*
Hampshire 81, 90, 97, 105, 123, 210, 225, 271, 304, 312 f. *324.3, 474.3*. Map *20*
Hanbury Map *28*
Hanover 278. Maps 15, 16, 17
Hanwell Maps *3, 6*
Hardingstone Map *22*
Hardown Hill Map *22*
Hare Island *374.3*
Harnham Hill Map *18*
Harrietsham Map *22*
Harrogate 314
Harrold Map *3* S
Harrow 492
Hartington Map *22*
Hartlepool Map *28*
Haslingfield 110, 293. Maps *6, 20*; see Eslingas S
Hassocks *492.1*. Map *22*
Hastings 470
Hatfield, Yorks *240.3*
— House 3
Hatheby; see Schleswig
Hatheloe 291
Hatton Map *6*
Haute Saône 383
Le Havre Maps 4, 19 B
Hawick *124.2*
Hawkshill Map *22* S
Hawnby Map *22*
Hay-on-Wye 126 f.
Hayle Bay 130
Hazebrouck Map 19 A
heafodgemacene *485.3*
Heberden 482, 498. *487.2*
Hedsor Map *21*
Helen of the Hosts 419
Helpstone Map *6*
Hemel Hempstead Map *22*
Hemingford Grey Map *21*
Hen; see Coel, Eudav, Llywarch, Riderch
East Hendred 299
Hengest 38, 42 f., 52, 56 f., 60 f., 73 f., 88, 90, 94, 106, 108, 110, 225, 266*f., 270 f., 293, 318, 512
Henley 8
Henocus; see Enoch
Henry I 313

INDEX (CORRECTED) TO *THE AGE OF ARTHUR*

Henry of Huntingdon 427
Hepple Map 22
Heraclius 514
hereditaria proclamatio 499
Hereford 227, 234, 365. *237.2*. Map 28
Herefordshire 310
Hereward 176
Heric 238
Hermenfred 291
Herpes 286*
Hertford 496. *110.1*. Map 6
Hertfordshire 136, 314, 475. *492.1*
Heruli 262 f.
Hervé 458 E
hestha 221.2; see *gwestva*
Heworth Map *3*
Hexham 396. Map 28
Heybridge Map *6*
Lower Heyford Map *21*
Heytesbury Map *5*
Hibernensis 446
Hickling 272
hide 483, 487*
Hieronymus; see Jerome E
High Cross Map *21*
High Down Map *6*
High King 161
High Wycombe Map *21* S
Hilary of Arles 343 E
Hilary of Poitiers 14, 353, 512 E
Pope Hilary 352 f., 513
Hilda 514 E
Hinckley Map *22*
Hinton St. Mary 347
Hippo Regius 339; see Augustine
Hisperic 415
Hitchin Map *22*
hlafæta 458.3, 486.3; see 'loaf-eater'
hlaford (lord) 485
Hnaef 266. *52.1*
Hocca *320.1*
Hockley Map *21*
Hoddam 219. Map 26
Holdenby Map *6*
Holderness Map *22*
Holland 402; see Netherlands
Hollingbourne Map *6*
Holme Map 28
Holme Pierrepoint Map *6*
Holstein 264, 270
Holyhead 353; see Caer Gybi
Holywell *462.1*
Holywell Row Map *6* S
honestiores 4
Honoratus 3, 38
(H)onoratus *124.2*
Honorius Augustus 21 f., 27, 29 f., 45, 48, 100, 518 T
Pope Honorius 514 E
Honorius of Gwent 202, 207
Hornsea Map *18*
Hornton 271 Maps *6*, *20*
Hors(a) 57, 81, 225, 270, 512. *266.3*
horse collar 437

Horseford; see Aylesford, Episford
horswealh 486.4
hostages 443
-hou Map *19* B
Hough-on-the-Hill; see Loveden Hill
Housesteads *51.1, 52.1*
Howards 198
Howel Dda 446
Howel; see Hueil
Howick Map *6*
Howletts Map *3*
Hoxne Map *3*
Hueil 121; see Cuill, Howel
Huelgoat Map 14, 11
Huga 482, 498
Huish Episcopi Map *21*
Humber 60, 218, 268 f., 271, 301
humiliores 4
Hundred 436, 451, 459, 491 f., 493*; see cantref, *tricha cét*
Hungary 198, 276, 402. *291.3*
Hungerford *125.1*
Huns 19 f., 22, 24, 80, 262, 266, 270, 279; see Attila
Hunton Map *5*
Hurbuck *51.1*. Map 22
Hurdlow Map 22
Hussa 234
Hwicce 310 f., 326, 496 f. *324.4, 390.1*. Map 23
hyrst 470
Hywel; see Howel

Iardomain 188 f.; see Western Isles
Íbar 352, 375, 383, 513. Map *9* E
Icel 271*f., 280, 283 f., 298, 325, 513
Iceland 355, 384, 433. *148.2*; see Isle of Delight P
Iceni 218. *192.2*. Map 2
Icht 155; see Wight, English Channel, Muir P
Ickleton 272
Icklingas 272, 281 f., 291, 325
Icklingham 272. Map *6*
Icknield Way 57, 60, 85, 102, 268 f., 293, 306, 442, 475. *314.3*. Maps 5, 10, 31 S
Ida 145, 231 f., 320, 515
Idon 229
Idris *240.4*
Ilam; see Musden
Ilchester 294 f., 308. Map *21*
Ile Tristan 258
Illan 125, 168. *158.2*
Ille Map 14
Illington Map *3*
Illtud 121, 205, 356 f., 370, 405, 408, 410, 432, 434, 439, 451, 513. Map 24 E
East Ilsley Map *21*
Imma *487.3*
Im(m)rama 355. *423.2*; see Voyages
Imperator 161, 329; see Emperor, *imperium*
imperium 317.1, 329.1; see Imperator
-in Map *17*
India 155

Ine 308, 313 f., 324, 421, 500, 517. *303.3, 309.2, 327.1, 486.4*
-ing- 279, 468*f., 472 f. Maps 19 A, 30 f.
Ingham Map *6*
Ingleton Map *22*
Inheritance 448, 485
—, Pictish *192.2*
Inishboffin *464.5*
Inis Cathaig 130, 174. Map *9*
Inn 53
Innocent I 336
Inverness 178 f., 188, 194, 197 f. Maps 10, 26
Iona 174 f., 181 f., 186, 378, 391 f., 397, 400, 426. *487.2*. Maps 10, 26; see Columba
Ippollits Map *22*
Ipswich 108, 282 f., 298, 322. Map *23*; see Gippingas
Irchester Map *21*
Ireland, Irish, especially 142 f., 345 f., 422 f., 445 f., Maps 9, 27
Irenaeus 12
Irish colonies 16 f., 64 f., 125, 129, 158 f.; see Crimthann, Demetia, Dergind, Scots
Irish Picts *64.2*
Irish Sea 31, 147
Iseult 118
Isidore of Seville 420, 446
Isle(s); see Delight, Man, Mevanian, Promise, Western, Wight
Islip Map *6*
Istria *441.2*
Íta 385, 440, 442. *432.2* E
Long Itchington Map *18*
-itz Map *17*
Iudeu; see Atbret, Giudi, Stirling
Iudicael 259, 402 E
Iudoc 259 E
Iudual 257, 361 f.
iugum 5, 487
Iuniauus 361 E
ius perpetuum, etc. 463 f., 498
Iuthael 259
iuventus 69
Ivel Map *31*
Ixworth Map *3*

K.H. Jackson 150, 322, 407
James the Deacon 391 E
jarl; see earl
Jarrow 397, 516. Map *28*
Jerome 23 f., 137, 148, 406, 408 f. *144.2* E
Jerusalem 250, 382 f., 409, 514
'Joab' 333
Jocelyn of Furness 215. *164.2*
John the Almsgiver 441
— Cassian 338, 356 E
— of Chinon 383 E
— Chrysostom *341.2*
— o'Groats Map *10*
— Reith 92; see Riothamus
Jonah 207

Jonas 165, 361
Josse 259; see Iudoc
Mount Jove 250
Jovian 512
Julianus of Aeclanum *342.3*
— Augustus 14, 20, 23, 26, 512
Jura 338
Justin I 513
— II 514
Justina 10, 19, 28, 343
Justinian Augustus 513
— Hermit 458 E
Jutes 41, 58, 85, 108, 111, 261 f., 272 f., 281 f., 304, 318. *41.3*. Map 15 P
Jutland 261, 278, 287 S

K-; see C-
Kassanauth *210.3*
West Keal Map *3*
Kebi (Cybi) 352 f., 513. *412.2* E
keels 57*
Keidyaw 214
Kells *374.3*. Map 27
Kelvedon Map *3*
Kemble Map *18*
Kempsford Map *21*
Kempston 60, 136. Maps *3, 20* S
Kemp Town (Brighton) Map *22*
Kenchester Map *7*
Kengar (Docco) 353; see Cyngar E
Kenneth m Alpin 196 f., 517
J.F.Kenney 350. *457.2*
Kent 8, 17, 39, 60, 74 f., 95, 99, 100, 103 f., 136, 138, 218, 226, 269, 271 f., 281 f., 293 f., 299 f., 306 f., 318 f., 325 f., 347, 389 f., 421, 440 f., 466 f., 470, 474*, 482 f., 493, 515, 518. *266.3, 323.1, 392.2, 394.5, 494.2*. Maps 13, 23, *20*
Kentigern 146, 182, 215, 219, 370 f., 513, 514. *432.2*. Map 26; see Conotigirnus E
ker- 459. *364.2*; see caer
Kerbschnitt 51
Kesteven 272, 282
Kettering Maps *3, 20*
'Keys' 221
Kidwelly 66, 123, 158, 207; see Cetgueli, Ystrad Tywi
Kiel 278. Map 15
Kiev 403
Kildare 351, 375, 385 f., 399, 434. *351.2, 374.3*. Maps 9, 27
Killabban Map 27
Killala Map 27
Killaloe 435; see Flannán
Killaspugbone Map *9*
Killeevy Map 9
Killian 516 E
kilns, corn 433 f.
kin 447, 484
Kincardine 178
Kingarth Map 26
king-lists 147
Kingsey Map *21*
kingship 219

INDEX (CORRECTED) TO *THE AGE OF ARTHUR* 139

Kings Newton Map *18*
Kings Walden Maps *20*, *21*
Kingston-on-Soar Map *6*
Kingthorpe Map *18*
Kinross Map *26*
Kintyre 124, 168, 180 f., 195, 223, 441. Map *10*
Kirkby Overblow *314.2*
Kirkby Thore *219.2*
Kirkliston *124.2*
Kirton-in-Lindsey Map *3*
Kitchen End Map *31*
Knook Map *5*
Kynan; see Cynan
Kynvelin 409
— 215 f.
— Drysgl *234.3*

Labraid 128
Lackford 271. Map *3* S
læt 313, 486
laeti 10, 52, 110, 273. *313.3*; see *Gentiles*
Laigin 154, 168. *158.2*; see Leinster
Lakenheath Map *20*
Lambourn Map *21*
Lancashire 17, 50, 156, 214 f. *51.1*, *310.2*, *494.2*. Map *23*
Lancaster 214. *156.3*. Map *6*
Lanchester *51.1*. Map *21*
Lancing; see Wlencing
land 474
Land of Promise 355, 384 f.
Landerneau Map *14*, 14
Landévennec *314.3*. Map *14*, *15*; see Winwaloe
landhæbbende 486.4
Landivisiau Map *14*, *16*
Langford Map *21* S
Langobards 261 f., 276, 292; see Lombards P
Lark 271 f.
Lasrian (Mo-Laisse)
— of Devenish 169, 174, 378, 385, 434. Map *27* E
— of Leighlin *432.2*. Map *27* E
Lastingham 395 f. Map *28*; see Chad
Lathes 474, 493
Lauhir(Longhand); see Aircol, Catwallaun, Ligessauc
Launceston 309
Laval Map *14*, 13
Lavington 482
Law 442 f., 445 f., 467*
-leah 474
Leamna *455.1*
-leben 292
Lebor Gabála 147.3
Leckhampton Map *22*
Ledinghem 287
Leeds 238 f. *314.2*
Leeuwarden 266. Map *15*
Legio XX 21
Legionensis pagus; see Léon
Legionum Urbs III; see Caerleon, Chester

Le Havre Maps 4, *19* B
Leicester 111, 125, 218, 296. *386.2*. Maps 2, 28, *3*
Leicestershire 116, 136, 281, 312
Leif Erikson 385
Leighlin *432.2*. Map *27*
Leighton Buzzard *299.3* S
Loch Léin *455.1*
Leinster 148 f., 160 f., 167, 191, 227, 351 f., 375, 386, 398 f. *116.2*, *166.2*, *351.2*, *410.2*. Maps 9, 27; see Laigin
Leintwardine Map *7*
Leis des Bretons 118
Leithrig 183 P
Leitrim 464 f.
Lenham Map *22*
Lennox 215, 455*
Lens Map *19* A
Leo I Augustus 513
Pope Leo I 349 f., 513 E
lleod 487. *485.2*; see *wergild*
leode 320, 490; see *gesith*
Leominster 310
Léon 138, 250 f. Map *14*
Leonorus 357 f., 363, 432. *412.2*; see Lunaire E
Lérins 338 f. *397.1*
Lesser Britain; see Brittany
Letavia *159.2*; see Llydaw
Letha *159.2*; see Llydaw
Le Touquet 250. Map *19* A
Leudonus 215
-lev Map *17*
Leven, Yorks Map *22*
Leven 234 f.
Lewes Map *6*; see Malling, Saxonbury
Liathán; see Uí Liatháin
Liberius 146
Lichfield 230, 242, 286, 308, 396 f., 493. *303.2*. Maps 13, 28
Liddel Water 67. *124.2*
Lidlington Map *31* S
Lighthorne Map *22*
Ligessauc Lauhir 120
Lilla 32
Lilla Howe Map *22*
Lille 287. Maps *19* A, B
Limbury Map *20*
Limoges *314.1*
Limpsfield Map *21* S
Lincoln 5, 76*, 111 f., 218, 271 f., 296. Maps 2, 20, 23, 28, *3*
Lincolnshire 60, 82, 111, 113, 136, 211, 306, 394 f., 397. *15.3*, *301.3*, *492.1*; see Kesteven, Lindsey
Lindenses 112
Lindisfarne 234, 321, 440, 515. *435.2*. Map 28; see Metcaud
Lindissi 306. Map 13
Lindsey 76, 112, 211, 272, 282, 296 f., 326, 466. Map 23; see Linnuis
Lin Garan *303.2*
Loch Linnhe 184
Linnuis 112; see Lindsey
Linton Map *20*

Lir *416.3*
Lismore, Ireland Map 27
—, Scotland Map 26
Litorius 146
Little; see Oakley, Rollright, Weldon, Willbraham
Littlehampton Map 22
litus 313.3, 485.2
Llan- 253, 364, 367, 370
Llanbadarn Fawr 120, 370, 397. Map 24
Llancarfan 126, 227, 367. Map 24; see Book, Nantcarfan
Llandaff 227 f., 397. Map 24; see Book
Llanddewi Brefi; see Brefi
Llandeilo Fawr 366 f. Map 24; see Book of Teilo
Llandough 350
Llandudno *210.1*
Llandovery 126. Map 7
Llanelwy *158.2, 432.2*; see St. Asaph
Llanfor *124.2*
Llangollen 63 f., 370. Map 24
Llangybi 353; see Caer Gybi
Llanilltud Fawr 357, 367. Map 24
Llanmaes *127.1*. Map 7, 7
Llanmarchell 127*. Map 7, 7
Llanrwst *127.1*
Llansemin *127.1*. Map 7, 3
Llantwit; see Llanilltud
Llan-y-Mawddwy *124.2*
Llevelys 418
Llewellyn 19, 176
Lleyn 125, 168, 240. *158.2*
Lloegr 420
Llongborth 104 f., 116
Lludd 418
Llwyfain 234; see Argoed Llwyfain
Llwyfennydd *219.2*
Llydaw *159.2, 249.1*; see Brittany, Letavia, Letha **P**
Llywarch Hen 216, 231 f.
'loaf-eater' 486; see *hlafæta*
'loaf-keeper' 485; see *hlaford*
Loanland *501.1*
Loch; see Léin, Linnhe, Ness, Tay
Lockinge Map *21*
locus 253
Loddington Map *21*
Loegaire 64, 159, 166 f., 375, 441, 512
'Loegrius' 420, 427
Loida, Loidis *314.2*; see Leeds
Loire 90*f., 251, 274. Maps 14, 29
Lombards 174, 485 f., 514; see Langobards
Lombardy 261, 376, 383, 402
London 5, 14 f., 60, 80 f., 94 f., 100, 108 f., 112, 136 f., 206, 211, 226, 293 f., 306f., 314, 327 f., 335, 350, 390, 392, 407, 409, 418, 442 f., 475, 492, 507. *200.2, 323.1* f., *441.2, 487.3, 493.1*. Maps 2, 13, 20, 23, 28, *21* **P, S**
Londonderry; see Derry
Long; see Compton, Itchington, Wittenham
Longbridge Map *18*
Longhand; see Lauhir

lord 485*; see *hlaford*
lordship 483
Lord of the Isles 157
Lorrha; see Lothra
Lossio Veda *186.3*
Lothians 17, 67, 124, 170, 177, 183, 190, 215 f. *314.2* Maps 13, *11*
Lothra 413. Map 27; see Ruadán
Loughborough Map *18*
Lough Ree 169, 376. Map 27
Louth 352 f. Maps 9, 27; see Mocteus
Lovan 235 f.
Loveden Hill *492.1*. Map *3*
River Low 236
Low Burrow Bridge *51.1*
Lowbury Map *21*
Low Countries 1, 287
Lower Heyford Map *21*
Lowick Map *21*
Ludgate 427
Ludlow 310
North Luffenham Map *3*
Lug 148
Lugaid 167, 435, 513
Lugdunensis III 250
Lugid *432.2* **E**
luidt 461
Luitcoet; see Caer Luitcoet, Lichfield, Wall **P**
Lullingstone 347
Lunaire; see Leonorus
St Lunaire Map 14, *12*
Lupicinus *338.3*
Lupus 63, 343, 346 f. **E**
Lurgan; see Fiachna
Lusk Map 9
Luton 60, 211, 269. Maps 13, *3, 20* **S**
Luxeuil 376. *440.2*
Lyme Regis 5
Lyminge *392.2* Map *6*
Lympne Map *6*
Lyneham Map *6*
Lyon 10, 496, 501. *12.3*
Lyonesse 137; see Léon

Maban 313
Mac Airt 118; see Cormac
Macbeth 198, 455
Mac Caille Map *9* **E**
Mac Cáirthinn Map *9* **E**
Mac Críche 353 **E**
Mac Cuilín Map *9* **E**
Mac Duff 455
Macedonia 430
Mac Erca (Muirchetach) 124, 167 f., 172 f., 176, 513
MacFirbis 423
Macha 434; see Armagh
Macliavus 250, 256 f.
Macliauus; see Malo **E**
Eoin MacNeill 457
MacNissi Aengus Maps *9, 27* **E**
Madehurst 482
Maeatae; see Meatae

INDEX (CORRECTED) TO *THE AGE OF ARTHUR* 141

Maedóc of Ferns (Aedán) 227, 398, 514. *351.2, 432.2* E
mægas 485
-maegl 409
Maegia 104; see Maglos
Mael (Mel) 372, 469. *351.1*. Map *9* E
Maeldubh 386; see Malmesbury E
Maelgwn 42 f., 66, 141, 145, 168, 192, 203 f., 216, 219 f., 228, 231 f., 250, 329 f., 365, 367, 370, 415 f., 443, 513, 518. *210.1, 410.2* L
Mael Odur *464.5*
Mael Suthain; see Calvus Perennis
Mael Uma 238
maenol 459, 462; see *mainaur*
Maes Cogwy (Maeserfelth) 241 f.; see Oswestry P
Maeserfelth; see Maes Cogwy
Maes Garmon *63.1*
Magdeburg Map 16
Mag Dergind 158. *455.1* P
Magiovinium 137 P
Magister Militum 5, 56, 121
Maglos 104, 252, 409; see Mael E
Magnentius 10 f., 19 f., 512
Magonsæte 310
Mag Roth 183 P
Maiden Castle Map 22
Maidenhead 324
Maidstone Map 22
mainaur 459; see *maenol*
Maine *455.1*; see Uí Maine
Mainz 10, 402, 516
Malcolm II 198
Malcolm III Canmore 198 f.
Malling Map 6
Malmesbury 386. *309.2*. Map *28*; see Aldhelm, Maeldubh, William
Malo 259, 384 f., 411, 434, 459. *412.2* E
St Malo Map 14, 17
Malory 118 f.
Malton 16, 213
Malvinus 313
Mamertinus 53
Isle of Man 239 f., 349. *191.1, 487.2*; see Mevania
Manann 194; see Manau, Mevania, Mynaw
Manannán *416.3*
Manapii 149
Manau Gododdin 17, 66 f., 195, 215; see Gododdin P
Manawydan 416.3
Manchester 137. *51.1*, Map *6*
manentes 502
Manocan 416
Mansuetus *90.5* E
manor *459.3*
Marcella *127.1*
Marcellinus (Dalmatia) 88. *53.1*
Marcellinus comes 28
Marcellus 126 f. *127.1*; see Marchell
Marchell 256. *127.1*. Map *7*
Marcianus 208

Marcianus Augustus 240, 513
Marcomanni *18.2*
Marculf 383
Marcus 257; see Mark Conomorus
Queen Margaret 198
Marianus 204, 210
Marianus Scottus 402 E
Mark 55, 118, 137, 257 f., 363, 366; see Conomorus
Market Harborough Map *21*
Market Overton Map *20*
Market Weighton 77, 217, 282
Markshall Map *3* S
Marlow 102
Maro; see Virgilius Maro
Maroboduus 158
Marseille 343. *397.1*
Marske Map *18*
Marston St. Lawrence Maps *6, 20*
Martin of Tours 23, 26*f., 146, 165, 191, 335 f., 356, 372 f., 405 f., 410, 419, 512 E
Martin Vicarius 11
Maserfelth; see Maes Cogwy
Masuna 132
Matière de Bretagne 118
Matching Map *5*
Maucennus 357. *410.2* E
Maudetus 432. *412.2* E
Maun 55
Mauri *52.1*
Maurice 514
Maxen Wledic 418 f.; see Maximus
Maxentius 130 f., 256
Magnus Maximus 20, 26 f., 30, 37, 63, 90, 141, 250, 419, 512
Mayo 435. Map *27*
'Mearc Redes Burna' 94
Mearns *455.1*
Meatae 188; see Circin, Maeatae, Miathi P
Meath 151, 155, 160 f., 167 f., 355, 375, 441. *303.2*. Maps *9, 27*
Meaux *90.5*. Map *4*
Mecklenberg 265, 269, 279
Medbourne Map *21*
Medmerry Map *22*
Medraut 140*, 283
Medway 82, 109, 226, 273, 306
St.-Méen Map *14, 19*
Meicen *240.3*; see Welshpool
Meidrim Map *7, 4*
Meifod Map *24*
Meilochon; see Maelgwn
Mel; see Mael E
Meliau 250, 256 f.
meliores 368
Melor 250, 256 f.
Melrose Map *28*
Melverley 243
Menai 216; see Bangor
Menevia (St. David's) *367.3*
Meonwara *474.3*
Merchiaun; see Marcianus

Mercia 42, 76, 184, 229 f., 240 f., 272, 283, 291, 296 f., 303, 306 f., 325 f., 475. *272.3, 283.2, 487.2, 494.2*
Mercians 195, 229 f., 240 f., 265 f., 270, 391 f., 421, 466 f., 518. *300.3, 303.3, 307.3, 309.2, 310.2, 323.1 f.* Map 23
Meriadauc; see Cynan
Merioneth 66 f., 124, 141, 204, 240. *214.4.* Map 13
Merlin; see Myrddin
Merovingians 3, 258, 400 f., 507
Mersey 314
Merthyr- *337.2*
Merthyr Tydfil 126
Mesioc 464
Mesopotamia 15
Metcaud, Metgoit; see Lindisfarne P
Methrum *127.1.* Map 7,4; see Meidrim
Metz *12.3*
Meuric; see Mouric
Meuse 402
Mevanian Islands 240; see Anglesey, Man, Manann P
Meven 259 E
Miathi; see Meatae P
Micheldever 3, 13. Map 6
Michomerus *65.2* E
Middle Angles; see Angles
— Saxons; see Middlesex, Saxons
Middlesex 94, 136, 307, 475. *323.1, 493.1, 494.2*
migrations 261
Mil 148
Milan 24
Mildenhall Map *21*
mills 433, 439
Milton, Northants Map 6
—, Kent Map 3
— Abbas Maps *22, 28*
Minden *442.2*
Minety Map *18*
minister 324.4
'Minocynus' *416.3*
Minster Lovell Map *21*
Mitcham 109, 226. Maps *3, 20* S
Mobhí Cláraineach *169.4* E
Mo-Choe Maps *9, 27* E
Mo-Choemóg 440. *433.2* E
Mo-Chua Map *27* E
Mocteus 352, 374, 411. *351.1, 432.2* Maps *9, 27* E
Mocu- names 161
modius 459 f.
Moel Fenlli 64 P
Moel-y-Geraint 64 P
Moggerhanger Map *21* S
Mog Nuadat 154
Mo-Laisse; see Lasrian
Mold *63.1*
Moling *433.2* E
Molt; see Ailill
Monaghan 149
Monasterboice Maps 9, 27
monastic numbers *432.2*

money 443
Mongfind 157. *160.1*
Mongols 403
'Moni Iudeorum' *367.3*; see David, Giudi
monks, especially 24 f., 335 f., 518. Maps 24–29
Monmouthshire 207, 229. *190.4*
Mons; see Mount
Mont St.-Michel Map 14, 18
Montagnes Noires Map 14
Montalembert 338
Monte Cassino 361, 365
Montgomery; see Powys
Montmartre 287
Montreuil *314.3.* Map *4*
Monts d'Arrée Map 14
Moors 3, 133
Morava Map 16
Moravia Map *29*; see Bohemia
Moray 454
Morcant Bu(i)lc 215 f., 513
— Hen 208, 230
— m Athruis 229 f., 309, 517
— m Coledauc 234 f.
Gwlad Morcant; see Glamorgan
Mordaf 216
Moresby Map *22*
Moreton-in-the-Marsh Map *28*
Morfael 243, 308
Morgan of Moray 454
Morgan; see Morcant
Mori Marusa 408
Morken; see Morcant Bulc
Morlaix 254. Map 14
mormaers 197
Moselle 406
South Moulescombe Map *22*
Mount Badon; see Badon
Mount Jove 250
Mouric 228 f., 232, 259, 515
Moville Map *27*; see Finnian
Moyarney Map *9*
-moydir Map *7*
Mucking Map *3*
mug 452
Mugny 375
Muinmon 148
Muirbolc Map *9*
Muirchetach; see Mac Erca
Muirchú 161, 175, 358, 441 E, T
Muiredach, Connacht 157, 512
— Leinster 375
— (Marianus) 402
Muir nIcht 155; see English Channel
Mul 31
Munster 126, 151 f., 167, 352, 367, 375, 433, 455, 513. Maps 9, 27
Mureston 183
Mursa 10, 14
Musden Map *22*
Mynaw; see Manaw, Menevia
Mynydawc 237
Myrddin 219
Myrgingas 261. Map *15* P

INDEX (CORRECTED) TO *THE AGE OF ARTHUR*

Nadottus 130
Nafferton Map *21*
Namur *383*.2. Map 4
Nantcarfan 369; see Llancarfan
Nantes 255 f., 274, 441. *314.1*. Map 14
Napton-on-the-Hill Map *21*
Naseby Map *21*
Nassington Maps *3, 20*
Natalis 411 E
Nath-Í 44, 65, 159, 166, 168, 512
Navan 151. *147.3, 157.3*; see Emain
St.-Nazaire Map 14, 20
Nechtansmere 186. *303.2*
Nectan Morbet 191 f.
Nectaridus 15
Néill; see Niall, Uí Néill
Neisse Map 16
nemed 499
Nemidh 154
Nendrum Maps 9, 27
Nennius 37, 49, 63, 200, 231, 234, 271, 399, 416, 520. *147.3, 408.3* E
Loch Ness 193
Netherby 218, 234
Netherlands 262 f., Map 15; see Holland
Newark 370. Map *3*
Newbold-on-Stour Map *28*
North Newbold Map *22*
Newbottle Maps *35, 36*
Newcastle-upon-Tyne 67, 69
Newcastleton *124.2*
Newfoundland 385
Newham Map *21*
Newhaven House Map *22*
Newmarket 85
Newnham Map *21*
Newport 208
Newport Pagnell Map *21*
Newton-le-Willows Map *6*
Niall 44, 157 f., 160, 167 f., 174, 511. *161.2*
Nicaea 13
Nile 53
Ninian 146*, 191, 337 f., 345, 411. Map 26 E
Nithard *415.3*
Nodens 148, 154; see Nuada
No Man's Land 482
Nordmanni (Danes) *276.1*
Nominoe 249
Nonn(ita) *314.1*; see David, Nun E
Norfolk 3, 57, 60 f., 85, 103, 108, 136 f., 198, 268, 271 f., 282 f., 287, 298, 312, 314, 370. *494.2*
Noricum 53, 78, 437; see Severinus
Norman Conquest 19, 42
Norman Romances 100, 116 f., 137, 177
Normandy 103, 250 f., 290 f. *90.5, 116.2, 146.2, 383.2*. Map 19
Normans 6, 198, 313, 315, 332, 398, 499 f., 503. *190.4*
'Norrey' *323.1*
Norse 193, 197 f., 309, 315, 321, 332, 385, 403, 489. *68.1, 146.2*; see Scandinavians

North; see Bradley, Downs, Elmham, Elmsall, Frodingham, Leigh, Luffenham, Newbold, Riding, Runcton
Northampton 211, 271, 392. Map *21*
Northamptonshire 106, 136, 286
Northfleet Map *6*
North Leigh 73. Map *22*
Northmen 258, 291, 421; see Danes, Nordmanni, Normans, Norse
Northolt Map *21*
North Sea 106
Northumberland 61, 221, 231 f. *17.3, 51.1*
Northumbria(ns) 41, 76, 141, 143, 145, 177, 184, 195 f., 206, 217, 231 f., 270, 291, 302 f., 311, 314, 317, 320 f., 326 f., 390 f., 461 f., 475, 489, 499 f., 517, 518. *310.2, 323.1, 440.2, 494.2*. Map 23
Norton (Daventry) Map *21*
Norton Disney *15.3*
Norway 283
Norwegians 385
Norwich 270, 272, 298. *314.3*. Maps 23, *3, 28*
Notitia Dignitatum 49 T
Nottingham 272. Map *22* S
Nottinghamshire 111, 281. *15.3*
Nouantae Map 2
Nuada Silverhand 148
Nubians 3
Nud 216 G
Nun Map *25*; see Nonn
Nunechi-a, -ius *314.1*
Nunna 314, 482, 498. *487.2*
Nuremberg, Nürnberg 403. Maps 16, 17
Nursia; see Benedict
Nursling *415.3*
Nuthamstead *314.3*. Map *28*
Nyni(g)a 337. *314.1*; see Ninian

Little Oakley Map *3* S
Oakley Down Map *22* S
oba 497
Obroditi *276.1*
Occaney Beck Map *22*
Ocha 167
Ocklynge Map *21*
Octha 61, 68, 75, 213, 271
Oddington Map *22*
Oder 274. Map 16
Odet Map 14
Odovacer 27 f., 91 f., 108, 131, 256, 274, 292, 506, 513 L
Odsey Map *20*
Odysseus *335.2*
Oesc 106, 113, 272, 318
Oescingas 272, 281, 318
Offa of Angel 265, 272, 282, 326
— of Essex *382.5* E
— of Mercia 303, 310, 317, 321, 331, 334, 398, 503, 512, 517. *494.2*
Offaly Map 9
ogams 191*. 422*, *57.2*
Ogma 148
Old; see Carlisle, Penrith, Sarum, Saxons, Yeavering

'Old King Cole' 54, 118
Olympiodorus *44.1*
Ombersley Map *5*
Omer 402 E
Ordovices 210. Map *2*
Oriel 157
Orkneys 61, 180 f., 188*f., 193 f. *195.1.* Map *10*
Orléans 91 f.
Orosius 410
Orpington Map *3*
Orwell 109. Map *20*
Osismii 363
Osney Map *3*
Osric, Hwicce 496 f. *324.4*
—, Northumbria *195.2*
Ossory 182, 352. Map *9*
Ostrogoths; see Goths
Oswald, Hwicce 497. *324.4*
—, Northumbria 184, 195, 302 f., 320 f., 329, 391, 515. *302.4, 421.5*
Oswestry 198, 241; see Maes Cogwy
Oswini 240 f.
Oswy 184, 195, 241 f., 302 f., 308, 317, 320 f., 326, 394, 443, 489, 515, 517
Othona 398; see Bradwell
Ouen (Dado) 259, 402 E
Oughteragh 464
Great Ouse 52, 268, 272. Map *31*
Sussex Ouse 103, 281
(O)utigirn 232
Oviliava (Wels) *437.4*
Oving Map *21*
-ow Map *17*
Owain 234 f., 443, 515
Oxford 112, 226, 268 f., 273, 293 f. *303.3, 474.3.* Maps *20, 6* S 206
Oxfordshire 136, 298. Map *20*
Oxton Map *22*

Pabo 214 f. *116.2, 234.3*
Pachomius *364.2*
Padstow 130, 361 f., 366, 441. Map *25* P
pagenses; see Powys
Pagham Map *22*
pagi 2
Painsthorpe Wold Map *22*
Palladius 64, 66, 345 f. E
Pannonia *18.2*
Paris 290, 318, 357, 361 f., 370, 402, 411. *12.3, 49.4.* Maps *4, 19* B
Parisii Map *2*
Park Street *15.3*
Parrett 296, 308 f.
Partholon 148
Partition 136 f., 513. Map *8*
Partney Map *28*
Pascent 236
Passau 53
'passive' princes 216, 233
Patching Map *22*
Paternus Pesrut 17, 19, 66
Paternus of Llanbadarn 120, 370. *432.2* E
patres 286

patricii, patricians 324, 327
Patrick 18, 26, 44, 55, 64 f., 95, 127, 146, 159 f., 164 f., 175, 188, 191, 193, 215, 337 f., 345 f., 361, 374 f., 399 f., 408, 411, 441, 513. *35.2, 228.1, 335.2, 367.3, 422.3.* Maps *9, 27* E
St Paul 146, 193
Paul Aurelian 252 f., 357, 363, 410, 432 f., 458. *353.3, 412.2, 432.2* E
Count Paul 91
Paul the Secretary 11, 512
Paulinus of Nola 410
— 'of Pella' *430.3*
— of Penychen 320, 399 f.; see Poulentus
— of Pumpsaint 367 f., 408, 410 f.
— of York 390 E
Pavia 403
Peada 241 f.
Peak District *300.3, 307.3.* Map *13*
Peebles 215, 219, 235
Pegsdon Map *21* E
Pehtland 195; see Pentland
Pelagianism 62, 71 f., 370, 394
Pelagius, monk 71 f., 338 f., 405, 408 f., 512 E
Pope Pelagius I 172, 514
— II 514
Pembroke 49
Pembrokeshire 125, 207, 441 f.; see Demetia
Penda 184, 240 f., 302 f., 308, 320, 325 f., 427, 443, 508, 515, 518. *303.3, 337.2, 342.3*
Pengwern 241; see Shrewsbury
Pointe de Penmarc Map *14, 24*
penncenedl 440, 461
Pennines 5, 6, 50, 52, 54, 96, 111, 197, 206, 213 f., 235 f., 298 f., 304 f., 314, 429, 475. *116.2, 494.2.* Map *20*
Penrith *219.2*
Old Penrith *156.3*
Penselwood 308; see Peonna P
Pensthorpe Map *3*
Pentland Firth *191.1*
Pentland Hills 177, 195
Penychen 208 P
Pen-y-Darren Map *7*
Penzance Map *25*
Peonna 308; see Penselwood P
Pepin I 514
— II, III 516
Perceval 118; see Peredur
Peredur 54, 118, 214, 219, 233, 515. *309.2*
Permin Map *29*
Péronne 402
Perran 355; see Ciarán E
Pershore 496. Map *28*
Persians 3, 265
Perth 178, 183. Map *10*
St Peter 146, 165
Peter of Demetia *116.2, 170.3*
Peterborough 3, 14. Maps *3, 28*

Petersfinger Map *18*
Villa Petri 252
Petroc 361, 366. Map 25 E
Pevensey 94. *49.4*. Map *20*
'Philibert' 253. *363.3*; see Childebert
Philemon *408.3*
Philo 4
Phocas 514
Phoenician language 406
Picardy 290, 402. *314.3*, Map 19 A
Picts 1, 15 f., 20 f., 39, 42 f., 54 f., 60 f., 71 f., 124, 142 f., 168, 174, 177 f., 186 f., 216, 302 f., 337, 396 f., 412, 426, 438, 455, 506, 515, 517, 518. *157.3*, *188.2*, *195.1*, *364.2*, *422.3*. Maps 2, 11, 12, 23 P
Pictland 306
'Irish Picts' *64.2*
'Pillar of Britain' 214, 234; see Kynvelyn Drysgl, Pabo, Post Prydein, Urien
Pir(r)an; see Perran E
Piro 357 f., 410
Pitney Map *21*
Pitsford Map *6*
Place-Names, English 468 f.
— Welsh; see Caer, Llan, Pleu-, Tre-
Placidia; see Galla Placidia
Plague 91, 142, 145, 169, 222 f., 435, 513, 517, 518
'plebeian kings' 240
Plettke 32*
Pleu-, Plou- 253, 364*, 459
Ploermel Map 14, 23
Plou Dalmazeau 250, 252. *364.2*. Map 14, 22
Ploueneur Menez 258
Plou Fragan 252. *364.2*
plwyf 459
Plymouth 51. Map 25
Pointe; see Penmarc, Raz
Poitiers 14, 26, 383, 514, 516; see Hilary
Poland 265, 279, 402
Pomerania 108, 265, 274 f.
Pompeius 8, 208
Pompeius Regalis 251; see Riwal
Pontefract Map *22*
Pontifex Maximus 24
Pontivy Map 14, 25
Poole 296
Pope 23; see Celestine, Damasus, Gregory, Hilary, Honorius, Innocent, Leo, Pelagius, Sixtus
population *430.3*
'Port' 104
Portchester 104 f. *49.4*. Maps 3, 6
Porthmawr 126 f., 441. *127.1*. Map 7, 5; see Whitesands Bay P
Portland 296
Portskewett *208.3*
Portsmouth 60, 104, 111, 210, 271, 513
Posbury, Posentesburh 308 f.
Posidonius *422.2*
Post Prydein 234; see Pabo, Pillar, Urien
Poulentus 121; see Paulinus
Powys 63 f., 69, 124, 210 f., 228, 232, 241 f., 310, 366, 370, 397. Maps 13, 23

Praefectus Gentium 18
— *Praetorio* 5, 19, 24
— *Urbi* 24
Praepositi 434
Praetextatus 24
Prague 265, 279. Maps 16, 17
Preshaw Map *22*
Preshute Map *21*
Preston Candover Map *22*
Priestholm 240
Prince 327
Prince of Wales 19
priodaur 450, 461
Pritani 149
Prittlewell Map *22*
Procopius 272, 279, 281, 287, 291
procurator 64. *491.4*
Land of Promise 355, 384 f.
Prosper 62, 72, 345 f.
Protector 18, 125, 127
Provence 12. *12.3*
provincia 493.1
Provincial Governors 5, 18, 133; see *rectores*
Ptolemy 149, 159
'Pubeus' 353 f; see Kebi
Puddlehill (Dunstable) Map *5* S
Puffin Island 240
Pumpsaint 368
Purton Map *21*
Pyd 242
Pyran 355; see Perran
Pyrenees 22, 114, 127
Pyro; see Piro

Quadi 265
Queen Camel Map *21*
Quentovic 250
Quiberon Map 14, 26
Quimper 91, 130 f., 228, 254 f. Map 14
Quimperlé Map 14, 27
Quintilian 9, 410
Quintilius Clemens 17 f.
Quonomorius 363; see Conomorus

Radegund 383, 404, 514 E
Radiger 287 f.
Raeti Gaesati *17.3*
Rafferty; see Domnall m Robartaig
Ragley Park Map *21*
Rahan Map 27
Rainham Map *21*
Ramsey Island 458
Rance Map 14
Rapes 475, 493
Raphoe Map 27
rath 436*. *431.3*, *433.2*. Map 7
Rathmor Map 9
Ravenna 22, 141, 394
Ravensford, Ravensworth *476.1*
Pointe du Raz Map 14, 29
reachtaire 157; see *rectores*
Reading Map *3* S
rectores 18, 132 f.

Reculver 266.3. Map 20
Redbourn 492.1. Map 22
Redon Map 14, 28
Redwald 239, 301, 322 f., 329. 493.1
Lough Ree 169, 376. Map 27
reeves 491*
Referendarius 320
Regalis; see Riwal
Reged 105, 214 f., 228, 232 f., 284, 515. Map 13; see Urien P
Regensburg 402 f. Maps 16, 17
reges, especially 201, 324
regnator 329.2
Regnenses 324.3
Regula; see Reith, Riothamus
Reith; see Riothamus
Reims 12.3
Rendlesham 283
Rennes 251 f. Map 14
Repton Map 28
Rhaetia 21; see Raeti
Rhenen 287
Rhine 3, 10, 16 f., 148, 264 f., 287, 405, 518. 12.3, 49.4, 291.2, 474.3. Maps 29, 4
Rhineland 10, 12, 14
Rhiwallon of Dol 198.3
Rhodri Mawr 517
Rhône Map 29
Rhun m Maelgwn 192, 206, 216 f., 240, 515
Rhun m Neithon 235
Ribble 314. 494.2
Ribchester 214. 51.1. Maps 2, 6
Ricemarchus 368.2
Richborough 15, 81, 83, 430, 513. 49.4, 442.2
Richmond 137. Map 22
Ricimer 88
Riderch 182, 216, 220, 234, 515
Riding (East, North, West); see Yorkshire
Riez; see Faustus
rígdomna 455.3
Rigohene 124.2
Rimini 13 f., 24, 512. 335.1
Rioc 412 E
Riothamus 90 ff., 251, 256 f.
Ripon 395. Maps 28, 22
Risely Map 3
Risingham 17.3
Rithergabail (Horseford) 81; see Aylesford, Episford
Rivalen 257.1
Riwal 251 f.
roads 442
Robert Stewart 199
Robin Hood's Bay Map 22
Roche Court Down Map 5
Rochester 307. 17.3. Map 28
Rodmead Down Map 22
Little Rollright Map 22
'Romania' 36 f.
Romanus 338.3 E
Roscoff 253
Roscrea Map 27

Rosnat 337, 352; see Whithorn P
Rothere 431.3
Rothley Temple Map 18
Rothwell Map 6
Rouen 26. 12.3, 90.5, 383.2. Maps 4, 19 B; see Victricius
Roundaway Down Map 22
Roxburgh 124.3
Royden Map 5
Royston 110, 441. 314.3. Map 6
Ruadán 170 f., 413, 442. 432.2. Map 27 E
Rudstone Map 6
Rugii 262 f., 270
North Runcton Map 6
Ruoihm 57; see Thanet
Rushford Map 6
Ruthin 64
Ruthwell 421.4

Saale Map 16
Saesneg 41
Saffron Walden Maps 22, 28
Saigir 130, 166. Maps 9, 27 (Seirkieran)
St Albans 265, 337, 344, 372, 397, 512. 15.3. Maps 2, 28; see Verulamium
— Andrews Map 26
— Asaph 397. 146.2, 432.2; see Llan Elwy
— Brieuc 251 f. 364.2. Map 14; see Brioc
— David's 126, 366, 397, 441, 458. Map 24; see Menevia
— Germain-des-Prés 249.2
— Germans Map 25
— Gildas-de-Rhuys Map 14, 9
— Ives 130
— John's, Cambridge Map 3
— Kew 350, 361. Map 25; see Docco, Iuniauus
— Lunaire Map 14, 12; see Leonorus
— Malo Map 14, 17
— Martha's 337.2
— Méen Map 14, 19; see Meven
— Nazaire Map 14, 20
— Omer Map 19 A
— Pancras, Chichester 94
— Pol (Dunkirk) 383.2
— Pol-de-Léon 253, 363. 383.2. Map 14
Saints' Island Map 27
Saints' Lives, especially 146, 164*f., 201, 223, 249 f., 347, 357, 363, 367, 403, 424, 439, 443
Salisbury 106, 225, 230, 286, 293 f., 308, 515. 226.2. Maps 13, 20
Salisbury Plain 97
Salmonsbury Map 22
Salomon 249
Saltburn Map 18
Saltford Map 22
Salvianus of Caer Gai 124.2
— of Marseille 343
Salzburg 402. Map 29; see Virgilius
Samson 383.2
Samson 146, 165, 249 f., 356 f., 370, 375, 410, 440, 458, 513. 432.2. Map 28 E
Samuel 214

INDEX (CORRECTED) TO *THE AGE OF ARTHUR*

Sancton 77, 390. Maps *3, 6*
Sandy 60, 109. Map *3* S
Sarmatians 52, 110, 265; see *laeti*
Sarre Map *3*
Old Sarum Map *5*
Sasanach 41
Saul 166. Map *9*
Saulcy 383
Savoy 137
Saxby Map *6*
Saxonbury Map *6*
Saxon Chronicle, especially 145, 233, 273, 468 A
Saxonia 41
Saxon Revolts, especially 43, 51, 53
— Raids on Ireland 65, 93
Saxons 1, 10, 16 f., 21 f., 37 f., 52, 56 f., 61, 65, 75 f., 223 f., 256 f., 272 f., 293 f., 311, 318, 512, 513, 518. Map 15; see Angles, 'Anglo-Saxons', English, etc. P
— East 307, 313, 322, 392, 398, 466 f., 490, 493. *311.2, 323.1, 324.3, 493.1.* Map 23; see Essex
— Middle *311.2*; see Middlesex
— Old 270, 291 f., 318, 437, 482, 486, 494. *324.3*
— South 100, 296, 309, 386, 466 f., 493. Maps 13, 23; see Sussex
— West 41*f., 103 f., 113, 296, 302, 307, 315, 323 f., 386, 392, 412, 421, 493, 498, 515, 517, 518. *300.3, 309.2, 311.2, 390.1.* Map 23; see Gewissae, Wessex
— of Bayeux 291
— of Egwin 287
— of the Loire 91 f., 274
Saxon Shore 5, 36, 49*, 52
Saxony 41, 261, 291 f.
Scandinavia(ns) 6, 33*, 41, 106, 148, 175, 197, 230, 241 f., 264, 291 f., 303, 318, 325, 332, 402, 484 f., 503, 517, 518. *190.4, 430.3, 494.2.* Map *4*; see Danes, Norse
Scarborough 5, 51; see Crossgates
Scattery Island Map *9* (Inis Cathaig)
Schleswig 106, 261, 265, 282. Maps 15, 16; see Hatheby
Schools 409 f.
Schottenklöster 403
Scotland, especially 17, 41 f., 62, 121, 124 f., 177*f., 198, 219, 259, 387, 441, 504 P
Scots xiii, 1, 42*, 64, 180 f., 190, 197, 218 f., 302, 398, 454, 483, 517, 518. *56.2, 161.2, 441.2*; see Irish
Scots Corner 234 f.
Scythians 19
Sea Mills (Bristol) Map *22*
Secundani 49.4
Segontium (Caernarfon) 419
Seine 290, 402. Map *4*
Seirkieran (Saigir) Map *27*
Selgouae *124.2.* Maps *2*; see Selkirk
Selim; see Solomon
Selkirk 17, 235. Map 13; see Selgouae

Selmeston Map *6*
Selsey 80, 94. *421.5.* Map 28
Selune Map *14*
Senán 130, 355, 424. Map *9* E
Senchus Fer nAlban 451. *180.3*
Seniargus *124.2*
senleithi 450
Senlis 380. *90.5.* Map *4*
Sens 10. *12.3*
Serach, Serigi 168 L (Serygei)
Servanus 411 E
servi 458
Severinus 54, 78 f.
Severn 63, 68, 100, 126, 210, 239 f., 293, 303, 310, 326, 361 f., 374
Severn Estuary, Sea 5 f., 36, 57, 157, 223, 227 f., 232, 268, 308, 350, 355, 429. *390.1*
Severus; see Sulpicius Severus
Severus Augustus 155 f.
Sewerby Map *21*
Shaftesbury *309.2*
Shalcombe Down Map *21*
Shannon 130, 355
Shannon Saints Map *25*
Shapwick Map *22*
Shawell Map *21*
Shefford Map *21* S
East Shefford 225. *125.1*, Maps *6*, *20* S
Shepperton Map *3* S
sheriff *491.4, 494.2*
Sherborne Map 28
Sherrington Map *22*
Shetlands *191.1*
shire 492, 494*
Shrewsbury 68, 241; see Pengwern
Shrewton Map *22*
Shropham Map *3*
Shropshire 210, 232. Map *20*
Sicilian Briton 23, 46, 48, 340 f., 356, 405, 408 f., 512. *35.2, 337.2, 342.3* E
Sicily 8, 119, 148, *45.2*
Sidonius Apollinaris 90 f., 96 f., 251, 407, 513 E
Sigambri 21
Sigbert 229
signal towers 16, 57
sil 160
Silchester 125*, 137*, 211, 296. Maps 2, 13, *21* P
Silures 150, 207, 366. *190.4.* Map *2*
Silvanus *52.2*
Silvius *420.2*
sixhynde 488
Sixtus III 513
W.F.Skene 457. *177.1, 196.3, 417.1*
Skye 180 f., 190, 193, *188.2, 191.1.* Map 10
Slane Map *9*
slaves; see *caeth, cumal, esne, mug, servi, taeog, theow*
Slavs 265, 272, 278 f., 405, 413, 437, 510. *190.4–5, 276.1, 292.2, 437.3, 458.2.* Map 17 P

Sleaford Map *6*
Sletty 175, 399. Maps 9, 27
Sliabh Mis 441
Slovakia 279
Smeath Map *22*
Snape Map *6*
Snettisham Map *6*
Snodland Map *22*
Snowdon(ia) 221, 408, 418, 506. *48.3*; see Gwynedd
Soemil 77. *213.3*
soer 449
Soissons 95, 513. Map *4*
Solinus *192.2*
Solomon of Powys 232; see Selim
Solsbury Hill 113
Solway 152, 177. *232.3*
Somerset 68, 121, 137, 221, 230, 294 f., 302, 308 f., 350, 441. *324.3*. Maps *20, 23, 28*
Somersham Map *6*
Somerton 294, 309
Somme 290
Sonning Map *3*
Souldern Map *6*
South; see Cadbury, Downs, Elkington, Ferriby, Moulscombe, Muskham, Saxons
Southampton 80, 104, 106, 370. *415.3*. Map *2*
Southampton Water 49, 106
Spelsbury Map *22*
Staffordshire 5, 210, 310, 474
Stainmore 234; see Brough
Stalmine Moss Map *22*
Great Stambridge Map *3*
Stamford 60
Standard Hill *492.1*
Standlake Map *21*
Standlow Map *22*
Stane Street 482
Stanwick 237
Statio Derventio 158
Steep Lowe Map *22*
Stettin Maps *16, 17*
Stevenage Map *6*
Stewarts 198 f.; see Stuarts
Stilicho 21 f., 30, 37, 49, 70, 108
Stirling 17, 183, 188, 194, 196 f., 215. *302.4, 367.3*. Map *10*; see Giudi, Iudeu **P**
stirrup 437
Stockbridge Map *18*
Stoke Golding Map *22*
Stone Map *21*
Stonehaven 178
West Stow Map *6*
'Stradwawl' 213
Strasbourg 10
Stratford-on-Avon 284. Map *18*
Strathclyde 219, 239, 314; see Alclud, Clyde, Dumbarton
Strathmore 178, 183, 188, 195, 306
Stratton (Cirencester) Map *22*
Stretton, Staffs. Map *22*

Stretton-on-the-Fosse Map *18*
Strongbow 149
Stuarts 259, 330; see Stewarts
Sturmer Map *22*
Suebi, Suevi 22, 261, 266, 292
Suffolk 140, 271, 283, 298. *140.3, 494.2*
sule 497
Sulpicius Severus 10, 15, 26 f., 335, 406, 419
Supervenientes 16.3; see 'Anticipators'
Surrey 109, 226, 269, 273, 307, 322, 493*. *323.1, 492.1*. Map *23*
Sussex 3, 84, 90, 93 f., 103 f., 113, 136, 225, 271, 298, 307, 325 f., 482, 492. *272.3, 324.3, 487.2, 492.1, 494.2*; see South Saxons
Sutherland *191.1*
Sutton Bonnington Map *6*
Sutton Courtenay Map *6*
Sutton Hoo 322, 467
Swallowcliffe Map *22*
Swarkeston Map *18*
Sweden 261. *148.2*
Sweethope Map *22*
Swindon 137, 225
Swords Map *27*
Syagrius 54, 91 f., 95, 114, 291, 513
Syagrius seals 95
Symmachus 19
Syracuse 516
Syria 25, 202. *5.1*

Tacitus of Kent 17
Cornelius Tacitus xiv, 16, 389. *190.4*
taeog 460*. *458.3*
Taeppa 322*f. *493.1*
Taghmon Map *27*
Talgarth Map *7, 1*
Talhearn Tataguen 232, 416
Taliesin 231 f., 242 f., 416*
'Taliesin' 426
Talorcan *195.3, 303.2*
Tamworth 243. Maps *23, 22*
Tancorix *51.1*
tanist 455.3
Taplow 322, 467. Map *22* **S**
Tara 155, 157, 170 f., 193, 349, 375, 435, 441. Map *9*; see Temoria **P**
Tara Feast 171 f.
Tarsus; see Theodore
Tataguen; see Talhearn
Tatheus 458. *207.5, 208.3* **E**
Taunton 308 f.
Taurus 13
Loch Tay 150
River Tay 190 f.
Teddington *472.2*
Te Deum 25
Tees 16
Tegeingl 442. *210.1, 462.1*; see Flint
Teilo 208, 363, 366, 397, 411 f. Map *24* **E**
Teltown 378 **P** (Tailtiu)
Temoria (Tara) *161.2* **P**
Temple Down Map *21*

INDEX (CORRECTED) TO *THE AGE OF ARTHUR* 149

Tenbury 310
Ternóc 384 E
Terryglass 375. Map 27; see Columba
Tethba Map 9
Teuyth 462
Great Tew Map 22
Thakeham Map 22
Thames 52, 60, 82, 100, 109 f., 136, 213, 225 f., 240, 268f., 271 f., 280 f., 290, 293, 299 f., 306 f., 322, 475. *324.2*, *493.1*. Map 20
Thanet 57, 60, 81, 85 f., 267. *487.2*; see Ruoihm
Thaw 208
Themistius 409
Theodore of Canterbury 327, 395 f., 414, 496, 498 f., 517, 518. *303.2* E
Theodoric of Bernicia 234
— of Ravenna 114, 141, 513. *114.3*
— I (Frank) 291
— f Budic 131, 228, 256 f.
— f Theudebald 126 f., 228. Map 7 L
Theodosius I 15, 19 f., 26, 30, 37, 84, 100, 512
Theodosius II 250, 343, 512
Count Theodosius 15 f.
Theodulf 234
Theod-; see also Theud-
theologoi 421
theow 315, 486
Thérouanne 402
Thessalonica 26
Thetford Map 3
Theudebald 127; see Theodoric
Theudebald (Frank) 513
Theudebert I 287, 513
Theud-; see also Theod-
Thorpe Malsor Map 21
Thorsberg 492
Throwley, Kent Map 21
Throwley, Staffs. Map 22
Thruxton Map 6
Thucydides 389
Thuriau *357.1* E
Thuringia 89, 265, 274 f., 291 f., 437, 482, 486
Thurmaston Map 3
Thurso Map 10
Tiberius II 514
Tickford Map 21
Tideover *314.2*
Tigernach *147.3*
Tigernach 352, 411. Map 27 E
Tigernmas *450.4*
Tigernomaglus *363.2*
Tigirnicus *124.2*
Tilbury *94.3* Map 28
Till 177
Tilshead Map 22
Timagenes *422.2*
Tintagel 439, 456. Map 25
Tintern 228 f., 515. Map 20
Tirconnel 160, 162, 169, 172. Map 9
tir cyvriv 448 f., 462

Tírechán 399. *464.5* E
Tír Eogain (Tyrone) Map 9
tir kyllidus 460.2
Tissington Map 22
Toddington Map 3 S
Toki 499
Tomen-y-mur *124.2*
Tory Island Map 27
Great Tosson Map 22
Totternhoe 8. *299.3* S
Toul *90.5*. Map 4
Toulouse *12.3*
Tours 26, 146, 165, 250, 258, 331, 335 f., 386, 516; see Gregory, Martin
Tractus Armoricanus 90, 250; see Brittany, Normandy, Picardy
trade 441 f.
Traprain Law 67 f., 215 P
Traval 241
Tre(f)- 364, 449 f., 459 f., 470
Tredunnock (Tref Redinauc) *120.3*. Map 7, 10
Trégastel Map 14, 31–32
Tréguier Map 14, 30
Tre'r Ceiri 461
Tren 241 f.
Trent 5, 136, 211, 213 f., 243, 284, 298, 303, 306, 322, 325, 398, 467, 493. *303.2*, *494.2*
'Tribal Hidage' 213, 298, 492*. *430.3*, *487.2* T
Tribes 252, 364, 453 f., 459
Tribruit *111.5*
tribunes 18, 125, 127. *52.1*
Tribunus 125
tributarii 482 f., 487, 502
Tribute 220, 434, 443, 458
tricha cét 156
Tricurium 361; see Trigg
trientes 257
Trier 9, 80, 405, 407, 409. *12.3*
Trieux Map 14
Trigg 130, 361. Map 25
Trim 468, 498. Map 9
Trinouantes *324.3*. Map 2
Triphun; see Tribunus
Tripontium Map 21
Tristan 118, 257
Ile Tristan 258. Map 14, 33
Trodwy 241
Troyes; see Lupus
Trumpington Map 3
tuath 282, 436 f., 449 f., 470
Tuathal Maelgarb 168 f., 375, 513
—Teachtmar 151 ff., 160
Tuda 395 E
Tuddenham Map 20
Tudwal *432.2* E
-tun 315, 450, 470*, 491. *364.2*. Maps 19 A, 20
tunc 460.3
Turpilius 208
Tuxford Map 21
Tweed 17, 67 f., 177, 198, 214 f, 233

Tweedmouth 17
twelfhynde, twyhynde 488
-ty *364.2*
Tyne 66, 152, 177, 214, 233 f., 282, 314, 392, 470, 475
Tynemouth Map 22
Tyningham Map 28
Tyrone 160; see Tír Eogain
Tyrrhene Sea *148.2*
Tyssilio 397, 434. Map 24 E
Tywardreath 257

uchelwr, uchelwyr 458, 460*
Uffa 298
Uffingas 298
Uffington Map 5
Ufford Map 6
Uí-names 160 f.
Uí Bairrche Map 9
— Bressail Map 9
— Chennselaig Map 9
— Chrimthann Map 9
— Dúnlange Map 9
— Fiachrach Aidni Map 9
— Liatháin 158*, 384. *125.3*. Map 9
— Maine 170. Map 9
— Néill 160, 167 f., 175, 182, 377 f. *167.4*. Maps 9, 27
Uisnech Map 9
Ukraine 403
Ulaid 124, 151 f., 160, 165 f., 172, 183, 349. *147.3*. Maps 9, 27; see Dál Araide, Dál Fiatach, Ulster
Ulph 234
Ulster 151 f., 161, 183, 235, 441. *442.2*; see Ulaid
Ultán 434. *162.1* E
Umbrafel 356
uncia 459 f., 487
Uncleby Map 22
underkings *324.3*
Undley Map 6
Upton Snodsbury Map 21
Urbgen *234.3*; see Urien
Urbs Legionis 111, 125; see Caerleon, Chester
Urien 219, 228, 232 f., 247, 258, 321, 329, 417, 490, 515. *234.2*
Urquhart *193.2*
Ushant Map 14, 21
Usk 121 f., 126, 207 f. Map 7

Valens Augustus 15, 19, 512
Bishop Valens 10 E
Valentia 16 f., 50, 214 P
Valentinian I 15 f., 26, 66, 215, 512. *50.4, 52.1*
— II 19 f., 512
— III 27, 40, 86, 98, 114
Valerianus 201
St Valéry 402
Vandals 21 f., 56, 74, 88, 114, 265 f., 274, 506. *100.2*
St Vandrille 402 E

Vannes 250 f. Map 14
Vannetais Map 14
Varni 261 f., 272 f., 287 f., 318. Map 15 P
vates 422; see *fáith*
Uenedotia 210; see Gwynedd
Uennianus; see Finnian E
Uepogenus, Uepoguenech *186.3*
Vercelli 25. *137.1*
Uerturiones; see Fortrenn
Verulamium 61, 79, 95, 137, 211, 335, 350, 372. *200.2*. Maps 13, 22
Vesuvius *441.2*
Ve(ttia?) Maia *124.2*
Vicars 5, 9
vicarium 497
vice-comes 491.4, 494.2
vici 2; see -wic
Victor (Wittur) 253
Vict(o?)r *124.2*
Victor Caesar *419.2*
Victoricus 348 E
Victricius 25, 33, 56, 345, 348, 356, 372, 405, 512; see Vict(o?)r E
Vienna 403
Vienne *12.3*
Vilaine Map 14
villa 470
Villa Banhedos 257
— Petri 252
— Wormavi 252
village 451, 459, 472, 491
Vinland 385
Uinnianus 379; see Finnian E
'Uinta' 298; see Creoda
Virgilius Maro 415 E
Virgilius of Salzburg 402. Map 29 E
Uirolec *193.2*
Visigoths; see Goths
Vitalinus 55 f., 73 f., 202
Vitalis (Vitalinus) 55
Vitalis of Fleury *164.2*
Volga 19
Völkerwanderung 261
Vortigern 35, 38, 44, 48 f., 55 f., 87 f., 110, 118, 124, 137, 158, 166, 179, 188, 191, 207, 213, 267 f., 271, 286, 347, 375, 388, 506, 512, 518. *63.2, 166.2* L
Uortimer 80 f. *95.2*
Uortipor 125, 203, 207, 513
Vosges 383, 414
Uotadini 17, 66 f., 124, 214 f. Map 2; see Gododdin, Manau P
Voyages 383*f.; see *Im(m)rama*
Uriconium; see Wroxeter
Vulgate 24, 172

Great Wakering Map 22
Waldringfield Map 6
Wall; see Antonine Wall, Hadrian's Wall
Wall-by-Lichfield 243; see Caer Luitcoet
Wallace 176. *215.2*; see Guallauc
Wallerwente 314
Wallingford 102. Maps 5, 6
Wallop 73, 513; see Guoloppum P

INDEX (CORRECTED) TO *THE AGE OF ARTHUR* 151

Wallsend 50
Walsingham Map *6*
Walter of Oswestry 198*f.
Walter Map 427
Waltham Cross Map *22*
Walthamstow Map *5*
Walton, name 482
Walton, Warwicks. Map *22*
Walton Head *314.2*
Wanborough Map *21*
Wansdyke 210, 246, 299. Map 13 P
Wansum 81
Wantage 299
-wardine 472
War Ditches Map *5*
Ware Map *6*
Warmark Map *3* S
Warni; see Varni
Waroc 258 f.
Warrington *370.3*
Warwick 284. Map *18*
Warwickshire 442
Wash 49
Watling Street 111, 442. Map *31*
Watlington Map *20*
Weald 94, 306 f., 472 f.
wealh 41, 312 f.
Wearmouth 397, 516. Map *28*
Weeting *57.2*
Weimar 278. Maps *16, 17*
Little Weldon Map *6*
Welhisc 313
Welkechildeland 474
Wels *437.4*; see Ovilava
Welsh, especially 41 f., 66 f., 307*f., 325 f., 347, 457 f., 466 f., 482, 493, 515, 518 P
Welsh poems 54, 64, 96, 104, 111, 116 f., 162, 218 f., 231 f., 416 f. T
Welshpool *127.1, 240.3*; see Meicen
Welton Map *6*
Wendens Ambo Maps *22, 28*
Wenefred 462 E
Wenlock Map *28*
Wentloog Map *7*; see Gwynlliauc
Wereham *314.3*. Map *28*
wergild 485*
Weser 278. *291.2*. Maps *15, 16*
Wessex 41 f., 104 f., 240, 303, 317 f., 324*, 431 f., 442, 451 f., 467 f., 488, 492. *323.1 f., 433.2, 494.2*. Map *20*; see West Saxons
West; see Angles, Bergholt, Keal, Riding, Saxons, Stow, Wickham
Westbere Map *6*
Westbury Map *22*
Western Isles 157, 181, 185, 188, 197
Wester Wanna 291 S
Westham Map *20*
Westmorland 50, 214, 219, 474. *51.1, 494.2*
Weston-under-Penyard 366; see Ariconium
Westwell Map *22*
Wethenoc 366 E

Wettenhall Map *28*
Wetton Map *22*
Wexford 441. Map *9*
Wheathampstead Map *22*
Wheatley Map *3*
Whitby 309, 315, 394, 421, 514, 516. Map *28*
White Horse Hill Map *5*
White Lowe Map *22*
Whitesands Bay 126, 441. Map *7, 5*; see Porth Mawr
Whitford *462.1*. Map *24*
Whithorn 141, 191, 337 f., 351, 357, 392, 397, 410 f., 512. *336.1, 440.2*. Map *26*; see Candida Casa, Rosnat P
Wibbandun 515
Wibtoft Map *22*
-wic; see *vici*
Wichnor 243. Map *21*
Wick Map *10*
West Wickham Map *21*
Wickham Bishops Map *5*
Widsith 421. *261.2*
Wigan Map *22*
Wigber Low Map *22*
Wigesta 311
Isle of Wight 155, 270, 303, 309, 492. *474.3, 487.2*; see Icht
Wiglaet 265
Wigston Magna Map *6*
Little Wilbraham Map *6*
Wilcote Map *22*
Wilfred 314, 321, 372, 394 f., 416, 498. *421.5* E
William I 198, 259. *116.2, 430.3*
— II 198
— III 456
— Fitzalan 198
— of Malmesbury 141, 427
Willibrord 402, 516. *412.2*. Map *29* E
Willoughby-on-the-Wolds Map *6*
Wilton Map *21*
Wiltshire 102, 210, 226, 256. *309.2, 324.3, 325.1*
Wimpole 109. Map *6*
Winchendon Map *21*
Winchester 80, 104, 106, 125, 225, 271, 293, 299, 309. *226.2*. Maps *2, 13, 20, 23, 28*
Windisch Map *17*
Winfrith *415.3*; see Boniface E
Wing 394. Map *28*
Wingham Map *6*
Winkburn Map *22*
Winkelbury Map *22*
Winnal *314.3*; see Winwaloe E
Winninus *412.2* E
Winniocus *440.2* E
Winnoc of Tours *383.1* E
Winnoc of Wormhout 259 E
Winnold House *314.3*
Winterbourne Gunner Map *21*
Winterslow Map *21*
Winwaed 241. *302.4* P

Winwaloe 252, 363, 386, 411, 459. *223.2*, *314.3*, *432.3*. Maps 28, *4* E
Wippedsfleot 81 f., 86
Wissa 281
witan 504
Witham 112, 282
Withington 499. Map *22*
Long Wittenham Map *3* S
Witto 333; see Candidus
Wittur; see Victor
Wixna 281
Wledic; see Gwledic
Wlencing 94
Woden 298
Woden's Barrow 299
Wolterton Map *6*
Womersley Map *22*
Woodbridge 282
Woodchester 73
Woodcuts *431.3*
Woodston Map *3*
Woodyates *431.3*. Map *22*
Wooler 214. Map *21*
Wootton Pillinge Map *31* S
Wor Map *22*
Worcester 499. Maps 23, 28
Worcestershire 298, 496. Map *20*
Worle Hall Map *22*
Villa Wormavi 252
Wormhoult 259
Worms (Germany) 10
-worth(y) 279, 472 f. Maps 32 f.
Worthy End Map *31*
Worthy Park Map *6*
Wrdesten *92.3*
Dinlle Wrecon   *245.2*;   see   Wrekin, Wroxeter
Wrekin 241; see Dinlle Wrecon
Wrmonoc 253, 363
Wrocensætna 243, 493
Wrotham Map *22*
Wroxeter (Vriconium) 5, 63, 68, 76, 126, 137, 202, 212, 225, 241, 286, 493. Maps 2, 13, 24
Wulfhere 241 f., 303, 308 f., 327, 492, 517. *310.2*, *321.3*, *493.1*
Würzburg 516

Wyaston Map *22*
Wycombe; see High Wycombe
Wye, Kent 326. Map *22*
River Wye 229, 259, 365 f.
Wykeham Map *18*
wylisc 41, 312
wynebwerth 485, 496; see face-payment
Wynewalestrete *314.3*; see Winwaloe
Wynnel's Grove *314.3*; see Winwaloe
Wyre Piddle Map *22*

xenodochia *383.1*

Yare 61
Yarmouth 61, 82, 392
Yeadon 314
Yearsley Map *22*
Yeavering Bell 67, 214 f. P
Old Yeavering 320 f. Map *21*
Yelford Map *22*
Yeovil 137
Ynyr 207; see Honorius
Ynys Pyr; see Caldey Island, Piro
York 5, 9, 49 f., 60 f., 68, 77, 118, 136 f., 177, 214 f., 220, 233 f., 268, 284, 300 f., 314, 331, 370, 394 f., 403, 513, 515, 516. *311.2*, *440.2*, *494.2*. Maps 2, 13, 23, 28, *3*, *22* P
Vale of York 5
Yorkshire 16, 32, 60, 72, 82, 214. *51.2*, *430.3*, *494.2*
— East Riding 17, 51, 60 f., 77, 112, 136, 213 f., 233, 304, 314, 390, 475. *370.3*; see Deira
— North Riding 314
— West Riding 50, 234, 310, 314 f., 472, 482
— Signal Towers 16, 57
Youlgreave Map *22*
Yoxall 243. Map *21*
Ypres Map *19* A
Ystrad Marchell *127.1*
Ystrad Tywi 397; see Cetgueli, Kidwelly
Ytene *474.3*

Zeno 513
Zuyder Zee 261